JEFFERSON DAVIS AND THE CONFEDERACY

Jefferson Davis

AND TREATIES CONCLUDED BY

and the Confederacy
THE CONFEDERATE STATES WITH INDIAN TRIBES

Edited by

RONALD GIBSON

1977

OCEANA PUBLICATIONS, INC.
Dobbs Ferry, New York

Library of Congress Cataloging in Publication Data
Main entry under title:

Jefferson Davis and the Confederacy and treaties concluded
  by the Confederate States with Indian tribes.

(The Presidential chronology series)
  Bibliography: p.
  1. Indians of North America — Confederate States of
America — Treaties. 2. Davis, Jefferson, 1808-1889 —
Biography. 3. Statesmen — Confederate States of
America — Correspondence. 4. Confederate States of
America — History. I. Gibson, Ronald V. II. Confederate
States of America. President.
KFZ9105.J44   341.42   77-10189
ISBN 0-379-12095-1

Manufactured in the United States of America

TABLE OF CONTENTS

INTRODUCTION

Nineteen hundred and seventy-seven is the year of years in which to bring out a book on the life of Jefferson Davis for in 1977 the United States Senate, of which Jefferson Davis had been a proud and influential member, resolved that United States citizenship should be posthumously restored to this great Southern statesman.

How came that this brave and principled American has been deprived of his citizenship for so long, his name almost forgotten by his own countrymen?

Jefferson Davis was a loser and Americans hate a loser whatever the contest, a game, an election, a war. Davis's failure in war even more than the issues on which that civil war was fought explains the low regard in which he has been held for more than a hundred years by most Americans living north of the Mason-Dixon line.

The issues of the Civil War - slavery and states' rights - were supremely important ones. Yet Thomas Jefferson owned slaves; John Calhoun fought persistently for states' rights; and Jefferson and Calhoun are lauded as statesmen. Whereas Jefferson Davis has been nudged into near-oblivion.

In American history, Jefferson Davis is our legendary loser, the forgotten man.

Davis possessed outstanding talents and achieved much that is noble in the course of his long, hazardous and tragic life. Wounded, he went on fighting at Buena Vista. Morally brave, he held on till his death to the principles of political action he considered to be fundamental. For this faith in principle, Davis was vilified, imprisoned, ostracized and shorn of his dearly cherished American citizenship.

Jefferson Davis knew every word of the American Constitution; few understood the document better. He had defendable reasons for his views on states' rights nor did his opinions derive in any way from political opportunism or the desire to advance himself.

Is it not fair to claim that the life of Jefferson Davis, though he lost a civil war, was an heroic one? Life breeds many kinds of heroes and that proud title can surely not be refused a man who persisted in a doomed struggle for a cause in which he believed regardless of danger and defeat and the North's purposeless revenge.

President Davis's heroic qualities were put to harsh test
for four tormenting years. Come wind, come weather he stuck
to his beliefs, fought on till captured and during his years in
jail soared unsoured above its trials, quietly returning on
release to the care of his family and the immense task of writing
the history of the Civil War.

To honor Jefferson Davis and to signal in 1977 an historic
gesture to restore his citizenship, we have assembled this
tribute to his name. The book tells in detailed chronological
form the eighty-year story of his private and public life. It
contains a score of documents chosen to light up the devotion
and poetry of his family affections as well as to expose how
he responded to the momentous demands of the Civil War.

It is our hope that the publicity we are now giving to the
hitherto neglected letters and messages of Jefferson Davis
will do much to rebuild his reputation and to unfold the lifework
of a long unjustly ignored American.

CHRONOLOGY

CHRONOLOGY

1808	Born, Fairview, Christian County, Kentucky, June 3
1815	At age 7, rode nearly 1000 miles on horseback from Mississippi to St. Thomas's College, Washington County, Kentucky
1821	Entered Transylvania University, Lexington Kentucky
1824	Accepted for U. S. Military Academy, West Point, New York
1828	Graduated, 2nd Lieutenant
1828-29	Stationed at Fort Crawford, Illinois
1829-31	Stationed at Fort Winnebago, Wisconsin
1832	Fought in Black Hawk War (in which Abraham Lincoln also fought)
1834	Adjutant, First Dragoons, Fort Gibson, Arkansas
1835	Resigned military commission, June 30 Married Sarah Knox Taylor at Beechland, Kentucky (his wife died of malaria three months later) Bought 14 slaves Began to cultivate his 1000-acre cotton plantation, Warren County, Mississippi
1835-36	Built Brierfield, his plantation home
1835-45	Lived in seclusion, worked hard outdoors by day, read deeply at night (The Federalist, Adam Smith, Congressional Debates, etc.)
1845	Married Varina Howell, Natchez, February 26 Elected to U. S. House of Representatives, November
1846	Maiden speech on the Oregon Territory, February 6 Resigned seat in House, June

Appointed Commander of a regiment of Volunteers, the Mississippi Rifles, June

Fought in the war against Mexico
Took part in the attack on Monterey, September 21-23

1847   Wounded at Buena Vista, February 23
Lauded for bravery by General Taylor, March 6
Resigned from Army
Appointed Senator from Mississippi, December

1848   Elected U. S. Senator by Mississippi Legislature, January

1850   Re-elected to Senate
Chairman, Senate Military Committee
Advocated extension of Missouri Compromise line to Pacific
Death of John C. Calhoun
The Texas Compromise

1851   Resigned from Senate
Ran for Governor of Mississippi; narrowly defeated

1852   At home, Brierfield

1853-57   U. S. Secretary of War
Raised Army strength from 11,000 to 15, 500
Proposed use of camels on Western plains
Member, President Pierce's Cabinet, the only Cabinet in U. S. history to continue for four years without a single change in personnel

1854-57   Dred Scott case

1857   Re-elected Senator from Mississippi, March 4

1857-60   Oratorical battles with Senator Douglas on the issues of slavery and states' rights

1859   John Brown's raid into Virginia, October

1860   South Carolina secession crisis, November 13-December 24

1861   Resigned from Senate on secession of Mississippi, January 21
Provisional Confederate Government set up, Montgomery, Alabama, February 4-8

1861   Confederate Constitution adopted, February 8
              Elected Provisional President, February 9
              Inaugural address, February 18
              Fort Sumter, shore batteries opened fire,
                Civil War began, April 12
              Confederate capital moved to Richmond, May 29
              First Battle of Bull Run, July 21
              Elected President, October 6

1862   Inaugurated President, February 22
              Fall of New Orleans, April
              Battle of Shiloh, April 6-7
              Death of General Albert Sidney Johnston
              General Thomas J. ('Stonewall') Jackson
                died of wounds, May 10
              Sinking of the Arkansas, August 5
              Second Battle of Bull Run, August 29-30
              Lee's Proclamation to the People of Mary-
                land, September 8
              Battle of Antietam, September 17
              Battle of Fredericksburg, December 13

1862-64   The Alabama case

1863   Lincoln's Emancipation Proclamation, January 1
              Message on allowing minors to hold Army
                commissions, Richmond, April 16
              Battle of Gettysburg, July 1-3

1864   Battle of the Wilderness, May 5-6
              Battle of Cold Harbor, June 1-3
              Battle of Petersburg, June 15-18
              March through Georgia, May-September
              Surrender of Atlanta, September 2
              Evacuation of Atlanta began, September 5
              March to the Sea (Sherman), November-December
              Approved arming of slaves, November 7
                (not approved by Confederate Congress
                till March 20, 1865)

1865   Hampton Roads Conference, February 3
              Message on Lincoln's refusal to enter into
                peace negotiations, February 6
              Last message to the People of the Con-
                federacy, April 4
              Lee's surrender at Appomatox Courthouse,
                April 9
              Assassination of Lincoln, April 14
              Final Cabinet meeting of the Confederate
                Government, April 24
              Captured at Irwinville, Georgia, May 10
              Imprisoned (at first in irons), Fort Monroe

1866	Indicted for treason, May
1867	Released from prison, May 13 Left for Canada, May
1868	In England and France; accorded tumultuous welcome Indictment quashed by Chief Justice, December 5 Amnesty Proclamation by President Johnson, December 25
1869-73	President, Carolina Insurance Company, Memphis
1870	Death of General Robert E. Lee, Oct. 12
1877	Second visit to England
1878	Settled at Beauvoir, on the Gulf, Mississippi
1878-81	Wrote Rise and Fall of the Confederate Government
1879	Bequeathed Beauvoir by his benefactress, Mrs. Sarah Dorsey
1884	Honored at Capitol by Mississippi Legislature Slanderous attacks by General Sherman
1885	Death of Ulysses S. Grant, July 23 Repudiated Theodore Roosevelt's public association of his name with that of Benedict Arnold
1886	Triumphal tour of Alabama and Georgia
1889	Died, New Orleans, December 6 Buried, New Orleans, December 11
1893	Re-interred, Richmond, Virginia
1977	U.S. Senate resolution to restore posthumously, United States citizenship

JEFFERSON DAVIS: AN ESSAY

"It is our duty to keep the memory of our heroes green.
Yet they belong not to us alone; they belong to the whole
country; they belong to America."

Jefferson Davis
April 1882

Had there been no Civil War, would Jefferson Davis have become President of the United States?

Perhaps not. Yet in 1853 who at the political card table held a more regal hand of cards? Jefferson Davis was riding high, a valiant soldier, a personable man of 45, the broom-sweeping Secretary of War in President Pierce's cabinet. Might the odds not then have seemed low against the fulfillment of so glittering a prospect?

Consider the points in Jefferson Davis's favor. He came from Mississippi, in those days an influential political state. He was a graduate of West Point. His courage at Buena Vista had been attested to by a future President. He had attended a prestigious Southern university, and — much more important — for ten years on his isolated cotton plantation he had schooled himself through study of the American political classics for whatever opportunities of statesmanship might come his way.

As to his personal qualities, they were many: a good mind, a dignified presence, eloquence in speech, a cultivated and considerate manner and, above all, the high seriousness of purpose that must precede readiness for any exalted responsibility. Indeed, Jefferson Davis's energies, talents, attainments and all-round preparedness were universally acknowledged.

Of Davis's many qualifications for high office, his military achievements must be placed first since throughout American history, from Washington to Grant and from Grant to Eisenhower, Americans have acclaimed and rewarded their leaders in battle.

Jefferson Davis had the courage of a fighting man. He also had a soldier's swiftness to obey. When Mississippi seceded from the Union, he instantly forsook the United States Senate to report for duty in the South. He had hoped to command the Confederate forces, but when the summons came to serve less glamourously as Confederate President his response was soldierly — he accepted at once.

In grappling with this unique, unassessable assignment the whole course of Davis's life was to change. From secure, slow-paced, hierarchical Washington he was pitchforked into a gabbling southern maelstrom. He arrived in Montgomery, the provisional Confederate capital, and discovered — nothing. Enthusiasm, yes; organization, no. No civil service, no revenue, no currency, no supplies, no army. The seceders from the United States army were magnificent, but the more numerous volunteers were another story, eager but untrained and unaccustomed to discipline.

And where would their arms and uniforms come from? The South had no factories and no allies and a naval blockade was to cut off the South from whatever aid might be had from overseas. New Orleans, the South's principal port, fell to the enemy.

President Davis toiled like a trinity of titans at his task but even he could not perform the feats of Superman. Endlessly harassed and interrupted, he had no time to plan and establish an efficient form of government. He tried to do far too much himself. He kept too close an eye on his generals in the field, peppering them with bulletins of advice, dashing off to see for himself how the battle fared. And in so doing he perforce neglected his own gigantic problems of central control and assurance of essential supplies.

Under this impossible load, the President's health deteriorated and with it his firm grip on events. He became irritable, stubborn and opinionated, quarrelling with aides and advisers whose guidance he could not afford to discourage.

Even so, with these and so many other handicaps, and with the money, industry and manpower of the North against him, Davis slogged miraculously on, never doubting the righteousness of the Confederate stand and that the Confederacy would ultimately win.

Had Jefferson Davis combined in his person the genius of Napoleon and Franklin Roosevelt the result would have been the same. The logistics of war were overwhelmingly against him. Nevertheless, for four years, under hopelessly antagonistic circumstances this brave man strove without ceasing for the cause in which he believed. Throughout the long, bloody, fratricidal conflict President Davis continued with much reason to see himself as a loyal American faithful to the Constitution whose clauses and meanings he had studied as closely as any man in the land. He was never a traitor as Theodore Roosevelt was so shamefully to allege.

Knowing President Davis's noble, unvengeful character, one can be sure that in victory he would never have treated the North as the North treated the South. Davis, like Lincoln, was blessed with the heaven-kissed quality of magnanimity. (How sad for the South that Lincoln did not live. Lincoln assuredly would not have permitted Sherman's savagery, nor would he have suffered Davis to rot for two years in jail.)

After his release from prison, where he had been kept at first in chains, Davis travelled to Canada and then on to England and France. Everywhere the Confederate President received a hero's welcome. Yet he came home a year later to a still hostile America. He had been deprived of his American citizenship, of which he was so proud, and never in his lifetime was it to be restored.

Powerful Northern interests frustrated his attempts to obtain aid in England to succour the ravaged South and only with difficulty did he raise money to maintain his family and to restore his plantation at Brierfield.

Through the benefaction of Mrs. Sarah Dorsey, Davis was able to retire to her estate, Beauvoir, on the Gulf of Mexico, and there he began to write the story of the Civil War, an undertaking in which Sarah and later his wife, Varina, acted as his amanuensis.

It took more than three years to write this long, two-volume history of the Civil War, an effort of sustained will by a seventy-year-old man impossible to overpraise, impeded as he was by ill-health, by family and financial troubles and by frequent unannounced visits from well-meaning strangers, many from the North. The last of Jefferson Davis's four sons was to die and he often received news of the deaths of old comrades in the war, one of the first to fall being his stalwart ally, Robert E. Lee.

Jefferson Davis's great work, *The Rise and Fall of the Confederacy,* was not well received and did little to restore his financial well-being. True, the history is not easy to read; it requires a concentration appropriate to the grave issues discussed. Only slowly did the *Rise and Fall,* like its distinguished author himself, come to be fairly valued throughout America.

The life and record of Jefferson Davis has to be assessed not by our current standards but according to the views of a considerate and contemplative Southerner of his time.

Jefferson Davis believed in slavery. He treated his 36 slaves at Brierfield well by the measures of the day. They were encouraged to operate their own domestic government and to settle disputes through trial by jury; Davis reserving only the right to pardon.

Davis was a staunch upholder of states' rights. He held consistently to his beliefs both before and after the Civil War and was well able to argue his case against the brightest constitutional lawyers in America. After all, who has the right to pronounce in this subtle, disputatious area that Davis was wrong and his opponents in the right?

Not for the first time in world history, good men like Davis and Lincoln found themselves enmeshed in a conflict of principle out of which emerged the tragedy of America's Civil War.

Lincoln, for his immortal role in that conflict, has long been revered by the American people. It is now time to grant due respect to Jefferson Davis, the man who lost the war but who, in losing, triumphed no less than did Lincoln at the moment of his death.

DOCUMENTS

INTRODUCTION TO THE DOCUMENTS

These documents range in time from the outbreak of
the Civil War in 1861 to 1881, eight years before
Jefferson Davis's death. Most of the documents have
been chosen for their political and constitutional
importance. Thus the little known Constitution of the
Confederate States of America is printed alongside the
Constitution of the United States in order to facilitate
close comparison of these two gravely considered
statements.

President Jefferson Davis's two Inaugural Addresses
are reproduced, the first delivered in Montgomery, the
provisional capital, ten days after the establishment
of the Confederate government. His second Inaugural took
place in Richmond a year later.

In April 1861, the month in which the Civil War
began, President Davis somehow found the time to speak
at length to the Confederate Congress in special
session and he then most carefully analyzed the meaning
and limitations of the concept of Union, defending the
constitutional right of states to secede. This masterly
Message to Congress is set forth in full.

Letters exchanged between Jefferson Davis and Robert
E. Lee are included. These relate to the handling of
army deserters and the use of Negroes as soldiers.
There is also a letter from Davis to Abraham Lincoln in
which the Confederate President in noble language
appeals to Lincoln to ensure the humane treatment of
prisoners of war.

In the course of his two-volume The Rise and Fall
of the Confederate Government, which took three years
to write, the former president challenges the existence
of any constitutional right to abolish slavery. A long
passage has been extracted from the book detailing
his reasons for this view.

The private side of Jefferson Davis's life is
touchingly illustrated in two letters written to his
wife, Varina, from jail; in a romantic letter from
Scotland describing the beauties and historic wonders
of the Walter Scott countryside; and in a moving letter
of sympathy to Varina on the feared death at sea of her
youngest brother.

Right up to his death Jefferson Davis wrote love letters to Varina (he was sixty years old when he wrote so endearingly to her from Scotland) and during his travels it was his charming habit to place within the pages of his letters fresh meadow flowers.

His letters, too, are meadow fresh and tender and beautifully written, an outpouring from the mind and soul of a gentle and great man.

Inaugural Address of the President of the Provisional Government, Montgomery, February 18, 1861[1]

Gentlemen of the Congress of the Confederate States of America, Friends, and Fellow-citizens: Called to the difficult and responsible station of Chief Magistrate of the Provisional Government which you have instituted, I approach the discharge of the duties assigned to me with humble distrust of my abilities, but with a sustaining confidence in the wisdom of those who are to guide and aid me in the administration of public affairs, and an abiding faith in the virtue and patriotism of the people. Looking forward to the speedy establishment of a permanent government to take the place of this, which by its greater moral and physical power will be better able to combat with many difficulties that arise from the conflicting interests of separate nations, I enter upon the duties of the office to which I have been chosen with the hope that the beginning of our career, as a Confederacy, may not be obstructed by hostile opposition to

[1] The ceremonies connected with the first inauguration of President Davis were held in front of the Capitol at Montgomery, Alabama.

our enjoyment of the separate existence and independence we have asserted, and which, with the blessing of Providence, we intend to maintain.

Our present political position has been achieved in a manner unprecedented in the history of nations. It illustrates the American idea that governments rest on the consent of the governed, and that it is the right of the people to alter or abolish them at will whenever they become destructive of the ends for which they were established. The declared purpose of the compact of the Union from which we have withdrawn was to "establish justice, insure domestic tranquillity, provide for the common defense, promote the general welfare, and secure the blessings of liberty to ourselves and our posterity;" and when, in the judgment of the sovereign States composing this Confederacy, it has been perverted from the purposes for which it was ordained, and ceased to answer the ends for which it was established, a peaceful appeal to the ballot box declared that, so far as they are concerned, the Government created by that compact should cease to exist. In this they merely asserted the right which the Declaration of Independence of July 4, 1776, defined to be "inalienable." Of the time and occasion of its exercise they as sovereigns were the final judges, each for itself. The impartial and enlightened verdict of mankind will vindicate the rectitude of our conduct; and He who knows the hearts of men will judge of the sincerity with which we have labored to preserve the Government of our fathers in its spirit.

The right solemnly proclaimed at the birth of the United States, and which has been solemnly affirmed and reaffirmed in the Bills of Rights of the States subsequently admitted into the Union of 1789, undeniably recognizes in the people the power to resume the authority delegated for the purposes of government. Thus the sovereign States here represented have proceeded to form this Confederacy; and it is by abuse of language that their act has been denominated a revolution. They formed a new alliance, but within each State its government has remained; so that the rights of person and property have not been disturbed. The agent through which they communicated with foreign nations is changed, but this does not necessarily interrupt their international relations. Sustained by the consciousness that the transition from the former Union to the present Confederacy has not proceeded from a disregard on our part of just obligations, or any failure to perform every constitutional duty, moved by no interest or passion to invade the rights of others, anxious to cultivate peace and commerce with all nations, if we may not hope to avoid war, we may at least expect that posterity will acquit us of having needlessly engaged in it. Doubly justified by the absence of wrong on our part, and by wanton aggression on the part of others, there can be no cause to doubt that the courage and patriotism of the people of the Confederate States will be found equal to any measure of defense which their honor and security may require.

An agricultural people, whose chief interest is the export of commodities required in every manufacturing country, our true policy is peace, and the freest trade which our necessities will permit. It is alike our interest and that of all those to whom we would sell, and from whom we would buy, that there should be the fewest practicable restrictions upon the interchange of these commodities. There can, however, be but little rivalry between ours and any manufacturing or navigating community, such as the Northeastern States of the American Union. It must follow, therefore, that mutual interest will invite to good will and kind offices on both parts. If, however, passion or lust of dominion should cloud the judgment or inflame the ambition of those States, we must prepare to meet the emergency and maintain, by the final arbitrament of the sword, the position which we have assumed among the nations of the earth.

We have entered upon the career of independence, and it must be inflexibly pursued. Through many years of controversy with our late associates of the Northern States, we have vainly endeavored to secure tranquillity and obtain respect for the rights to which we were entitled. As a necessity, not a choice, we have resorted to the remedy of separation, and henceforth our energies must be directed to the conduct of our own affairs, and the perpetuity of the Confederacy which we have formed. If a just perception of mutual interest shall permit us peaceably to pursue our separate political career, my most earnest desire will have been fulfilled. But if this be denied to us, and the integrity of our territory and jurisdiction be assailed, it will but remain for us with firm resolve to appeal to arms and invoke the blessing of Providence on a just cause.

As a consequence of our new condition and relations, and with a view to meet anticipated wants, it will be necessary to provide for the speedy and efficient organization of branches of the Executive department having special charge of foreign intercourse, finance, military affairs, and the postal service. For purposes of defense, the Confederate States may, under ordinary circumstances, rely mainly upon the militia; but it is deemed advisable, in the present condition of affairs, that there should be a well-instructed and disciplined army, more numerous than would usually be required on a peace establishment. I also suggest that, for the protection of our harbors and commerce on the high seas, a navy adapted to those objects will be required. But this, as well as other subjects appropriate to our necessities, have doubtless engaged the attention of Congress.

With a Constitution differing only from that of our fathers in so far as it is explanatory of their well-known intent, freed from sectional conflicts, which have interfered with the pursuit of the general welfare, it is not unreasonable to expect that States from which we have recently parted may seek to unite their fortunes to ours under the Government which we have instituted. For this your Constitution makes adequate provision; but beyond this, if I mistake not the judgment and will of the people, a reunion with the States from which we have separated is neither practicable nor desirable. To increase the power, develop the resources, and promote the happiness of the Confederacy, it is requisite that there should be so much of homogeneity that the welfare of every portion shall be the aim of the whole. When this does not exist, antagonisms are engendered which must and should result in separation.

Actuated solely by the desire to preserve our own rights, and promote our own welfare, the separation by the Confederate States has been marked by no aggression upon others, and followed by no domestic convulsion. Our industrial pursuits have received no check, the cultivation of our fields has progressed as heretofore, and, even should we be involved in war, there would be no considerable diminution in the production of the staples which have constituted our exports, and in which the commercial world has an interest scarcely less than our own. This common interest of the producer and consumer can only be interrupted by exterior force which would obstruct the transmission of our staples to foreign markets—a course of conduct which would be as unjust, as it would be detrimental, to manufacturing and commercial interests abroad.

Should reason guide the action of the Government from which we have separated, a policy so detrimental to the civilized world, the Northern States included, could not be dictated by even the strongest desire to inflict injury upon us; but, if the contrary should prove true, a terrible responsibility will rest upon it, and the suffering of millions will bear testimony to the folly and wickedness of our aggressors. In the meantime there will remain to us, besides the ordinary means before suggested, the well-known resources for retaliation upon the commerce of an enemy.

Experience in public stations, of subordinate grade to this which your kindness has conferred, has taught me that toil and care and disappointment are the price of official elevation. You will see many errors to forgive, many deficiencies to tolerate; but you shall not find in me either want of zeal or fidelity to the cause that is to me the highest in hope, and of most enduring affection. Your generosity has bestowed upon me an undeserved distinction, one which I neither sought nor desired. Upon the continuance of that sentiment, and upon your wisdom and patriotism, I rely to direct and support me in the performance of the duties required at my hands.

We have changed the constituent parts, but not the system of government. The Constitution framed by our fathers is that of these Confederate States. In their exposition of it, and in the judicial construction it has received, we have a light which reveals its true meaning.

Thus instructed as to the true meaning and just interpretation of that instrument, and ever remembering that all offices are but trusts held for the people, and that powers delegated are to be strictly construed, I will hope by due diligence in the performance of my duties, though I may dissappoint your expectations, yet to retain, when retiring, something of the good will and confidence which welcome my entrance into office.

It is joyous in the midst of perilous times to look around upon a people united in heart, where one purpose of high resolve animates and actuates the whole; where the sacrifices to be made are not weighed in the balance against honor and right and liberty and equality. Obstacles may retard, but they cannot long prevent, the progress of a movement sanctified by its justice and sustained by a virtuous people. Reverently let us invoke the God of our fathers to guide and protect us in our efforts to perpetuate the principles which by his blessing they were able to vindicate, establish, and transmit to their posterity. With the continuance of his favor ever gratefully acknowledged, we may hopefully look forward to success, to peace, and to prosperity.

Inaugural Address of the President of the Confederate Government, Richmond, February 22, 1862

(Richardson, ed. *Messages and Papers of the Confederacy*, Vol. I, p. 183 ff.)

Davis had been chosen provisional President of the Confederacy by the Montgomery Congress, and was formally inaugurated February 18. A regular election held in accordance with the Confederate Constitution, in October 1861, resulted in his election as President for a term of six years: his inaugural followed on the 22nd of February. On Davis, see his own *Rise and Fall of the Confederate Government*, 2 Vols.; W. E. Dodd, *Jefferson Davis;* A. Tate, *Jefferson Davis;* E. Cutting, *Jefferson Davis.* His writings can be found in D. Rowland, ed. *Jefferson Davis,* *Constitutionalist, His Letters, Papers and Speeches,* 10 vols.

FELLOW-CITIZENS: On this the birthday of the man most identified with the establishment of American Independence, and beneath the monument erected to commemorate his heroic virtues and those of his compatriots, we have assembled to usher into existence the permanent government of the confederate States. Through this instrumentality, under the favor of Divine Providence, we hope to perpetuate the principles of our Revolutionary fathers. The day, the memory and the purpose seem fitly associated. . . .

When a long course of class legislation, directed not to the general welfare, but to the aggrandizement of the Northern section of the Union, culminated in a warfare on the domestic institutions of the Southern States —when the dogmas of a sectional party, substituted for the provisions of the constitutional compact, threatened to destroy the sovereign rights of the States, six of those States, withdrawing from the Union, confederated together to exercise the right and perform the duty of instituting a government which would better secure the liberties for the preservation of which that Union was established.

Whatever of hope some may have entertained that a returning sense of justice would remove the danger with which our rights were threatened, and render it possible to preserve the Union of the Constitution, must have been dispelled by the malignity and barbarity of the Northern States in the prosecution of the existing war. The confidence of the most hopeful among us must have been destroyed by the disregard they have recently exhibited for all the time-honored bulwarks of civil and religious liberty. Bastiles filled with prisoners, arrested without civil process or indictment duly found; the writ of *habeas corpus* suspended by Executive mandate; a State Legislature controlled by the imprisonment of members whose avowed principles suggested to the Federal Executive that there might be another added to the list of seceded States; elections held under threats of a military power; civil officers, peaceful citizens and gentle women incarcerated for opinion's sake, proclaimed the incapacity of our late associates to administer a government as free, liberal and humane as that established for our common use.

For proof of the sincerity of our purpose to maintain our ancient institutions, we may point to the constitution of the Confederacy and the laws enacted under it, as well as to the fact that through all the necessities of an unequal struggle there has been no act on our part to impair personal liberty or the freedom of speech, of thought or of the press. The courts have been open, the judicial functions fully executed, and every right of the peaceful citizen maintained as securely as if a war of invasion had not disturbed the land.

The people of the States now confederated became convinced that the Government of the United States had fallen into the hands of a sectional majority, who would pervert that most sacred of all trusts to the destruction of the rights which it was pledged to protect. They believed that to remain longer in the Union would subject them to a continuance of a disparaging discrimination, submission to which would be inconsistent with their welfare, and intolerable to a proud people. They therefore determined to sever its bonds and establish a new confederacy for themselves.

The experiment instituted by our Revolutionary fathers, of a voluntary union of sovereign States for purposes specified in a solemn compact, had been perverted by those who, feeling power and forgetting right, were determined to respect no law but their own will. The Government had ceased to answer the ends for which it was ordained and established. To save ourselves from a revolution which, in its silent but rapid progress, was about to place us under the despotism of numbers, and to preserve in spirit, as well as in form, a system of government we believed to be peculiarly fitted to our condition, and full of promise for mankind, we determined to make a new association, composed of States homogeneous in interest, in policy and in feeling.

True to our traditions of peace and our love of justice, we sent commissioners to the United States to propose a fair and amicable settlement of all questions of public debt or property which might be in dispute. But the Government at Washington, denying our right to self-government, refused even to listen to any proposals for a peaceful separation. Nothing was then left to us but to prepare for war.

The first year in our history has been the most eventful in the annals of this continent. A new government has been established, and its machinery put in operation over an area exceeding seven hundred thousand square miles. The great principles upon which we have been willing to hazard everything that is dear to man have made conquests for us which could never have been achieved by the sword. Our Confederacy has grown from six to thirteen States; and Maryland, already united to us by hallowed memories and material interests, will, I believe, when able to speak with unstifled voice, connect her destiny with the South. . . .

The period is near at hand when our foes must sink under the immense load of debt which they have incurred, a debt which in their effort to subjugate us has already attained such fearful dimensions as will subject them to burthens which must continue to oppress them for generations to come.

We, too, have had our trials and difficulties. That we are to escape them in future is not to be hoped. It was to be expected when we entered upon this war that it would expose our people to sacrifices and cost them much, both of money and blood. But we knew the value of the object for which we struggle, and understood the nature of the war in which we were engaged. Nothing could be so bad as failure, and any sacrifice would be cheap as the price of success in such a contest. . . .

It was, perhaps, in the ordination of Providence, that we were to be taught the value of our liberties by the price which we pay for them.

The recollections of this great contest, with all its common traditions of glory, of sacrifice and of blood, will be the bond of harmony and enduring affection amongst the people; producing unity in policy, fraternity in sentiment, and joint effort in war.

Nor have the material sacrifices of the past year been made without some corresponding benefits. If the acquiescence of foreign nations in a pretended blockade has deprived us of our commerce with them, it is fast making us a self-supporting and an independent people. The blockade, if effectual and permanent, could only serve to divert our industry from the production of articles for export, and employ it in supplying commodities for domestic use.

It is a satisfaction that we have maintained the war by our unaided exertions. We have neither asked nor received assistance from any quarter. Yet the interest involved is not wholly our own. The world at large is concerned in opening our markets to its commerce. When the independence of the confederate States is recognized by the nations of the earth, and we are free to follow our interests and inclinations by cultivating foreign

trade, the Southern States will offer to manufacturing nations the most favorable markets which ever invited their commerce. Cotton, sugar, rice, tobacco, provisions, timber and naval stores, will furnish attractive exchanges. Nor would the constancy of these supplies be likely to be disturbed by war. Our confederate strength will be too great to tempt aggression; and never was there a people whose interests and principles committed them so fully to a peaceful policy as those of the confederate States. By the character of their productions they are too deeply interested in foreign commerce wantonly to disturb it. War of conquest they cannot wage, because the constitution of their confederacy admits of no coërced association. Civil war there can not be between States held together by their volition only. The rule of voluntary association, which cannot fail to be conservative, by securing just and impartial government at home, does not diminish the security of the obligations by which the confederate States may be bound to foreign nations. In proof of this it is to be remembered that, at the first moment of asserting their right of secession, these States proposed a settlement on the basis of a common liability for the obligations of the General Government.

Fellow-citizens, after the struggles of ages had consecrated the right of the Englishman to constitutional representative government, our colonial ancestors were forced to vindicate that birthright by an appeal to arms. Success crowned their efforts, and they provided for their posterity a peaceful remedy against future aggression.

The tyranny of an unbridled majority, the most odious and least responsible form of despotism, has denied us both the right and remedy. Therefore we are in arms to renew such sacrifices as our fathers made to the holy cause of constitutional liberty. At the darkest hour of our struggle the provisional gives place to the permanent government. After a series of successes and victories, which covered our arms with glory, we have recently met with serious disasters. But in the heart of a people resolved to be free, these disasters tend but to stimulate to increased resistance.

To show ourselves worthy of the inheritance bequeathed to us by the patriots of the Revolution, we must emulate that heroic devotion which made reverse to them but the crucible in which their patriotism was refined.

With confidence in the wisdom and virtue of those who will share with me the responsibility, and aid me in the conduct of public affairs; securely relying on the patriotism and courage of the people, of which the present war has furnished so many examples, I deeply feel the weight of the responsibilities I now, with unaffected diffidence, am about to assume; and, fully realizing the inequality of human power to guide and to sustain, my hope is reverently fixed on Him whose favor is ever vouchsafed to the cause which is just. With humble gratitude and adoration, acknowledging the Providence which has so visibly protected the Confederacy during its brief but eventful career, to Thee, O God! I trustingly commit myself, and prayerfully invoke thy blessing on my country and its cause.

Mississippi Resolutions on Secession, November 30, 1860

(Laws of Mississippi, 1860, p. 43 ff.)

On secession in Mississippi, see D. L. Dumond, *The Secession Movement,* ch. x; J. F. H. Claiborne, *Life and Correspondence of John A. Quitman;* J. F. Garner, "The First Struggle over Secession in Mississippi," Mississippi Hist. Soc., *Publications,* Vol. IV.

Whereas, The Constitutional Union was formed by the several States in their separate sovereign capacity for the purpose of mutual advantage and protection;

That the several States are distinct sovereignties, whose supremacy is limited so far only as the same has been delegated by voluntary compact to a Federal Government, and when it fails to accomplish the ends for which it was established, the parties to the compact have the right to resume, each State for itself, such delegated powers;

That the institution of slavery existed prior to the formation of the Federal Constitution, and is recognized by its letter, and all efforts to impair its value or lessen its duration by Congress, or any of the free States, is a violation of the compact of Union and is destructive of the ends for which it was ordained, but in defiance of the principles of the Union thus established, the people of the Northern States have assumed a revolutionary position towards the Southern States;

That they have set at defiance that provision of the Constitution which was intended to secure domestic tranquillity among the States and promote their general welfare, namely: "No person held to service or labor in one State, under the laws thereof, escaping into another, shall, in consequence of any law or regulation therein, be discharged from such service or labor, but shall be delivered up on claim of the party to whom such service or labor may be due;"

That they have by voluntary associations, individual agencies and State legislation interfered with slavery as it prevails in the slaveholding States;

That they have enticed our slaves from us, and by State intervention obstructed and prevented their rendition under the fugitive slave law;

That they continue their system of agitation obviously for the purpose of encouraging other slaves to escape from service, to weaken the institution in the slave-holding States by rendering the holding of such property insecure, and as a consequence its ultimate abolition certain;

That they claim the right and demand its execution by Congress to exclude slavery from the Territories, but claim the right of protection for every species of property owned by themselves;

That they declare in every manner in which public opinion is expressed their unalterable determination to exclude from admittance into the Union any new State that tolerates slavery in its Constitution, and thereby force Congress to a condemnation of that species of property;

That they thus seek by an increase of abolition States "to acquire two-thirds of both houses" for the purpose of preparing an amendment to the Constitution of the United States, abolishing slavery in the States, and so continue the agitation that the proposed amendment shall be ratified by the Legislatures of three-fourths of the States;

That they have in violation of the comity of all civilized nations, and in violation of the comity established by the Constitution of the United States, insulted and outraged our citizens when travelling among them for

pleasure, health or business, by taking their servants and liberating the same, under the forms of State laws, and subjecting their owners to degrading and ignominious punishment;

That to encourage the stealing of our property they have put at defiance that provision of the Constitution which declares that fugitives from justice (escaping) into another State, on demand of the Executive authority of that State from which he fled, shall be delivered up;

That they have sought to create domestic discord in the Southern States by incendiary publications;

That they encouraged a hostile invasion of a Southern State to excite insurrection, murder and rapine;

That they have deprived Southern citizens of their property and continue an unfriendly agitation of their domestic institutions, claiming for themselves perfect immunity from external interference with their domestic policy; . . .

That they have elected a majority of Electors for President and Vice-President on the ground that there exists an irreconcilable conflict between the two sections of the Confederacy in reference to their respective systems of labor and in pursuance of their hostility to us and our institutions, thus declaring to the civilized world that the powers of this Government are to be used for the dishonor and overthrow of the Southern Section of this great Confederacy. Therefore,

Be it resolved by the Legislature of the State of Mississippi, That in the opinion of those who now constitute the said Legislature, the secession of each aggrieved State is the proper remedy for these injuries.

President Davis's Message to the Confederate Congress, April 29, 1861

(Richardson, ed. *Messages and Papers of the Confederacy*, Vol. I, p. 63 ff.)

Davis called the Confederate Congress together in special session April 29, 1861. In his message he analyzed again the theory of the Union and the logic of secession. In this message he also asked for authority to prosecute the war: in response to his requests Congress at this session authorized him to use all the land and naval force of the Confederacy, to issue letters of marque, raise volunteers, make loans, etc. See, J. Davis, *Rise and Fall of the Confederate Government*, Vol. I, Part IV, ch. iv.

Gentlemen of the Congress. . . .

The declaration of war made against this Confederacy by Abraham Lincoln, the President of the United States, in his proclamation issued on the 15th day of the present month, rendered it necessary, in my judgment, that you should convene at the earliest practicable moment to devise the measures necessary for the defense of the country. The occasion is indeed an extraordinary one. It justifies me in a brief review of the relations heretofore existing between us and the States which now unite in warfare against us and in a succinct statement of the events which have resulted in this warfare, to the end that mankind may pass intelligent and impartial judgment on its motives and objects. During the war waged against Great Britain by her colonies on this continent a common danger impelled them to a close alliance and to the formation of a Confederation, by the terms of which the colonies, styling themselves States, entered "*severally* into a firm league of friendship with each other for their common defense, the security of their liberties, and their mutual and general welfare. binding themselves to assist each other against all force offered to or attacks made upon them, or any of them, on account of religion, sovereignty, trade, or any other pretense whatever." In order to guard against any misconstruction of their compact, the several States made explicit declaration in a distinct article—that "*each* State *retains its* sovereignty, freedom, and independence, and every power. jurisdiction, and right which is not by this Confederation *expressly delegated* to the United States in Congress assembled."

Under this contract of alliance, the war of the Revolution was successfully waged, and resulted in the treaty of peace with Great Britain in 1783, by the terms of which the several States were *each by name* recognized to be independent. The Articles of Confederation contained a clause whereby all alterations were prohibited unless confirmed by the Legislatures of *every State* after being agreed to by the Congress; and in obedience to this provision, under the resolution of Congress of the 21st of February, 1787, the several States appointed delegates who attended a convention "for the *sole and express purpose* of revising the Articles of Confederation and reporting to Congress and the several Legislatures such alterations and provisions therein as shall, when agreed to in Congress *and confirmed by the States,* render the Federal Constitution adequate to the exigencies of Government and the preservation of the Union." It was by the delegates chosen by the *several States* under the resolution just quoted that the Constitution of the United States was framed in 1787 and submitted to the *several States* for ratification, as shown by the seventh article. which is in these words: "The ratification of the *conventions of nine States* shall be sufficient for the establishment of this Constitution *between the States* so ratifying the same." . . . The Constitution of 1787, having, however, omitted the clause already recited from the Articles of Confederation, which provided in explicit terms that each State *retained* its sovereignty and independence, some alarm was felt in the States, when invited to ratify the Constitution, lest this omission should be construed into an abandonment of their cherished principle, and they refused to be satisfied until amendments were added to the Constitution placing beyond any pretense of doubt the reservation by the States of all their sovereign rights and powers not expressly delegated to the United States by the Constitution.

Strange. indeed, must it appear to the impartial observer, but it is none the less true that all these carefully worded clauses proved unavailing to prevent the rise and growth in the Northern States of a political school which has persistently claimed that the government thus formed was not a compact *between* States, but was in effect a national government, set up *above* and *over* the States. An organization created by the States to secure the blessings of liberty and independence against *foreign* aggression, has been gradually perverted into a machine for their control in their *domestic* affairs. The *creature* has been exalted above its *creators;* the *principals* have been made subordinate to the *agent* appointed by themselves. The people of the Southern States, whose almost exclusive occupation was agriculture, early perceived a tendency in the Northern States to render the common government subservient to their own purposes by imposing burdens on commerce as a protection to their manufacturing and shipping interests. . . . By degrees, as the Northern States gained preponderance in the National Congress, self-interest taught their people to yield ready assent to any plausible advocacy of their right as a majority to govern the minority without control. They learned to listen with impatience to the suggestion of any constitutional impediment to the exercise of their will, and so utterly have the principles of the Constitution been corrupted in the Northern mind that, in the inaugural address delivered by President Lincoln in March last, he asserts as an axiom, which he plainly deems to be undeniable, that the theory of the Constitution requires that in all cases the majority shall govern; . . . This is the lamentable and fundamental error on which rests the policy that has culminated in his declaration of war against these Confederate States. In addition to the long-continued and deepseated resentment felt by the Southern States at the persistent abuse of the powers they had delegated to the Congress, for the purpose of enriching the manufacturing and shipping classes of the North at the expense of the South, there has existed for nearly half a century another subject of discord, involving interests of such transcendent magnitude as at all times to create the apprehension in the minds of many devoted lovers of the Union that its permanence was impossible. When the several States .delegated certain powers to the United States Congress, a

large portion of the laboring population consisted of African slaves imported into the colonies by the mother country. In twelve out of the thirteen States negro slavery existed, and the right of property in slaves was protected by law. This property was recognized in the Constitution, and provision was made against its loss by the escape of the slave. The increase in the number of slaves by further importation from Africa was also secured by a clause forbidding Congress to prohibit the slave trade anterior to a certain date, and in no clause can there be found any delegation of power to the Congress authorizing it in any manner to legislate to the prejudice, detriment, or discouragement of the owners of that species of property, or excluding it from the protection of the Government.

The climate and soil of the Northern States soon proved unpropitious to the continuance of slave labor, whilst the converse was the case at the South. Under the unrestricted free intercourse between the two sections, the Northern States consulted their own interests by selling their slaves to the South and prohibiting slavery within their limits. The South were willing purchasers of property suitable to their wants, and paid the price of the acquisition without harboring a suspicion that their quiet possession was to be disturbed by those who were inhibited not only by want of constitutional authority, but by good faith as vendors, from disquieting a title emanating from themselves. As soon, however, as the Northern States that prohibited African slavery within their limits had reached a number sufficient to give their representation a controlling voice in the Congress, a persistent and organized system of hostile measures against the rights of the owners of slaves in the Southern States was inaugurated and gradually extended. A continuous series of measures was devised and prosecuted for the purpose of rendering insecure the tenure of property in slaves. . . . Emboldened by success, the theatre of agitation and aggression against the clearly expressed constitutional rights of the Southern States was transferred to the Congress; Senators and Representatives were sent to the common councils of the nation, whose chief title to this distinction consisted in the display of a spirit of ultra-fanaticism, and whose business was not "to promote the general welfare or insure domestic tranquillity," but to awaken the bitterest hatred against the citizens of sister States, by violent denunciation of their institutions; the transaction of public affairs was impeded by repeated efforts to usurp powers not delegated by the Constitution, for the purpose of impairing the security of property in slaves, and reducing those States which held slaves to a condition of inferiority. Finally a great party was organized for the purpose of obtaining the administration of the Government, with the avowed object of using its power for the total exclusion of the slave States from all participation in the benefits of the public domain acquired by all the States in common, whether by conquest or purchase; of surrounding them entirely by States in which slavery should be prohibited; of those rendering the property in slaves so insecure as to be comparatively worthless, and thereby annihilating in effect property worth thousands of millions of dollars. This party, thus organized, succeeded in the month of November last in the election of its candidate for the Presidency of the United States.

In the meantime, the African slaves had augmented in number from about 600,000, at the date of the adoption of the constitutional compact, to upward of 4,000,000. In moral and social condition they had been elevated from brutal savages into docile, intelligent, and civilized agricultural laborers, and supplied not only with bodily comforts but with careful religious instruction. Under the supervision of a superior race their labor had been so directed as not only to allow a gradual and marked amelioration of their own condition, but to convert hundreds of thousands of square miles of the wilderness into cultivated lands covered with a prosperous people; towns and cities had sprung into existence, and had rapidly increased in wealth and population under the social system of the South; the white population of the Southern slave-holding States had augmented from about 1,250,000 at the date of the adoption of the Constitution to more than 8,500,000, in 1860; and the productions in the South of cotton, rice, sugar, and tobacco, for the full development and continuance of which the labor of African slaves was and is indispensable, had swollen to an amount which formed nearly three-fourths of the exports

of the whole United States and had become absolutely necessary to the wants of civilized man. With interests of such overwhelming magnitude imperiled, the people of the Southern States were driven by the conduct of the North to the adoption of some course of action to avert the danger with which they were openly menaced. With this view the Legislatures of the several States invited the people to select delegates to conventions to be held for the purpose of determining for themselves what measures were best adapted to meet so alarming a crisis in their history. Here it may be proper to observe that from a period as early as 1798 there had existed in all of the States of the Union a party almost uninterruptedly in the majority based upon the creed that each State was, in the last resort, the sole judge as well of its wrongs as of the mode and measure of redress. . . .

. . . In the exercise of a right so ancient, so well-established, and so necessary for self-preservation, the people of the Confederate States, in their conventions, determined that the wrongs which they had suffered and the evils with which they were menaced required that they should revoke the delegation of powers to the Federal Government which they had ratified in their several conventions. They consequently passed ordinances resuming all their rights as sovereign and independent States and dissolved their connection with the other States of the Union.

Having done this, they proceeded to form a new compact amongst themselves by new articles of confederation, which have been also ratified by the conventions of the several States with an approach to unanimity far exceeding that of the conventions which adopted the Constitution of 1787. They have organized their new Government in all its departments; the functions of the executive, legislative, and judicial magistrates are performed in accordance with the will of the people, as displayed not merely in a cheerful acquiescence, but in the enthusiastic support of the Government thus established by themselves; and but for the interference of the Government of the United States in this legitimate exercise of the right of a people to self-government, peace, happiness, and prosperity would now smile on our land. . . .

Jefferson Davis.

Letter from Jefferson Davis to Abraham Lincoln on the Exchange and Treatment of Prisoners of War, July 6, 1861

RICHMOND, July 6, 1861.

To Abraham Lincoln, President and Commander in Chief of the Army and Navy of the United States.

Sir: Having learned that the schooner Savannah, a private armed vessel in the service, and sailing under a commission issued by authority of the Confederate States of America, had been captured by one of the vessels forming the blockading squadron off Charleston harbor, I directed a proposition to be made to the officer commanding that squadron for an exchange of the officers and crew of the Savannah for prisoners of war held by this Government "according to number and rank." To this proposition, made on the 19th ult., Captain Mercer, the officer in command of the blockading squadron, made answer on the same day that "the prisoners (referred to) are not on board of any of the vessels under my command."

It now appears by statements made without contradiction in newspapers published in New York, that the prisoners above mentioned were conveyed to that city, and have there been treated not as prisoners of war, but as criminals; that they have been put in irons, confined in jail, brought before the courts of justice on charges of piracy and treason, and it is even rumored that they have been actually convicted of the offenses charged, for no other reason than that they bore arms in defense of the rights of this Government and under the authority of its commission.

I could not, without grave discourtesy, have made the newspaper statements above referred to the subject of this communication, if the threat of treating as pirates the citizens of this Confederacy, armed for service on the high seas, had not been contained in your proclamation of the —— April last. That proclamation, however, seems to afford sufficient justification for considering these published statements as not devoid of probability.

It is the desire of this Government so to conduct the war now existing as to mitigate its horrors as far as may be possible; and, with this intent, its treatment of the prisoners captured by its forces has been marked by the greatest humanity and leniency consistent with public obligations; some have been permitted to return home on parôle, others to remain at large under similar conditions within this Confederacy, and all have been furnished with rations for their subsistence, such as are allowed to our own troops. It is only since the news has been received of the treatment of the prisoners taken on the Savannah that I have been compelled to withdraw these indulgences, and to hold the prisoners taken by us in strict confinement.

A just regard to humanity and to the honor of this Government now requires me to state explicitly that, painful as will be the necessity, this Government will deal out to the prisoners held by it the same treatment and the same fate as shall be experienced by those captured on the Savannah, and if driven to the terrible necessity of retaliation by your execution of any of the officers or the crew of the Savannah, that retaliation will be extended so far as shall be requisite to secure the abandonment of a practice unknown to the warfare of civilized man, and so barbarous as to disgrace the nation which shall be guilty of inaugurating it.

With this view, and because it may not have reached you, I now renew the proposition made to the commander of the blockading squadron to exchange for the prisoners taken on the Savannah, an equal number of those now held by us, according to rank. I am yours, etc.

JEFFERSON DAVIS,
President and Commander in Chief of the Army and Navy of the Confederate States.

Letter from General Robert E. Lee to President Davis Offering His Resignation, August 8, 1863

Camp Orange, Aug. 8, 1863.

Mr. President—Your letters of July 28 and August 2 have been received, and I have waited for a leisure hour to reply; but I fear that will never come. I am extremely obliged to you for the attention given to the wants of this army, and the efforts made to supply them. Our absentees are returning, and I hope the earnest and beautiful appeal made to the country in your proclamation may stir up the whole people, and that they may see their duty and perform it. Nothing is wanted but that their fortitude should equal their bravery, to insure the success of our cause. We must expect reverses, even defeats. They are sent to teach us wisdom and prudence; to call forth greater energies, and to prevent our falling into greater disasters. Our people have only to be true and united, to bear manfully the misfortunes incident to war, and all will come right in the end.

I know how prone we are to censure, and how ready to blame others for the non-fulfillment of our expectations. This is unbecoming in a generous people, and I grieve to see its expression. The general remedy for the want of success in a military commander is his removal. This is natural, and in many instances proper. For, no matter what may be the ability of the officer, if he loses the confidence of his troops, disaster must sooner or later come.

I have been prompted by these reflections more than once since my return from Pennsylvania to propose to Your Excellency the propriety of selecting another commander for this army. I have seen and heard of expressions of discontent in the public journals at the result of the expedition. I do not know how far this feeling extends in the army. My brother officers have been too kind to report it, and so far the troops have been too generous to exhibit it. It is fair, however, to suppose that it does exist, and success is so necessary to us that nothing should be risked to secure it. I, therefore, in all sincerity, request Your Excellency to take measures to supply my place. I do this with the more earnestness because no one is more aware than myself of my inability for the duties of my position. I can not even accomplish what I myself desire. How can I fulfil the expectations of others? In addition, I sensibly feel the growing failure of my bodily strength. I have not yet recovered from the attack I experienced the past spring. I am becoming more and more incapable of exertion, and am thus prevented from making the personal examinations and giving the personal supervisions to the operations in the field, which I feel to be necessary. I am so dull that in making use of the eyes of others I am frequently misled. Everything, therefore, points to the advantages to be derived from a new commander, and I the more anxiously urge the matter upon Your Excellency from my belief that a younger and abler man than myself can readily be obtained. I know that he will have as gallant and brave an army as ever existed to second his efforts, and it would be the happiest day of my life to see at its head a worthy leader; one that would accomplish more than I could perform, and all that I have wished. I hope that Your Excellency will attribute my request to the true reason, the desire to serve my country and to do all in my power to insure the success of her righteous cause.

I have no complaints to make of any one but myself. I have received nothing but kindness from those above me, and the most considerate attention from my comrades and companions in arms. To Your Excellency, I am specially indebted for uniform kindness and consideration. You have done everything in your power to aid me in the work committed to my charge, without omitting anything to promote the general welfare. I pray that your efforts may at length be crowned with success, and that you may long live to enjoy the thanks of a grateful people.

With sentiments of great esteem, I am very respectfully and truly yours,

R.E. Lee, General

Letter of President Davis to General Lee Rejecting Lee's Offer to Resign, August 11, 1863

General:

Yours of the 8th inst. has been received. I am glad to find that you concur so entirely with me as to the want of our country in this trying hour, and am happy to add that after the first depression consequent upon our disasters in the West, indications have appeared that our people will exhibit that fortitude which we agree in believing is alone needful to secure ultimate success.

It well became Sydney Johnston when overwhelmed by a senseless clamor to admit the rule that success is the test of merit, and yet there has been nothing which I have found to require a greater effort of patience than to bear the criticisms of the ignorant, who pronounce everything a failure which does not equal their expectations or desires, and can see no good result which is not in the line of their own imaginings. I admit the propriety of your conclusions, that an officer who loses the confidence of his troops should have his position changed, whatever may be his ability; but when I read the sentence, I was not at all prepared for the application you were about to make. Expressions of discontent in the public journals furnish but little evidence of the sentiment of an army. I wish I could feel that the public journals were not generally partisan or venal.

Were you capable of stooping to it, you could easily surround yourself with those who would fill the press with your laudations, and seek to exalt you for what you had not done rather than detract from the achievements which will make you and your army the subject of history and object of the world's admiration for generations to come.

I am truly sorry to know that you still feel the effects of the illness you suffered last Spring, and can readily understand the embarrassments you experience in using the eyes of others, having been so much accustomed to make your own reconnaissances. Practice will however do much to relieve that embarrassment, and the minute knowledge of the country which you have acquired will render you less dependent for topographical information.

But suppose, my dear friend, that I were to admit, with all their implications, the points which you present, where am I to find that new commander who is to possess the greater ability which you believe to be required. I do not doubt the readiness with which you would give way to one who could accomplish all that you have wished, and you will do me the justice to believe that if Providence would kindly offer such a person for our use, I would not hesitate to avail of his services.

My sight is not sufficiently penetrating to discover such hidden merit if it exists, and I have but used to you the language of sober earnestness, when I have impressed upon you the propriety of avoiding all unnecessary exposure to danger because I felt our country could not bear to lose you. To ask me to substitute you by some one in my judgment more fit to command, or who would possess more of the confidence of the army or of the reflecting men in the country is to demand for me an impossibility.

It only remains for me to hope that you will take all possible care of yourself, that your health and strength may be entirely restored, and that the Lord will preserve you for the important duties devolved upon you in the struggle of our suffering country, for the independence which we have engaged in war to maintain.

As ever very respectfully and truly yours,

Jeffn. Davis

Letter from General Lee to President Davis on the Punishment of Deserters, April 13, 1864

H^D Q^{RS} Army N. Va.

13th April 1864.

His Excy Jefferson Davis,
    Presdt. Confed. States,
        Richmond,

Mr. President,

I have the honor to acknowledge the receipt of the letter of Col Lee written by your directions, with reference to the case of Privt Jacob Shomore Co. B. 52nd Va. Regt. and requesting my views as to the policy of extending clemency to other offenders now in confinement, or undergoing punishment.[1] With regard to prvt. Shomore, my endorsement expressed the opinion I had formed from reading the application for pardon, and the endorsements of

Gens. Ewell & Early. I had not seen, nor have I yet read the record of the case, it being one of these tried by Gen Ewell's Military court before the late law requiring these proceedings to be reviewed by me. My views are based upon those considerations of policy which experience has satisfied me to be sound, and which are adverse to leniency, except in cases showing some reason for mitigation. The fact that prvt. Shomore had been a good soldier previous to his desertion, is insisted upon, as it frequently has been in like cases, as a ground of mitigation, and were he alone concerned, I would be disposed to give weight to it. But I am satisfied that it would be impolitic and unjust to the rest of the army to allow previous good conduct alone to atone for an offence most pernicious to the service,

---

[1] Not found.

and most dangerous as an example. In this connection, I will lay before your Excellency some facts
that will assist you in forming your judgment, and
at the same time, present the opinions I have formed
on the subject of punishment in the army. In re-
viewing Court Martial cases, it has been my habit
to give the accused the benefit of all extenuating
circumstances that could be allowed to operate in
their favor without injury to the service. In addition to those parties whose sentences I have remitted
altogether or in part, or whom, when capitally convicted, I have recommended to pardon or commuta-
tion of punishment, I have kept a list during the
past winter of certain offenders, whose cases while
they could not be allowed to go unpunished altogether, without injury to the service, had some extenuating features connected with them. I confirmed
the sentences, and all of them have undergone a
part of their punishment, but recently I remitted
the remainder in the order of which I enclose a copy.

Beyond this, I do not think it prudent to go,
unless some reason be presented which will enable
me to be lenient without creating a bad precedent,
and encouraging others to become offenders. I have
arrived at this conclusion from experience. It is
certain that a relaxation of the sternness of discipline
as a mere act of indulgence, unsupported by good
reasons, is followed by an increase of the number of
offenders. The escape of one criminal encourages
others to hope for like impunity, and that encourage-
ment can be given as well by a repetition of a general
act of amnesty or pardon, as by frequent exercise
of clemency towards individuals. If the convicted
offenders alone were concerned, there would be no
objection to giving them another trial, as we should
be no worse off if they again deserted than before.
But the effect of the example is the chief thing to be
considered, and that it is injurious, I have no doubt.
Many more men would be lost to the service if a
pardon be extended in a large number of cases, than
would be restored to it by the immediate effects of
that action.

The military executions that took place to such
an extent last autumn, had a very beneficial influence,
but in my judgment, many of them would have been
avoided had the infliction of punishment in such
cases uniformly followed the commission of the
offence. But the failure of courts to convict or
sentence to death, the cases in which pardon or com-
mutation of punishment had been granted upon my
recommendation, and the instances in which the
same indulgence was extended by your Excellency
upon grounds made known to you by others, had
somewhat relaxed discipline in this respect, and the
consequences became immediately apparent in the
increased number of desertions. I think that a
return to the current policy would inevitably be
attended with like results. Desertion and absence
without leave are nearly the only offences ever tried
by our Courts. They appear to be almost the only
vices in the army. Notwithstanding the executions
that have recently taken place, I fear that the number of those who have escaped punishment in some
one of the ways above mentioned has had a bad effect
already. The returns for the month of March show
5474 men absent without leave, and 322 desertions
during the month. There have been 62 desertions
within the present month specially reported, but
the whole number I fear considerably exceeds that
some of the large number absent without leave, are
probably sick men who have failed to report, and
some of the deserters are probably absent without
leave, but the number is sufficiently great to show
the necessity of adhering to the only policy that will
restrain the evil, and which I am sure will be found
to be truly merciful in the end.[3] Desertions and
absence without leave not only weaken the army by
the number of offenders not reclaimed, but by the
guards that must be kept over those who are arrested.
I think therefore that it would not be expedient to

---

[3] The abstracts of field returns printed in the *Official
Records* do not generally indicate the number absent without
leave, and group under the caption "total number absent"

pardon & return to duty any of those now under
sentence, or release those under charges, except for
good cause shown.

I have the honour to be

With great respect

Your obt. servt.

R. E. LEE

Genl.

Letter from General Lee to President Davis Advocating the Use of Negro Troops, March 10, 1865

[MS in Robert Edward Lee Papers,
Duke University Library]

H^D Q^{RS} ARMIES C S
10th March 1865

His Exc^y Jeffⁿ Davis
Presd^t C States
Richmond

MR PRESIDENT,

I do not know whether the law authorising the use of negro troops has received your sanction, but if it has, I respectfully recommend that measures be taken to carry it into effect as soon as practicable.[19]

It will probably be impossible to get a large force of this kind in condition to be of service during the present campaign, but I think no time should be lost in trying to collect all we can. I attach great importance to the result of the first experiment with these troops, and think that if it prove successful, it will greatly lessen the difficulty of putting the law into operation.

I understand that the Governor of Virginia is

---

[19] Three days later Davis replied (O. R., 46, 2, 1308) : "I am in receipt of your favor in regard to the bill for putting negroes in the army. The bill was received from the Congress to-day and was immediately signed. I shall be pleased to receive such suggestions from you as will aid me in carrying out the law, and I trust you will endeavor in every available mode to give promptitude to the requisite action." The law allowed Davis to requisition as many slaves as were needed to defend the country (with the reservation that not more than one fourth of the slaves of any state would be called). Although the bill made no promises of freedom, it was generally understood that slaves who served in the army would be manumitted by the states. Some Negro troops were raised, but the law came too late to be of any value.

prepared to do all that may be required of him under the authority he possesses.[20] I hope it will be found practicable to raise some negro companies in Richmond, and have written to Gen Ewell to do all in his power to get them, as soon as he shall be informed in what manner to proceed.[21] In the beginning it would be well to do everything to make the enlistment entirely voluntary on the part of the negroes, and those owners who are willing to furnish some of their slaves for the purpose, can do a great deal to inspire them with the right feeling to prepare them to become soldiers, and to be satisfied with their new condition. I have received letters from persons offering to select the most suitable among their slaves, as soon as Congress should give the authority, and think that a considerable number would be forthcoming for the purpose if called for.

I hope that if you have approved the law, you will cause the necessary steps to carry it into effect to be taken as soon as possible.[22]

With great respect
Your ob[t] serv[t]
R E LEE
Genl

---

[20] "The governor of Virginia calls my attention to the fact that he has not received a requisition for slaves, as provided for in the act of the General Assembly," Davis informed Lee on March 24. Lee immediately asked Davis to "call upon the governor . . . for the whole number of negroes, slave and free, between the ages of eighteen and forty-five, for service as soldiers. . . . The services of these men are now necessary to enable us to oppose the enemy." O. R., 46, 3, 1339.

[21] Unfit for further field service, Ewell was in command of the Richmond defenses.

[22] On April 1, Davis unhappily informed Lee (O. R., 46, 3, 1370): "I have been laboring, without much progress, to advance the raising of negro troops."

President Davis's Views on the Use of Negro Troops.

Subsequent events advanced my views from a prospective to a present need for the enrollment of negroes to take their place in the ranks. Strenuously I argued the question with Members of Congress who called to confer with me. To a member of the Senate I stated, as I had done to many others, the fact of having led negroes against a lawless body of armed white men, and the assurance which the experiment gave me that they might, under proper conditions, be relied on in battle, and finally used to him the expression which I believe I can repeat exactly: "If the Confederacy falls, there should be written on its tombstone, 'Died of a theory'." General Lee was brought before a committee to state his opinion as to the probable efficiency of negroes as soldiers, and disappointed the probable expectation by his unqualified advocacy of the proposed measure.

President Davis's Last Message to the People of the Confederacy, April 4, 1865

(Richardson, ed. *Messages and Papers of the Confederacy*, Vol. I, p. 568 ff.)

On April 2, the Confederate Government abandoned Richmond and fled to Danville; the following day Richmond fell. President Davis's last appeal to the Confederate people reveals a stubborn determination to continue the war, but in this decision in which he was not supported by Lee, he was overruled by the course of events.

Danville, Va. April 4, 1865.
To the People of the Confederate States of America.

The General in Chief of our Army has found it necessary to make such movements of the troops as to uncover the capital and thus involve the withdrawal of the Government from the city of Richmond.

It would be unwise, even were it possible, to conceal the great moral as well as material injury to our cause that must result from the occupation of Richmond by the enemy. It is equally unwise and unworthy of us, as patriots engaged in a most sacred cause, to allow our energies to falter, our spirits to grow faint, or our efforts to become relaxed under reverses, however calamitous. While it has been to us a source of national pride that for four years of unequaled warfare we have been able, in close proximity to the center of the enemy's power, to maintain the seat of our chosen Government free from the pollution of his presence; while the memories of the heroic dead who have freely given their lives to its defense must ever remain enshrined in our hearts; while the preservation of the capital, which is usually regarded as the evidence to mankind of separate national existence, was an object very dear to us, it is also true, and should not be forgotten, that the loss which we have suffered is not without compensation. For many months the largest and finest army of the Confederacy, under the command of a leader whose presence inspires equal confidence in the troops and the people, has been greatly trammeled by the necessity of keeping constant watch over the approaches to the capital, and has thus been forced to forego more than one opportunity for promising enterprise. The hopes and confidence of the enemy have been constantly excited by the belief that their possession of Richmond would be the signal for our submission to their rule, and relieve them from the burden of war, as their failing resources admonish them it must be abandoned if not speedily brought to a successful close. It is for us, my countrymen, to show by our bearing under reverses how wretched has been the self-deception of those who have believed us less able to endure misfortune with fortitude than to encounter danger with courage. We have now entered upon a new phase of a struggle the memory of which is to endure for all ages and to shed an increasing luster upon our country.

Relieved from the necessity of guarding cities and particular points, important but not vital to our defense, with an army free to move from point to point and strike in detail the detachments and garrisons of the enemy, operating on the interior of our own country, where supplies are more accessible, and where the foe will be far removed from his own base and cut off from all succor in case of reverse, nothing is now needed to render our triumph certain but the exhibition of our own unquenchable resolve. Let us but will it, and we are free; and who, in the light of the past, dare doubt your purpose in the future?

Animated by the confidence in your spirit and fortitude, which never yet has failed me, I announce to you, fellow-countrymen, that it is my purpose to maintain your cause with my whole heart and soul; that I will never consent to abandon to the enemy one foot of the soil of any one of the States of the Confederacy. . . . If by stress of numbers we should ever be compelled to a temporary withdrawal from her limits, or those of any other border State, again and again will we return, until the baffled and exhausted enemy shall abandon in despair his endless and impossible task of making slaves of a people resolved to be free.

Let us not, then, despond, my countrymen; but, relying on the never-failing mercies and protecting care of our God, let us meet the foe with fresh defiance, with unconquered and unconquerable hearts.

Jeff'n Davis.

Jefferson Davis's Letter to His Wife from Jail, Fortress Monroe, November 3, 1865

My dear Wife,
    Yours of the 23 Ulto. received this day and brought
the only cheering ray which can light up the gloom of
my imprisonment. When I grow restless from desire to
receive another letter from you I draw comfort from
reperusal of those preserved.

    I am sustained by a Power I know not of. When
Franklin was brought before the privy council of
George III, and a time-serving courtier heaped the
grossest indignities upon him, he bore them with com-
posure, and afterward attributed his ability to do so
to the consciousness of innocence in the acts which he
was reviled.

    What, under Providence, may be in store for us I
have no ability to foresee. I have tried to do my duty
to my fellowmen, and I have the sustaining belief that
He who is full of mercy, and knowing my inmost heart,
will acquit me, where man, blind man seeks to condemn.

Jefferson Davis's Letter to His Wife from Jail, November 21, 1865

F. Monroe 21 Nov. 65

My dear Wife

I have the happiness to acknowledge yours of the 7th Inst. God be praised for your welfare and for the kind friends He has drawn around you in the day of your affliction.

To make the best of the existing condition is alike required by patriotism and practical sense. The negro is unquestionably to be at last the victim; but it is possible to defer the conflict and to preserve a part of the kind relations heretofore existing between the races, when a life-long common interest united them. The object is worthy all the effort. To be successful, the policy must be as far removed from the conservatism that rejects everything new, as from the idealism which would retain nothing which is old. If catch-words determine who shall mould the institutions and administer the affairs of the Southern States - the deluge. Though neither a spectator nor an actor, a life spent more in the service of my country than in that of my family, leaves me now unable to disengage myself from the considerations of public interests.

Let me renew the caution against believing the statements of correspondents in regard to me. To calumniate a state prisoner and thus either gratify or excite hatred against him, is an old device, and never was a fairer opportunity presented to do so without the fear of contradiction than is offered in my case.

Letter from Robert E. Lee to Jefferson Davis, June 1, 1867, on the Occasion of the Former President's Release from Jail

Lexington, Va.
1 June 1867

My dear Mr. Davis,

You can conceive better than I can express the misery which your friends have suffered from your long imprisonment and the other afflictions incident thereto. To none has this been more painful than to me, and the impossibility of affording relief has added to my distress. Your release has lifted a load from my heart which I have not words to tell, and my daily prayer to the great Ruler of the World is that He may shield you from all future harm, guard you from all evil and give you that peace which the world cannot take away.

That the rest of your days may be triumphantly happy, is the sincere and earnest wish of your most obt. faithful friend and sevt.

R.E. Lee

Letter from Jefferson Davis to His Wife from Scotland, Summer 1869

The country above the Tweed, the Ettrick
and the Yarrow is the best combination of
the beautiful, the useful, and the grand
that I have beheld. There is in the people
the warmest hospitality and cheerful
greetings - Many ask for you and regret
your absence.

I send you a few sprigs only of interest
because of the localities where they were
gathered. The little daisy was plucked
from the ground near the depository of the
Heart of Bruce. The harebell grew near to
the Tomb of Scott. Another, the smallest,
from Arthur's seat. The little white
flower is from the plain where Lord
Marmion is described as pausing enraptured
with the beauties of the Firth of Forth
and the plains of Down Edin.

**Letter from Jefferson Davis to His Wife on the Feared Death at Sea of
   Her Youngest Brother, November 11, 1875**

(EXPLANATORY NOTE: A San Francisco news dispatch
announced the sinking of the steamship Pacific which
ran between that city and Seattle and which had been
rammed by a large sailing vessel in a dense fog. The
dispatch stated that its Captain, Jefferson Davis
Howell, was lost. The news was to prove true. Only
twenty-eight, the youngest of Varina's brothers was
the most promising and the only one who achieved even
the slightest success. After Captain Howell had seen
his three hundred passengers safely removed from the
sinking vessel, he stripped to his underclothes and
swam to a raft with an old lady clinging to him. After
three days and four nights of hunger and exposure to
cold, Jeffy D. slipped off the raft and was swallowed
up by the sea. Davis was as grieved as his wife, for
he regarded him as a son.)

My dear Wife,

> I have deferred writing you under the hope
> that an answer would come to a telegram I
> sent to William Howell in San Francisco
> asking for reliable information in regard to
> brother Jefferson.

> Though grievously anxious I am not despondent.
> ....Our dear boy was strong in body and
> in heart, he was skillful in all which was
> needful in case of a wreck. Too true to his
> trust to leave his ship while there was
> anything for the Capt. to do, he would see
> the danger and provide for it by constructing
> a raft which would live in ordinary weather
> for many days. His physical and moral strength
> would endure much, and in the thoroughfare of
> ships would be probably rescued. God grant
> that my hopes may soon be fulfilled and our
> sorrow turned to rejoicing. For you my dear
> Wife, my heart is sore, and I long to be with
> you in this day of trial.

> The pride I felt in the gallantry and success
> of our boy as a Sailor is both humbled and
> rebuked. Of all the earth you alone suffer as
> I do, and you I hope will feel the trust
> which supports me.

With love to our children and all a heart can
feel of devotion to you I am affectionately

Your Husband

Jefferson Davis's Dedication in His Two-Volume History of the Civil War, *The Rise and Fall of the Confederate Government,* to The Women of the Confederacy, June 1881

TO THE WOMEN OF THE CONFEDERACY, whose pious ministrations to our wounded soldiers soothed the last hours of those who died far from the objects of their tenderest love; whose domestic labors contributed much to supply the wants of our defenders in the field; whose zealous faith in our cause shone a guiding star undimmed by the darkest clouds of war; whose fortitude sustained them under all the privations to which they were subjected; whose annual tribute expresses their enduring grief, love, and reverence for our sacred dead; and whose patriotism will teach their children to emulate the deeds of our revolutionary sires; these pages are dedicated by their countryman,

JEFFERSON DAVIS

Conclusion of *The Rise and Fall of the Confederate Government,* June 1881

CONCLUSION.

MY first object in this work was to prove, by historical authority, that each of the States, as sovereign parties to the compact of Union, had the reserved power to secede from it whenever it should be found not to answer the ends for which it was established. If this has been done, it follows that the war was, on the part of the United States Government, one of aggression and usurpation, and, on the part of the South, was for the defense of an inherent, unalienable right.

My next purpose was to show, by the gallantry and devotion of the Southern people, in their unequal struggle, how thorough was their conviction of the justice of their cause; that, by their humanity to the wounded and captives, they proved themselves the worthy descendants of chivalric sires, and fit to be free; and that, in every case, as when our army invaded Pennsylvania, by their respect for private rights, their morality and observance of the laws of civilized war, they are entitled to the confidence and regard of mankind.

The want of space has compelled me to omit a notice of many noble deeds, both or heroic men and women. The roll of honor, merely, would fill more than the pages allotted to this work. To others, who can say *cuncta quorum vidi*, I must leave the pleasant task of paying the tribute due to their associate patriots.

In asserting the right of secession, it has not been my wish to incite to its exercise: I recognize the fact that the war showed it to be impracticable, but this did not prove it to be wrong; and, now that it may not be again attempted, and that the Union may promote the general warfare, it is needful that the truth, the whole truth, should be known, so that crimination and recrimination may for ever cease, and then, on the basis of fraternity and faithful regard for the rights of the States, there may be written on the arch of the Union, *Esto perpetua.*

The Presidency of the United States, a Comment by Jefferson Davis

I had been so near the office for four years, while in the Cabinet of Mr. Pierce, that I saw it from behind the scenes, and it was to me an office in no wise desirable. The responsibilities were great; the labor, the vexations, the disappointments, were greater. Those who have intimately known the official and personal life of our Presidents can not fail to remember how few have left the office as happy men as when they entered it, how darkly the shadows gathered around the setting sun, and how eagerly the multitude would turn to gaze upon another orb just rising to take its place in the political firmament.

Worn by incessant fatigue, broken in fortune, debarred by public opinion, prejudice, or tradition, from future employment, the wisest and best who have filled that office have retired to private life, to remember rather the failure of their hopes than the success of their efforts. He must, indeed, be a self-confident man that could hope to fill the chair of WASHINGTON with satisfaction to himself, with the assurance of receiving on his retirement the meed awarded by the people to that great man, that he had "lived enough for life and for glory," or even of feeling that the sacrifice of self had been compensated by the service rendered to his country.

The Emancipation Proclamation, January 1, 1863

(*U. S. Statutes at Large*, Vol. XII, p. 1268–9)

As early as July 22, 1862, Lincoln had read to his Cabinet a preliminary draft of an emancipation proclamation. At this time Secretary Seward suggested that the proclamation should not be issued until a military victory had been won. The battle of Antietam gave Lincoln his desired opportunity; on the 22 of September he read to his Cabinet a second draft of the proclamation. After some modifications this was issued as a preliminary proclamation; the formal and definite proclamation came January 1, 1863. The *Diaries* of Welles, Chase, and Bates give interesting records of the Cabinet meetings. This proclamation was particularly important in its effect upon European, especially English, public opinion. See E. D. Adams, *Great Britain and the American Civil War*, 2 Vols.; D. Jordan and E. J. Pratt, *Europe and the American Civil War;* W. R. West, *Contemporary French Opinion on the American Civil War.* On the con-

stitutionality of emancipation, see J. G. Randall, *Constitutional Problems Under Lincoln*, chs. xv–xvi.

BY THE PRESIDENT OF THE UNITED
STATES OF AMERICA:

A Proclamation.

Whereas on the 22d day of September, A.D. 1862, a proclamation was issued by the President of the United States, containing, among other things, the following, to wit:

"That on the 1st day of January, A.D. 1863, all persons held as slaves within any State or designated part of a State the people whereof shall then be in rebellion against the United States shall be then, thenceforward, and forever free; and the executive government of the United States, including the military and naval authority thereof, will recognize and maintain the freedom of such persons and will do no act or acts to repress such persons, or any of them, in any efforts they may make for their actual freedom.

"That the executive will on the 1st day of January aforesaid, by proclamation, designate the States and parts of States, if any, in which the people thereof, respectively, shall then be in rebellion against the United States; and the fact that any State or the people thereof shall on that day be in good faith represented in the Congress of the United States by members chosen thereto at elections wherein a majority of the qualified voters of such States shall have participated shall, in the absence of strong countervailing testimony, be deemed conclusive evidence that such State and the people thereof are not then in rebellion against the United States."

Now, therefore, I, Abraham Lincoln, President of the United States, by virtue of the power in me vested as Commander-in-Chief of the Army and Navy of the United States in time of actual armed rebellion against the authority and government of the United States, and as a fit and necessary war measure for suppressing said rebellion, do, on this 1st day of January, A.D. 1863, and in accordance with my purpose so to do, publicly proclaimed for the full period of one hundred days from the first day above mentioned, order and designate as the States and parts of States wherein the people thereof, respectively, are this day in rebellion against the United States the following, to wit:

Arkansas, Texas, Louisiana (except the parishes of St. Bernard, Plaquemines, Jefferson, St. John, St. Charles, St. James, Ascension, Assumption, Terrebonne, Lafourche, St. Mary, St. Martin, and Orleans, including the city of New Orleans), Mississippi, Alabama, Florida, Georgia, South Carolina, North Carolina, and Virginia (except the forty-eight counties designated as West Virginia, and also the counties of Berkeley, Accomac, Northhampton, Elizabeth City, York, Princess Anne, and Norfolk, including the cities of Norfolk and Portsmouth), and which excepted parts are for the present left precisely as if this proclamation were not issued.

And by virtue of the power and for the purpose aforesaid, I do order and declare that all persons held as slaves within said designated States and parts of States are, and henceforward shall be, free; and that the Executive Government of the United States, including the military and naval authorities thereof, will recognize and maintain the freedom of said persons.

And I hereby enjoin upon the people so declared to be free to abstain from all violence, unless in necessary self-defense; and I recommend to them that, in all cases when allowed, they labor faithfully for reasonable wages.

And I further declare and make known that such persons of suitable condition will be received into the armed service of the United States to garrison forts, positions, stations, and other places, and to man vessels of all sorts in said service.

And upon this act, sincerely believed to be an act of justice, warranted by the Constitution upon military necessity, I invoke the considerate judgment of mankind and the gracious favor of Almighty God.

Jefferson Davis's Denial of Any Constitutional Right to Abolish Slavery. *(The Rise and Fall of the Confederate Government,* vol. 2, pp. 158-161)

At the commencement of the year 1862 it was the purpose of the United States Government to assail us in every manner and at every point and with every engine of destruction which could be devised. The usual methods of civilized warfare consist in the destruction of an enemy's military power and the capture of his capital. These, however, formed only a small portion of the purposes of *our* enemy. If peace with fraternity and equality in the Union, under the Constitution as interpreted by its framers, had been his aim, this was attainable without war; but, seeking supremacy at the cost of a revolution in the entire political structure, involving a subversion of the Constitution, the subjection of the States, the submission of the people, and the establishment of a union under the sword, his efforts were all directed to subjugation or extermination. Thus, while the Executive was preparing immense armies, iron-clad fleets, and huge instruments of war, with which to invade our territory and destroy our citizens, the willing aid of an impatient, enraged Congress was invoked to usurp new powers, to legislate the subversion of our social institutions, and to give the form of legality to the plunder of a frenzied soldiery.

That body had no sooner assembled than it brought forward the doctrine that the Government of the United States was engaged in a struggle for its existence, and could therefore resort to any measure which a case of self-defense would justify. It pretended not to know that the only self-defense authorized in the Constitution for the Government created by it, was by the peaceful method of the ballot-box; and that, so long as the Government fulfilled the objects of its creation (see preamble of the Constitution), and exercised its delegated powers within their prescribed limits, its surest and strongest defense was to be found in that ballot-box.

The Congress next declared that our institution of slavery was the cause of all the troubles of the country, and therefore the whole power of the Government must be so directed as to remove it. If this had really been the cause of the troubles, how easily wise and patriotic statesmen might have furnished a relief. Nearly all the slaveholding States had withdrawn from the Union, therefore those who had been suffering vicariously might have welcomed their departure, as the removal of the cause which disturbed the Union, and have tried the experiment of separation. Should the trial have brought more wisdom and a spirit of conciliation to either or both, there might have arisen, as a result of the experiment, a reconstructed fraternal Union such as our fathers designed.

The people of the seceded States had loved the Union. Shoulder to shoulder with the people of the other States, they had bled for its liberties and its honor. Their sacrifices in peace had not been less than those in war, and their attachment had not diminished by what they had given, nor were they less ready to give in the future. The concessions they had made for many years and the propositions which followed secession proved their desire to preserve the peace.

The authors of the aggressions which had disturbed the harmony of the Union had lately aquired power on a sectional basis, and were eager for the spoil of their sectional victory. To conceal their real motive, and artfully to appeal to the prejudice of foreigners, they declared that slavery was the cause of the troubles of the country, and of the "rebellion" which they were engaged in suppressing. In his inaugural address in March, 1861, President Lincoln said: "I have no purpose, directly or indirectly, to interfere with the institution of slavery in the States where it exists. I believe I have no lawful right to do so, and I have no inclination to do so." The leader (Sumner) of the Abolition party in Congress, on February 25, 1861, said in the Senate, "I take this occasion to declare most explicitly that I do not think that Congress has any right to interfere with slavery in a State." The principle thus announced had regulated all the legislation of Congress from the beginning of its first session in 1789 down to the first session of the Thirty-seventh Congress, commencing July 4, 1861.

A few months after the inaugural address above cited and the announcement of the fact above quoted were made, Congress commenced to legislate for the abolition of slavery. If it had the power now to do what it before had not, whence was it derived? There had been no addition in the interval to the grants in the Constitution; not a word or letter of that instrument had been changed since the possession of the power was disclaimed; yet after July 4, 1861, it was asserted by the majority in Congress that the Government had power to interfere with slavery in the States. Whence came the change? The answer is, It was wrought by the same process and on the same plea that tyranny has ever employed against liberty and justice—the time-worn excuse of usurpers—necessity; an excuse which is ever assumed as valid, because the usurper claims to be the sole judge of his necessity.

The Constitutions of the United States and of the Confederate States of America

THE CONSTITUTION OF THE UNITED STATES[1]

WE the People of the United States, in Order to form a more perfect Union, establish Justice, insure domestic Tranquility, provide for the common defence, promote the general Welfare, and secure the Blessings of Liberty to ourselves and our Posterity, do ordain and establish this CONSTITUTION for the United States of America.

CONSTITUTION OF THE CONFEDERATE STATES OF AMERICA.[2]

WE, the people of the *Confederate* States, *each State acting in its sovereign and independent character, in order to form a permanent federal government,* establish justice, insure domestic tranquillity, and secure the blessings of liberty to ourselves and our posterity—*invoking the favor and guidance of Almighty God*—do ordain and establish this Constitution for the *Confederate* States of America.

ARTICLE I.

SECTION. 1. All legislative Powers herein granted shall be vested in a Congress of the United States,

ARTICLE I.

SECTION 1. All legislative powers herein *delegated* shall be vested in a Congress of the *Con-*

1. This is an exact copy, except that interlineations are indicated by enclosing them in angle brackets < >, taken from Max Farrand, ed., *The Records of the Federal Convention,* 3 volumes (New Haven: Yale University Press, 1911), II, 651-664.

2. This is an exact copy, except that italics are used to indicate the differences between this constitution and its parent document, taken from the *Journal of the Congress of the Confederate States of America, 1861-1865* (Washington: Government Printing Office, 1904-1905), I, 909-923.

which shall consist of a Senate and House of Representatives.

SECTION. 2. The House of Representatives shall be composed of Members chosen every second Year by the People of the several States, and the Electors in each State shall have [the] Qualifications requisite for Electors of the most numerous Branch of the State Legislature.

No Person shall be a Representative who shall not have attained to the Age of twenty five Years, and been seven Years a Citizen of the United States, and who shall not, when elected, be an Inhabitant of that State in which he shall be chosen.

Representatives and direct Taxes shall be apportioned among the several States which may be included within this Union, according to their respective Numbers, which shall be determined by adding to the whole Number of free Persons, including those bound to Service for a Term of Years, and excluding Indians not taxed, three fifths of all other Persons. The actual Enumeration shall be made within three Years after the first Meeting of the Congress of the United States, and within every subsequent Term of ten Years, in such Manner as they shall by Law direct. The Number of Representatives

federate States, which shall consist of a Senate and House of Representatives.

SECTION 2. 1. The House of Representatives shall be composed of members chosen every second year by the people of the several States; and the electors in each State shall *be citizens of the Confederate States, and* have the qualifications requisite for electors of the most numerous branch of the State Legislature; *but no person of foreign birth, not a citizen of the Confederate States, shall be allowed to vote for any officer, civil or political, State or Federal.*

2. No person shall be a Representative who shall not have attained the age of twenty-five years, and *be a citizen of the Confederate* States, and who shall not, when elected, be an inhabitant of that State in which he shall be chosen.

3. Representatives and direct taxes shall be apportioned among the several States, which may be included within this *Confederacy,* according to their respective numbers, which shall be determined, by adding to the whole number of free persons, including those bound to service for a term of years, and excluding Indians not taxed, three-fifths of all *slaves.* The actual enumeration shall be made within three years after the first meeting of the Congress of the *Confederate* States, and within every subsequent term of ten years, in such manner as they shall by law direct. The number of Representa-

shall not exceed one for every thirty thousand, but each State shall have at Least one Representative; and until such enumeration shall be made, the State of New Hampshire shall be entitled to chuse three, Massachusetts eight, Rhode-Island and Providence Plantations one, Connecticut five, New-York six, New Jersey four, Pennsylvania eight, Delaware one, Maryland six, Virginia ten, North Carolina five, South Carolina five, and Georgia three.

When vacancies happen in the Representation from any State, the Executive Authority thereof shall issue Writs of Election to fill such Vacancies.

The House of Representatives shall chuse their Speaker and other Officers; and shall have the sole Power of Impeachment.

SECTION. 3. The Senate of the United States shall be composed of two Senators from each State, chosen by the Legislature thereof, for six Years; and each Senator shall have one Vote.

Immediately after they shall be assembled in Consequence of the first Election, they shall be divided as equally as may be into three Classes. The Seats of the

tives shall not exceed one for every *fifty* thousand, but each State shall have at least one Representative; and until such enumeration shall be made, the State of *South Carolina* shall be entitled to choose *six, the State of Georgia ten, the State of Alabama nine, the State of Florida two, the State of Mississippi seven, the State of Louisiana six, and the State of Texas six.*

4. When vacancies happen in the representation from any State, the Executive authority thereof shall issue writs of election to fill such vacancies.

5. The House of Representatives shall choose their Speaker and other officers; and shall have the sole power of impeachment, *except that any judicial or other Federal officer, resident and acting solely within the limits of any State, may be impeached by a vote of two-thirds of both branches of the Legislature thereof.*

SECTION 3. 1. The Senate of the *Confederate* States shall be composed of two Senators from each State, chosen for six years by the Legislature thereof, *at the regular session next immediately preceding the commencement of the term of service;* and each Senator shall have one vote.

2. Immediately after they shall be assembled, in consequence of the first election, they shall be divided as equally as may be into three classes. The seats of the

Senators of the first Class shall be vacated at the Expiration of the second Year, of the second Class at the Expiration of the fourth Year, and of the third class at the Expiration of the sixth Year, so that one third may be chosen every second Year; and if Vacancies happen by Resignation, or otherwise, during the Recess of the Legislature of any State, the Executive thereof may make temporary Appointments until the next Meeting of the Legislature, which shall then fill such Vacancies.

No Person shall be a Senator who shall not have attained to the Age of thirty Years, and been nine Years a Citizen of the United States, and who shall not, when elected, be an Inhabitant of that State for which he shall be chosen.

The Vice President of the United States shall be President of the Senate, but shall have no Vote, unless they be equally divided.

The Senate shall chuse their other Officers, and also a President pro tempore, in the Absence of the Vice President, or when he shall exercise the Office of President of the United States.

The Senate shall have the sole Power to try all Impeachments. When sitting for that Purpose, they shall be on Oath or Affirmation. When the President of the United States [is tried,] the Chief Justice shall preside: And no Person shall be convicted without the Concurrence of two-thirds of the Members present.

Senators of the first class shall be vacated at the expiration of the second year; of the second class at the expiration of the fourth year; and of the third class at the expiration of the sixth year; so that one-third may be chosen every second year; and if vacancies happen by resignation, or otherwise, during the recess of the Legislature of any State, the Executive thereof may make temporary appointments until the next meeting of the Legislature which shall then fill such vacancies.

3. No person shall be a Senator who shall not have attained the age of thirty years, and *be a citizen of the Confederate* States; and who shall not, when elected, be an inhabitant of *the* State for which he shall be chosen.

4. The Vice President of the *Confederate* States shall be President of the Senate, but shall have no vote unless they be equally divided.

5. The Senate shall choose their other officers; and also a President *pro tempore* in the absence of the Vice President, or when he shall exercise the office of President of the *Confederate* States.

6. The Senate shall have the sole power to try all impeachments. When sitting for that purpose, they shall be on oath or affirmation. When the President of the *Confederate* States is tried, the Chief Justice shall preside; and no person shall be convicted without the concurrence of two-thirds of the members present.

Judgment in Cases of Impeachment shall not extend further than to removal from Office, and disqualification to hold and enjoy any Office of honor, Trust or Profit under the United States: but the Party convicted shall nevertheless be liable and subject to Indictment, Trial, Judgment and Punishment, according to Law.

SECTION. 4. The Times, Places and Manner of holding Elections for Senators and Representatives, shall be prescribed in each State by the Legislature thereof; but the Congress may at any time by Law make or alter such Regulations, except as to the places of chusing Senators.

The Congress shall assemble at least once in every Year, and such Meeting shall be on the first Monday in December, unless they shall by Law appoint a different Day.

SECTION. 5. Each House shall be the Judge of the Elections, Returns and Qualifications of its own Members, and a Majority of each shall constitute a Quorum to do Business; but a smaller Number may adjourn from day to day, and may be authorized to compel the Attendance of absent Members, in such Manner, and under such Penalties as each House may provide.

Each House may determine the Rules of its Proceedings, punish its Members for disorderly Behaviour, and, with the Concur-

7. Judgment in cases of impeachment shall not extend further than to removal from office, and disqualification to hold and enjoy any office of honor, trust, or profit, under the *Confederate* States; but the party convicted shall, nevertheless, be liable and subject to indictment, trial, judgment and punishment according to law.

SECTION 4. 1. The times, place, and manner of holding elections for Senators and Representatives, shall be prescribed in each State by the Legislature thereof, *subject to the provisions of this Constitution;* but the Congress may, at any time, by law, make or alter such regulations, except as to the *times and* places of choosing Senators.

2. The Congress shall assemble at least once in every year; and such meeting shall be on the first Monday in December, unless they shall, by law, appoint a different day.

SECTION 5. 1. Each House shall be the judge of the elections, returns, and qualifications of its own members, and a majority of each shall constitute a quorum to do business; but a smaller number may adjourn from day to day, and may be authorized to compel the attendance of absent members, in such manner and under such penalties as each House may provide.

2. Each House may determine the rules of its proceedings, punish its members for disorderly behavior, and, with the concur-

rence of two-thirds, expel a Member.

Each House shall keep a Journal of its Proceedings, and from time to time publish the same, excepting such Parts as may in their Judgment require Secrecy; and the Yeas and Nays of the Members of either House on any question shall, at the Desire of one fifth of those Present, be entered on the Journal.

Neither House, during the Session of Congress, shall, without the Consent of the other, adjourn for more than three days, nor to any other Place than that in which the two Houses shall be sitting.

SECTION. 6. The Senators and Representatives shall receive a Compensation for their Services, to be ascertained by Law, and paid out of the Treasury of the United States. They shall in all Cases, except Treason, Felony and Breach of the Peace, be privileged from Arrest during their Attendance at the Session of their respective Houses, and in going to and returning from the same; and for any Speech or Debate in either House, they shall not be questioned in any other Place.

No Senator or Representative shall, during the Time for which he was elected, be appointed to any civil Office under the Authority of the United States, which shall have been created, or the Emoluments whereof shall have encreased during such time; and no Person holding any Office under the United States, shall be

rence of two thirds of the whole number, expel a member.

3. Each House shall keep a journal of its proceedings, and from time to time publish the same, excepting such parts as may in their judgment require secrecy; and the yeas and nays of the members of either House, on any question, shall, at the desire of one fifth of those present, be entered on the journal.

4. Neither House, during the session of Congress, shall, without the consent of the other, adjourn for more than three days, nor to any other place than that in which the two Houses shall be sitting.

SECTION 6. 1. The Senators and Representatives shall receive a compensation for their services, to be ascertained by law, and paid out of the Treasury of the *Confederate* States. They shall, in all cases, except treason, felony and breach of the peace, be privileged from arrest during their attendance at the session of their respective Houses, and in going to and returning from the same; and for any speech or debate in either House, they shall not be questioned in any other place.

2. No Senator or Representative shall, during the time for which he was elected, be appointed to any civil office under the authority of the *Confederate* States, which shall have been created, or the emoluments whereof shall have been increased during such time; and no person holding any office under the *Confederate* States shall

a Member of either House during his Continuance in Office.

be a member of either House during his continuance in office. *But Congress may, by law, grant to the principal officer in each of the executive departments a seat upon the floor of either House, with the privilege of discussing any measures appertaining to his department.*

SECTION. 7. All Bills for raising Revenue shall originate in the House of Representatives; but the Senate may propose or concur with Amendments as on other Bills.

Every Bill which shall have passed the House of Representatives and the Senate, shall, before it become a Law, be presented to the President of the United States; If he approve he shall sign it, but if not he shall return it, with his Objections to that House in which it shall have originated, who shall enter the Objections at large on their Journal, and proceed to reconsider it. If after such Reconsideration two thirds of that House shall agree to pass the Bill, it shall be sent, together with the Objections, to the other House, by which it shall likewise be reconsidered, and if approved by two thirds of that House, it shall become a Law. But in all such Cases the Votes of both Houses shall be determined by yeas and nays, and the Names of the Persons voting for and against the Bill shall be entered on the Journal of each House respectively. If any Bill shall not be returned by the President within ten Days (Sundays

SECTION 7. 1. All bills for raising revenue shall originate in the House of Representatives; but the Senate may propose or concur with amendments, as on other bills.

2. Every bill which shall have passed *both Houses*, shall, before it becomes a law, be presented to the President of the *Confederate* States; if he approve, he shall sign it; but if not, he shall return it, with his objections, to that House in which it shall have originated, who shall enter the objections at large on their journal, and proceed to reconsider it. If, after such reconsideration, two-thirds of that House shall agree to pass the bill, it shall be sent, together with the objections, to the other House, by which it shall likewise be reconsidered, and if approved by two-thirds of that House, it shall become a law. But, in all such cases, the votes of both Houses shall be determined by yeas and nays, and the names of the persons voting for and against the bill shall be entered on the journal of each House respectively. If any bill shall not be returned by the President within ten days (Sundays excepted) after it shall have been presented to

excepted) after it shall have been presented to him, the Same shall be a law, in like Manner as if he had signed it, unless the Congress by their Adjournment prevent its Return, in which Case it shall not be a Law.

Every Order, Resolution, or Vote to which the Concurrence of the Senate and House of Representatives may be necessary (except on a question of Adjournment) shall be presented to the President of the United States; and before the Same shall take Effect, shall be approved by him, or being disapproved by him, shall be repassed by two thirds of the Senate and House of Representatives, according to the Rules and Limitations prescribed in the Case of a Bill.

SECTION. 8. The Congress shall have Power

To lay and collect Taxes, Duties, Imposts and Excises, to pay the Debts and Provide for the common Defence and general Welfare of the United States; but all Duties, Imposts and Excises shall be uniform throughout the United States;

him, the same shall be a law, in like manner as if he had signed it, unless the Congress, by their adjournment, prevent its return; in which case it shall not be a law. *The President may approve any appropriation and disapprove any other appropriation in the same bill. In such case he shall, in signing the bill, designate the appropriations disapproved; and shall return a copy of such appropriations, with his objections, to the House in which the bill shall have originated; and the same proceeding shall then be had as in case of other bills disapproved by the President.*

3. Every order, resolution or vote, to which the concurrence of *both Houses* may be necessary (except on a question of adjournment), shall be presented to the President of the *Confederate* States; and, before the same shall take effect, shall be approved by him; or, being disapproved by him, shall be repassed by two-thirds of *both Houses,* according to the rules and limitations prescribed in case of a bill.

SECTION 8. The Congress shall have power—

1. To lay and collect taxes, duties, imposts, and excises, *for revenue necessary* to pay the debts, provide for the common defence, *and carry on the Government of the Confederate* States; *but no bounties shall be granted from the Treasury; nor shall any duties or taxes on im-*

To borrow Money on the credit of the United States;

To regulate Commerce with foreign Nations, and among the several States, and with the Indian Tribes;

To establish an uniform Rule of Naturalization, and uniform Laws on the subject of Bankruptcies throughout the United States;

To coin Money, regulate the Value thereof, and of foreign Coin, and fix the Standard of Weights and Measures;

To provide for the Punishment of counterfeiting the Securities

portations from foreign nations be laid to promote or foster any branch of industry; and all duties, imposts, and excises shall be uniform throughout the Confederate States:

2. To borrow money on the credit of the *Confederate* States:

3. To regulate commerce with foreign nations, and among the several States, and with the Indian tribes; *but neither this, nor any other clause contained in the Constitution, shall ever be construed to delegate the power to Congress to appropriate money for any internal improvement intended to facilitate commerce; except for the purpose of furnishing lights, beacons, and buoys, and other aid to navigation upon the coasts, and the improvement of harbors and the removing of obstructions in river navigation, in all which cases, such duties shall be laid on the navigation facilitated thereby, as may be necessary to pay the costs and expenses thereof:*

4. To establish uniform *laws* of naturalization, and uniform laws on the subject of bankruptcies, throughout the *Confederate* States; *but no law of Congress shall discharge any debt contracted before the passage of the same:*

5. To coin money, regulate the value thereof and of foreign coin, and fix the standard of weights and measures:

6. To provide for the punishment of counterfeiting the securi-

and current Coin of the United States;

To establish Post Offices and post Roads;

To promote the Progress of Science and useful Arts, by securing for limited Time to Authors and Inventors the exclusive Right to their respective Writings and Discoveries;

To constitute Tribunals inferior to the supreme Court;

To define and punish Piracies and Felonies committed on the high Seas, and Offences against the Law of Nations;

To declare War, grant Letters of Marque and Reprisal, and make Rules concerning Captures on Land and Water;

To raise and support Armies, but no Appropriation of Money to that Use shall be for a longer Term than two Years;

To provide and maintain a Navy;

To make Rules for the Government and Regulation of the land and naval Forces;

To provide for calling forth the Militia to execute the Laws of the Union, suppress Insurrections and repel Invasions;

To provide for organizing, arming, and disciplining, the Militia, and for governing such Part of them as may be employed in the Service of the United States, reserving to the States respectively,

ties and current coin of the *Confederate* States:

7. To establish post-offices and post-*routes; but the expenses of the Post-office Department, after the first day of March, in the year of our Lord eighteen hundred and sixty-three, shall be paid out of its own revenues:*

8. To promote the progress of science and useful arts, by securing for limited times to authors and inventors the exclusive right to their respective writings and discoveries:

9. To constitute tribunals inferior to the Supreme Court:

10. To define and punish piracies and felonies committed on the high-seas, and offences against the law of nations:

11. To declare war, grant letters of marque and reprisal, and make rules concerning captures on land and on water:

12. To raise and support armies, but no appropriation of money to that use shall be for a longer term than two years:

13. To provide and maintain a navy:

14. To make rules for the government and regulation of the land and naval forces:

15. To provide for calling forth the militia to execute the laws of the *Confederate* States, suppress insurrections, and repel invasions:

16. To provide for organizing, arming, and disciplining the militia, and for governing such part of them as may be employed in the service of the *Confederate* States, reserving to the States,

the Appointment of the Officers, and the Authority of training the Militia according to the discipline prescribed by Congress;

To exercise exclusive Legislation in all Cases whatsoever, over such District (not exceeding ten Miles square) as may, by Cession of particular States, and the Acceptance of Congress, become the Seat of the Government of the United States, and to exercise like Authority over all Places purchased by the Consent of the Legislature of the State in which the Same shall be, for the Erection of Forts, Magazines, Arsenals, dock-Yards, and other needful Buildings;—And

To make all Laws which shall be necessary and proper for carrying into Execution the foregoing Powers, and all other Powers vested by this Constitution in the Government of the United States, or in any Department or Officer thereof.

SECTION. 9. The Migration or Importation of such Persons as any of the States now existing shall think proper to admit, shall not be prohibited by the Congress prior to the Year one thousand eight hundred and eight, but a Tax or duty may be imposed on such Importation, not exceeding ten dollars for each Person.

The Privilege of the Writ of Habeas Corpus shall not be sus-

respectively, the appointment of the officers, and the authority of training the militia according to the discipline prescribed by Congress:

17. To exercise exclusive legislation in all cases whatsoever, over such district (not exceeding ten miles square) as may, by cession of *one or more* States and the acceptance of Congress, become the seat of the Government of the *Confederate* States: and to exercise like authority over all places purchased by the consent of the Legislature of the State in which the same shall be, for the erection of forts, magazines, arsenals, dockyards, and other needful buildings: and

18. To make all laws which shall be necessary and proper for carrying into execution the foregoing powers, and all other powers vested by this Constitution in the Government of the *Confederate* States, or in any department or officer thereof.

SECTION 9. 1. The importation of *negroes of the African race, from any foreign country other than the slave-holding States or Territories of the United States of America, is hereby forbidden; and Congress is required to pass such laws as shall effectually prevent the same.*

2. *Congress shall also have power to prohibit the introduction of slaves from any State not a member of, or Territory not belonging to, this Confederacy.*

3. The privilege of the writ of *habeas corpus* shall not be sus-

pended, unless when in Cases of Rebellion or Invasion the public Safety may require it.

No Bill of Attainder or ex post facto Law shall be passed.

No Capitation, or other direct, Tax shall be laid, unless in Proportion to the Census or Enumeration herein before directed to be taken.

No Tax or Duty shall be laid on Articles exported from any State.

No Preference shall be given by any Regulation of Commerce or Revenue to the Ports of one State over those of another: nor shall Vessels bound to, or from, one State, be obliged to enter, clear, or pay Duties in another.

No Money shall be drawn from the Treasury, but in Consequence of Appropriations made by Law; and a regular Statement and Account of the Receipts and Expenditures of all public Money shall be published from time to time.

pended, unless when in case of rebellion or invasion the public safety may require it.

4. No bill of attainder, *ex post facto law, or law denying or impa[i]ring the right of property in negro slaves shall be passed.*

5. No capitation or other direct tax shall be laid, unless in proportion to the census or enumeration hereinbefore directed to be taken.

6. No tax or duty shall be laid on articles exported from any State *except by a vote of two-thirds of both Houses.*

7. No preference shall be given by any regulation of commerce or revenue to the ports of one State over those of another.

8. No money shall be drawn from the treasury, but in consequence of appropriations made by law; and a regular statement and account of the receipts and expenditures of all public money shall be published from time to time.

9. *Congress shall appropriate no money from the treasury except by a vote of two-thirds of both Houses, taken by yeas and nays, unless it be asked and estimated for by some one of the heads of departments, and submitted to Congress by the President; or for the purpose of paying its own expenses and contingencies; or for the payment of claims against the Confederate States, the justice of which shall have*

been judicially declared by a tribunal for the investigation of claims against the Government, which it is hereby made the duty of Congress to establish.

10. All bills appropriating money shall specify in federal currency the exact amount of each appropriation, and the purposes for which it is made; and Congress shall grant no extra compensation to any public contractor, officer, agent or servant, after such contract shall have been made or such service rendered.

No Title of Nobility shall be granted by the United States: And no Person holding any Office of Profit or Trust under them, shall, without the Consent of the Congress, accept of any present, Emolument, Office, or Title, of any kind whatever, from any King, Prince, or foreign State.

11. No title of nobility shall be granted by the *Confederate* States; and no person holding any office of profit or trust under them, shall, without the consent of the Congress, accept of any present, emolument, office or title of any kind whatever, from any king, prince, or foreign state.

12. Congress shall make no law respecting an establishment of religion, or prohibiting the free exercise thereof; or abridging the freedom of speech, or of the press; or the right of the people peaceably to assemble and petition the government for a redress of grievances.

13. A well-regulated militia being necessary to the security of a free state, the right of the people to keep and bear arms shall not be infringed.

14. No soldier shall, in time of peace, be quartered in any house without the consent of the owner; nor in time of war, but in a manner to be prescribed by law.

15. The right of the people to

be secure in their persons, houses, papers, and effects, against unreasonable searches and seizures, shall not be violated; and no warrants shall issue but upon probable cause, supported by oath or affirmation, and particularly describing the place to be searched, and the persons or things to be seized.

16. No person shall be held to answer for a capital or otherwise infamous crime, unless on a presentment or indictment of a grand jury, except in cases arising in the land or naval forces, or in the militia, when in actual service in time of war or public danger; nor shall any person be subject, for the same offence, to be twice put in jeopardy of life or limb; nor be compelled, in any criminal case, to be a witness against himself; nor be deprived of life, liberty, or property, without due process of law; nor shall private property be taken for public use without just compensation.

17. In all criminal prosecutions, the accused shall enjoy the right to a speedy and public trial, by an impartial jury of the State and district wherein the crime shall have been committed, which district shall have been previously ascertained by law, and to be informed of the nature and cause of the accusation; to be confronted with the witnesses against him; to have compulsory process for obtaining witnesses in his favor; and to have the assistance of counsel for his defence.

18. In suits at common law,

where the value in controversy shall exceed twenty dollars, the right of trial by jury shall be preserved; and no fact *so* tried by a jury shall be otherwise re-examined in any court of the *Confederacy*, than according to the rules of common law.

19. Excessive bail shall not be required, nor excessive fines imposed, nor cruel and unusual punishment inflicted.

20. *Every law, or resolution having the force of law, shall relate to but one subject, and that shall be expressed in the title.*

SECTION. 10. No State shall enter into any Treaty, Alliance, or Confederation; grant Letters of Marque and Reprisal; coin Money; emit Bills of Credit; make any Thing but gold and silver Coin a Tender in Payment of Debts; pass any Bill of Attainder, ex post facto Law, or Law impairing the Obligation of Contracts, or grant any Title of Nobility.

SECTION 10. 1. No State shall enter into any treaty, alliance, or confederation; grant letters of marque and reprisal; coin money; make anything but gold and silver coin a tender in payment of debts; pass any bill of attainder, or *ex post facto* law, or law impairing the obligation of contracts, or grant any title of nobility.

No State shall, without Consent of [the] Congress, lay any Imposts or Duties on Imports or Exports, except what may be absolutely necessary for executing its inspection Laws: and the net Produce of all Duties and Imposts, laid by any State on Imports or Exports, shall be for the Use of the Treasury of the United States; and all such Laws shall be subject to the Revision and Control of [the] Congress.

2. No State shall, without the consent of the Congress, lay any imposts or duties on imports or exports, except what may be absolutely necessary for executing its inspection laws; and the nett produce of all duties and imposts, laid by any State on imports or exports, shall be for the use of the Treasury of the *Confederate* States; and all such laws shall be subject to the revision and control of Congress.

No State shall, without the Consent of Congress, lay any Duty of Tonnage, keep Troops, or Ships of

3. No State shall, without the consent of Congress, lay any duty on tonnage, *except on sea-going*

War in time of Peace, enter into any Agreement or Compact with another State, or with a foreign Power, or engage in War, unless actually invaded, or in such imminent Danger as will not admit of delay.

vessels, for the improvement of its rivers and harbors navigated by the said vessels; but such duties shall not conflict with any treaties of the Confederate States with foreign nations; and any surplus revenue thus derived, shall, after making such improvement, be paid into the common treasury. Nor shall any State keep troops or ships-of-war in time of peace, enter into any agreement or compact with another State, or with a foreign power, or engage in war, unless actually invaded, or in such imminent danger as will not admit of delay. *But when any river divides or flows through two or more States, they may enter into compacts with each other to improve the navigation thereof.*

ARTICLE. II.

SECTION. 1. The executive Power shall be vested in a President of the United States of America. He shall hold his Office during the Term of four Years, and, together with the Vice President, chosen for the same Term, be elected, as follows

Each State shall appoint, in such Manner as the Legislature thereof may direct, a Number of Electors, equal to the whole Number of Senators and Representatives to which the State may be entitled in the Congress: but no Senator or Representative, or Person holding an Office of Trust or

ARTICLE II.

SECTION 1. 1. The executive power shall be vested in a President of the *Confederate* States of America. *He and the Vice President shall hold their offices for* the term of *six* years; *but the President shall not be re-eligible. The President and the Vice-President shall* be elected as follows:

2. Each State shall appoint, in such manner as the Legislature thereof may direct, a number of electors equal to the whole number of Senators and Representatives to which the State may be entitled in the Congress; but no Senator or Representative, or person holding an office of trust or

Profit under the United States, shall be appointed an Elector.

[3]The Electors shall meet in their respective States, and vote by Ballot for two Persons, of whom one at least shall not be an Inhabitant of the same State with themselves. And they shall make a List of all the Persons voted for, and of the Number of Votes for each; which List they shall sign and certify, and transmit sealed to the Seat of the Government of the United States, directed to the President of the Senate. The President of the Senate shall, in the Presence of the Senate and House of Representatives, open all the Certificates, and the Votes shall then be counted. The Person having the greatest Number of Votes shall be the President, if such Number be a Majority of the whole Number of Electors appointed; and if there be more than one who have such Majority and have an equal Number of Votes, then the House of Representatives shall immediately chuse by Ballot one of them for President; and if no Person have a Majority, then from the five highest on the List the said House shall in like Manner chuse the President. But in chusing the President, the Votes shall be taken by States, the Representation from each State having one Vote; a quorum for this Purpose shall consist of a Member or Members from two thirds of the States, and a Majority of all

profit under the *Confederate* States, shall be appointed an elector.

3. The electors shall meet in their respective States and vote by ballot for President and Vice President, one of whom, at least, shall not be an inhabitant of the same State with themselves; they shall name in their ballots the person voted for as President, and in distinct ballots the person voted for as Vice President, and they shall make distinct lists of all persons voted for as President, and of all persons voted for as Vice President, and of the number of votes for each, which lists they shall sign and certify, and transmit, sealed, to the seat of the government of the *Confederate* States, directed to the President of the Senate; the President of the Senate shall, in the presence of the Senate and House of Representatives, open all the certificates, and the votes shall then be counted, the person having the greatest number of votes for President shall be the President, if such number be a majority of the whole number of electors appointed; and if no person have such majority, then, from the persons having the highest numbers, not exceeding three, on the list of those voted for as President, the House of Representatives shall choose immediately, by ballot, the President. But in choosing the President, the votes shall be taken by States the representation from each State having one vote; a

3. Superseded by the twelfth amendment.

the States shall be necessary to a Choice. In every Case, after the Choice of the President, the Person having the greatest Number of Votes of the Electors shall be the Vice President. But if there should remain two or more who have equal Votes, the Senate shall chuse from them by Ballot the Vice President.

The Congress may determine the Time of chusing the Electors, and the Day on which they shall give their Votes; which Day shall be the same throughout the United States.

No Person except a natural born Citizen or a Citizen of the United States, at the time of the Adoption of this Constitution, shall be eligible to the Office of President;

quorum for this purpose shall consist of a member or members from two-thirds of the States, and a majority of all the States shall be necessary to a choice. And if the House of Representatives shall not choose a President, whenever the right of choice shall devolve upon them, before the fourth day of March next following, then the Vice-President shall act as President, as in the case of the death or other constitutional disability of the President.

4. The person having the greatest number of votes as Vice President, shall be the Vice President, if such number be a majority of the whole number of electors appointed; and if no person have a majority, then, from the two highest numbers on the list, the Senate shall choose the Vice President; a quorum for the purpose shall consist of two-thirds of the whole number of Senators, and a majority of the whole number shall be necessary to a choice.

5. But no person constitutionally ineligible to the office of President shall be eligible to that of Vice President of the *Confederate* States.

6. The Congress may determine the time of choosing the electors, and the day on which they shall give their votes; which day shall be the same through out the *Confederate* States.

7. No person except a natural born citizen of the *Confederate* States, or a citizen thereof at the time of the adoption of this Constitution, *or a citizen thereof born*

neither shall any person be eligible to that Office who shall not have attained to the Age of thirty five Years, and been fourteen Years a Resident within the United States.

In Case of the Removal of the President from Office, or of his Death, Resignation, or Inability to discharge the Powers and Duties of the said office, the Same shall devolve on the Vice President, and the Congress may by Law provide for the Case of Removal, Death, Resignation, or Inability, both of the President and Vice President, declaring what Officer shall then act as President, and such Officer shall act accordingly, until the Disability be removed, or a President shall be elected.

The President shall, at stated Times, receive for his Services, a Compensation, which shall neither be encreased nor diminished during the Period for which he shall have been elected, and he shall not receive within that Period any other Emolument from the United States, or any of them.

Before he enter on the Execution of his Office, he shall take the following Oath or Affirmation:—

"I do solemnly swear (or affirm) that I will faithfully execute the Office of President of the United States, and will to the best of my

in the United States prior to the 20th of December, 1860, shall be eligible to the office of President; neither shall any person be eligible to that office who shall not have attained the age of thirty-five years, and been fourteen years a resident within the limits of the Confederate States, as they may exist at the time of his election.

8. In case of the removal of the President from office, or of his death, resignation, or inability to discharge the powers and duties of the said office, the same shall devolve on the Vice President; and the Congress may, by law, provide for the case of removal, death, resignation, or inability, both of the President and Vice President, declaring what officer shall then act as President; and such officer shall act accordingly, until the disability be removed or a President shall be elected.

9. The President shall, at stated times, receive for his services a compensation, which shall neither be increased nor diminished during the period for which he shall have been elected; and he shall not receive within that period any other emolument from the Confederate States, or any of them.

10. Before he enters on the execution of his office, he shall take the following oath or affirmation:

"I do solemnly swear (or affirm) that I will faithfully execute the office of President of the Confederate States of America, and will, to the best of my ability, preserve,

Ability, preserve, protect and defend the Constitution of the United States."

SECTION. 2. The President shall be Commander in Chief of the Army and Navy of the United States, and of the Militia of the several States, when called into the actual Service of the United States; he may require the Opinion, in writing, of the principal Officer in each of the executive Departments, upon any Subject relating to the Duties of their respective Offices, and he shall have Power to grant Reprieves and Pardons for Offences against the United States, except in Cases of impeachment.

He shall have Power, by and with the Advice and Consent of the Senate, to make Treaties, provided two thirds of the Senators present concur; and he shall nominate, and by and with the Advice and Consent of the Senate, shall appoint Ambassadors, other public Ministers and Consuls, Judges of the supreme Court, and all other Officers of the United States, whose Appointments are not herein otherwise provided for, and which shall be established by Law: but the Congress may by law vest the Appointment of such inferior Officers, as they think proper, in the President alone, in the Courts of Law, or in the Heads of Departments.

protect, and defend the Constitution *thereof.*"

SECTION 2. 1. The President shall be commander-in-chief of the Army and Navy of the *Confederate* States, and of the militia of the several States, when called into the actual service of the *Confederate* States; he may require the opinion, in writing, of the principal officer in each of the executive departments, upon any subject relating to the duties of their respective offices, and he shall have power to grant reprieves and pardons for offences against the *Confederate States,* except in cases of impeachment.

2. He shall have power, by and with the advice and consent of the Senate, to make treaties; provided two thirds of the Senators present concur; and he shall nominate, and by and with the advice and consent of the Senate, shall appoint ambassadors, other public ministers and consuls, judges of the Supreme Court and all other officers of the *Confederate* States, whose appointments are not herein otherwise provided for, and which shall be established by law; but the Congress may, by law, vest the appointment of such inferior officers, as they think proper, in the President alone, in the courts of law, or in the heads of departments.

3. *The principal officer in each of the executive departments, and all persons connected with the diplomatic service, may be removed from office at the pleasure*

of the President. All other civil officers of the executive departments may be removed at any time by the President, or other appointing power, when their services are unnecessary, or for dishonesty, incapacity, inefficiency, misconduct, or neglect of duty; and, when so removed, the removal shall be reported to the Senate, together with the reasons therefor.

The President shall have Power to fill up all Vacancies that may happen during the Recess of the Senate, by granting Commissions which shall expire at the End of their next Session.

4. The President shall have power to fill up all vacancies that may happen during the recess of the Senate, by granting commissions which shall expire at the end of their next session; but no person rejected by the Senate shall be re-appointed to the same office during their ensuing recess.

SECTION. 3. He shall from time to time give to the Congress Information of the State of the Union, and recommend to their consideration such Measures as he shall judge necessary and expedient; he may, on extraordinary Occasions, convene both Houses, or either of them, and in Case of Disagreement between them, with Respect to the time of Adjournment, he may adjourn them to such Time as he shall think proper; he shall receive Ambassadors and other public Ministers; he shall take Care that the Laws be faithfully executed, and shall Commission all the officers of the United States.

SECTION 3. 1. *The President* shall, from time to time, give to the Congress information of the state of the *Confederacy*, and recommend to their consideration such measures as he shall judge necessary and expedient: he may, on extraordinary occasions, convene both Houses, or either of them; and in case of disagreement between them, with respect to the time of adjournment, he may adjourn them to such time as he shall think proper; he shall receive ambassadors and other public ministers; he shall take care that the laws be faithfully executed, and shall commission all the officers of the *Confederate* States.

SECTION. 4. The President, Vice President and all civil Officers of the United States, shall be

SECTION 4. The President, Vice President, and all civil officers of the *Confederate* States, shall be

removed from Office on Impeachment for, and conviction of, Treason, Bribery, or other high Crimes
and Misdemeanors.

ARTICLE. III.

SECTION. 1. The judicial Power
of the United States, shall be
vested in one supreme Court, and
in such inferior Courts as the Congress may from time to time
ordain and establish. The Judges,
both of the supreme and inferior
Courts, shall hold their offices
during good Behavior, and shall,
at stated times, receive for their
Services, a Compensation, which
shall not be diminished during
their Continuance in Office.

SECTION. 2. The judicial Power
shall extend to all Cases, in Law
and Equity, arising under this
Constitution, the Laws of the
United States, and Treaties made,
or which shall be made, under
their Authority;—to all Cases affecting Ambassadors, other public
Ministers and Consuls;—to all
Cases of admiralty and maritime
Jurisdiction;—to Controversies to
which the United States shall be a
Party;—to Controversies between
two or more States;—between a
State and Citizens of another
State;—between Citizens of different States;—between Citizens
of the same State claiming Lands
under Grants of different States,
and between a State, or the Citizens thereof, and foreign States,
Citizens or Subjects.

In 'all Cases affecting Ambassadors, other public Ministers and

removed from office on impeachment, for and conviction of, treason, bribery, or other high crimes
and misdemeanors.

ARTICLE III.

SECTION 1. 1. The judicial power of the *Confederate* States shall
be vested in one Supreme Court,
and in such inferior Courts, as the
Congress may, from time to time,
ordain and establish. The judges,
both of the Supreme and inferior
Courts, shall hold their offices
during good behavior, and shall,
at stated times, receive for their
services a compensation which
shall not be diminished during
their continuance in office.

SECTION 2. 1. The judicial power shall extend to all cases arising
under this Constitution, the laws
of the *Confederate* States, and
treaties made, or which shall be
made, under their authority; to
all cases affecting ambassadors,
other public ministers and consuls; to all cases of admiralty and
maritime jurisdiction; to controversies to which the *Confederate*
States shall be a party; to controversies between two or more
States; between a State and
citizens of another State, *where
the State is plaintiff;* between citizens claiming lands under grants
of different States; and between a
State or the citizens thereof, and
foreign states, citizens or subjects;
*but no State shall be sued by a
citizen or subject of any foreign
state.*

2. In all cases affecting ambassadors, other public ministers and

Consuls, and those in which a State shall be Party, the supreme Court shall have original Jurisdiction. In all the other Cases before mentioned, the supreme Court shall have appellate Jurisdiction, both as to Law and Fact, with such Exceptions, and under such Regulations as the Congress shall make.

The trial of all Crimes, except in Cases of Impeachment, shall be by Jury; and such Trial shall be held in the State where the said Crimes shall have been committed; but when not committed within any State, the Trial shall be at such Place or Places as the Congress may by Law have directed.

SECTION. 3. Treason against the United States, shall consist only in levying War against them, or in adhering to their Enemies, giving them Aid and Comfort. No Person shall be convicted of Treason unless on the Testimony of two Witnesses to the same overt Act, or on Confession in open Court.

The Congress shall have Power to declare the Punishment of Treason, but no Attainder of Treason shall work Corruption of Blood, or Forfeiture except during the Life of the Person attainted.

ARTICLE. IV.

SECTION. 1. Full Faith and Credit shall be given in each State to the public Acts, Records, and judicial Proceedings of every other State. And the Congress may by general Laws prescribe

consuls, and those in which a State shall be a party, the Supreme Court shall have original jurisdiction. In all the other cases before mentioned, the Supreme Court shall have appellate jurisdiction both as to law and fact, with such exceptions and under such regulations as the Congress shall make.

3. The trial of all crimes, except in cases of impeachment, shall be by jury, and such trial shall be held in the State where the said crimes shall have been committed; but when not committed within any State, the trial shall be at such place or places as the Congress may by law have directed.

SECTION 3. 1. Treason against the *Confederate* States shall consist only in levying war against them, or in adhering to their enemies, giving them aid and comfort. No person shall be convicted of treason unless on the testimony of two witnesses to the same overt act, or on confession in open court.

2. The Congress shall have power to declare the punishment of treason; but no attainder of treason shall work corruption of blood, or forfeiture, except during the life of the person attainted.

ARTICLE IV.

SECTION 1. 1. Full faith and credit shall be given in each State to the public acts, records, and judicial proceedings of every other State. And the Congress may, by general laws, prescribe the

the Manner in which such Acts, Records and Proceedings shall be proved, and the Effect thereof.

SECTION. 2. The Citizens of each State shall be entitled to all Privileges and Immunities of Citizens in the several States.

A Person charged in any State with Treason, Felony, or other Crime, who shall flee from Justice, and be found in another State, shall on Demand of the executive Authority of the State from which he fled, be delivered up, to be removed to the State having Jurisdiction of the Crime.

No Person held to Service or Labour in one State, under the Laws thereof, escaping into another, shall, in Consequence of any Law or Regulation therein, be discharged from such Service or Labour, but shall be delivered up on Claim of the Party to whom such Service or Labour may be due.

SECTION. 3. New States may be admitted by the Congress into this Union; but no new State shall be formed or erected within the Jurisdiction of any other State; nor any State be formed by the Junction of two or more States, or Parts of States, without the Consent of the Legislatures of the

manner in which such acts, records, and proceedings shall be proved, and the effect thereof.

SECTION 2. 1. The citizens of each State shall be entitled to all the privileges and immunities of citizens in the several States, *and shall have the right of transit and sojourn in any State of this Confederacy, with their slaves and other property; and the right of property in said slaves shall not be thereby impaired.*

2. A person charged in any State with treason, felony, or other crime *against the laws of such State,* who shall flee from justice, and be found in another State, shall, on demand of the Executive authority of the State from which he fled, be delivered up, to be removed to the State having jurisdiction of the crime.

3. *No slave or other* person held to service or labor *in any State or Territory of the Confederate States,* under the laws thereof, escaping *or lawfully carried* into another, shall, in consequence of any law or regulation therein, be discharged from such service or labor: but shall be delivered up on claim of the party *to whom such slave belongs, or* to whom such service or labor may be due.

SECTION 3. 1. *Other States may be admitted into this Confederacy by a vote of two-thirds of the whole House of Representatives and two-thirds of the Senate, the Senate voting by States;* but no new State shall be formed or erected within the jurisdiction of any other State; nor any State

States concerned as well as of the Congress.

The Congress shall have power to dispose of and make all needful Rules and Regulations respecting the Territory or other Property belonging to the United States; and nothing in this Constitution shall be so construed as to Prejudice any Claims of the United States, or of any particular State.

be formed by the junction of two or more States, or parts of States, without the consent of the legislatures of the States concerned, as well as of the Congress.

2. The Congress shall have power to dispose of and make all needful rules and regulations *concerning* the *property of the Confederate* States, *including the lands thereof.*

3. *The Confederate States may acquire new territory; and Congress shall have power to legislate and provide governments for the inhabitants of all territory belonging to the Confederate States, lying without the limits of the several States; and may permit them, at such times, and in such manner as it may by law provide, to form States to be admitted into the Confederacy. In all such territory, the institution of negro slavery, as it now exists in the Confederate States, shall be recognized and protected by Congress and by the territorial government: and the inhabitants of the several Confederate States and Territories shall have the right to take to such Territory any slaves lawfully held by them in any of the States or Territories of the Confederate States.*

SECTION. 4. The United States shall guarantee to every State in this Union a Republican Form of Government, and shall protect each of them against Invasion; and on Application of the Legisla-

4. The *Confederate* States shall guarantee to every State *that now is, or hereafter may become, a member of this Confederacy,* a republican form of government; and shall protect each of them against

ture, or of the Executive (when the Legislature cannot be convened) against domestic Violence.

ARTICLE. V.

The Congress, whenever two thirds of both Houses shall deem it necessary, shall propose Amendments to this Constitution, or, on the Application of the Legislatures of two thirds of the several States, shall call a Convention for proposing Amendments, which, in either Case, shall be valid to all Intents and Purposes, as Part of this Constitution, when ratified by the Legislatures of three fourths of the several States, or by Conventions in three fourths thereof, as the one or the other Mode of Ratification may be proposed by the Congress; Provided that no Amendment which may be made prior to the Year One thousand eight hundred and eight shall in any Manner affect the first and fourth Clauses in the Ninth Section of the first Article; and that no State, without its Consent, shall be deprived of its equal Suffrage in the Senate.

ARTICLE. VI.

All Debts contracted and Engagements entered into, before the Adoption of this Constitution, shall be as valid against the United States under this Constitution, as under the Confederation.

invasion; and on application of the legislature, (or of the executive when the legislature *is not in session*,) against domestic violence.

ARTICLE V.

SECTION 1. 1. *Upon the demand of any three States, legally assembled in their several conventions, the Congress shall summon a Convention of all the States, to take into consideration such amendments to the Constitution as the said States shall concur in suggesting at the time when the said demand is made; and should any of the proposed amendments to the Constitution be agreed on by the said Convention—voting by States—and the same be ratified by the legislatures of two-thirds of the several States, or by conventions in two-thirds thereof—as the one or the other mode of ratification may be proposed by the general Convention—they shall thenceforward form a part of this Constitution.* But no State shall, without its consent, be deprived of its equal *representation* in the Senate.

ARTICLE VI.

1. *The Government established by this Constitution is the sucessor of the Provisional Government of the Confederate States of America, and all the laws passed by the latter shall continue in force until the same shall be repealed or modified; and all the officers appointed by the same shall remain in office until their*

This Constitution, and the Laws of the United States which shall be made in Pursuance thereof; and all Treaties made, or which shall be made, under the Authority of the United States, shall be the supreme Law of the Land; and the Judges in every State shall be bound thereby, any thing in the Constitution or laws of any State to the Contrary notwithstanding.

The Senators and Representatives before mentioned, and the Members of the several State Legislatures, and all executives and judicial Officers, both of the United States and of the several States, shall be bound by Oath or Affirmation, to support this Constitution; but no religious Test shall ever be required as a Qualification to any Office or public Trust under the United States.

successors are appointed and qualified, or the offices abolished.

2. All debts contracted and engagements entered into before the adoption of this Constitution shall be as valid against the *Confederate* States under this Constitution as under the *Provisional Government.*

3. This Constitution, and the laws of the *Confederate* States made in pursuance thereof, and all treaties made, or which shall be made under the authority of the *Confederate* States, shall be the supreme law of the land; and the judges in every State shall be bound thereby, anything in the Constitution or laws of any State to the contrary notwithstanding.

4. The Senators and Representatives before mentioned, and the members of the several State legislatures, and all executive and judicial officers, both of the *Confederate* States and of the several States, shall be bound by oath or affirmation to support this Constitution; but no religious test shall ever be required as a qualification to any office or public trust under the *Confederate* States.

5. The enumeration, in the Constitution, of certain rights, shall not be construed to deny or disparage others retained by the people *of the several States.*

6. The powers not delegated to the *Confederate* States by the Constitution, nor prohibited by it to the States, are reserved to the States, respectively, or to the people *thereof.*

ARTICLE. VII.

The Ratification of the Conventions of nine States, shall be sufficient for the Establishment of this Constitution between the States so ratifying the Same.

ARTICLE VII.

1. The ratification of the conventions of *five* States shall be sufficient for the establishment of this Constitution between the States so ratifying the same.

2. *When five States shall have ratified this Constitution, in the manner before specified, the Congress under the Provisional Constitution shall prescribe the time for holding the election of President and Vice President; and for the meeting of the Electoral College, and for counting the votes, and inaugurating the President. They shall, also, prescribe the time for holding the first election of members of Congress under this Constitution, and the time for assembling the same. Until the assembling of such Congress, the Congress under the Provisional Constitution shall continue to exercise the legislative powers granted them; not extending beyond the time limited by the Constitution of the Provisional Government.*

Done in convention by the Unanimous Consent of the States present the Seventeenth Day of September in the Year of our Lord one thousand seven hundred and eighty seven and of the Independence of the United States of America the Twelfth In Witness whereof We have hereunto subscribed our Names,

Go. Washington—
Presdt.
and deputy from
Virginia

Adopted unanimously by the Congress of the Confederate States of South Carolina, Georgia, Florida, Alabama, Mississippi, Louisiana and Texas, sitting in Convention at the capitol, in the city of Montgomery, Alabama, on the Eleventh day of March, in the year Eighteen Hundred and Sixty-One.

Howell Cobb,
President of the
Congress.

THE TREATIES CONCLUDED BY THE CONFEDERATE STATES WITH INDIAN TRIBES

Note: The following pages have been reproduced from THE STATUTES AT LARGE OF THE PROVISIONAL GOVERNMENT OF THE CONFEDERATE STATES OF AMERICA, 1864. Because of age, the readability has been affected in some of the documents.

INDIAN TREATIES.

TREATY WITH THE CREEK NATION.

JULY 10TH, 1861.

A TREATY OF FRIENDSHIP AND ALLIANCE,

Made and concluded at the North Fork Village, on the North Fork of the   July 10, 1861.
Canadian river, in the Creek Nation, west of Arkansas, on the tenth
day of July, in the year of our Lord, one thousand eight hundred
and sixty-one, between the Confederate States of America, by Albert
Pike, Commissioner, with plenary powers, of the Confederate States,
of the one part, and the Creek Nation of Indians, by its Chiefs, Head
Men and Warriors in General Council assembled, of the other part.

The Congress of the Confederate States of America, having, by "An   Preamble.
act for the protection of certain Indian tribes," approved the twenty-
first day of May, in the year of our Lord, one thousand eight hundred
and sixty-one, offered to assume and accept the protectorate of the
several nations and tribes of Indians occupying the country west of
Arkansas and Missouri, and to recognize them as their wards, subject to
all the rights, privileges and immunities, titles and guarantees with
each of said nations and tribes under treaties made with them by the
United States of America; and the Creek Nation of Indians having
assented thereto upon certain terms and conditions:

Now, therefore, the said Confederate States, by Albert Pike, their
Commissioner, constituted by the President under authority of the act
of Congress in their behalf, with plenary powers for these purposes, and
the Creek Nation, in General Council assembled, have agreed to the
following articles, that is to say:

ARTICLE I. There shall be perpetual peace and friendship, and an   Peace and friend-
alliance offensive and defensive, between the Confederate States of ship perpetual.
America, and all of their States and people, and the Creek Nation of
Indians, and all its towns and individuals.

ARTICLE II. The Creek Nation of Indians acknowledges itself to be   Terms upon
under the protection of the Confederate States of America, and of no which the Confed-
other power or sovereign whatever; and doth hereby stipulate and agree erate States assume
with them that it will not hereafter, nor shall any of its towns or indi- tectorate of the
viduals, contract any alliance or enter into any compact, treaty or agreement Creek nation.
with any individual State or with a foreign power: *Provided,* That it
may make such compacts and agreements with neighboring nations and
tribes of Indians for their mutual welfare and the prevention of difficulties

as may not be contrary to this treaty, or inconsistent with its obligations to the Confederate States; and the said Confederate States do hereby assume and accept the said protectorate, and recognize the said Creek Nation as their ward; and by the consent of the said Creek Nation, now here freely given, the country whereof it is proprietor in fee, as the same .s hereinafter defined, is annexed to the Confederate States, in the same manner and to the same extent as it was annexed to the United States of America before that government was dissolved, with such modifications, however, of the terms of annexation, and upon such conditions, as are hereinafter expressed, in addition to all the rights, privileges, immunities, .titles and guarantees with or in favor of the said nation, under treaties made with it, and under the statutes of the United States of America.

Boundaries ARTICLE III. The following shall constitute and remain the boundaries of the Creek country,.viz: Beginning at the mouth of the North Fork of the Canadian river, and running northerly four miles; thence running a straight line so as to meet a line drawn from the south bank of the Arkansas river, opposite the east or lower bank of Grand river, at its junction with the Arkansas, and which runs a course south forty-four degrees west, one mile, to a post placed in the ground, thence along said line to the Arkansas and up the same to the Verdigris river, to where the old territorial line crosses it; thence along said line north to a point twenty-five miles from the Arkansas river where the old territorial line crosses the same; thence running west with the southern line of the Cherokee country to the North Fork of the Canadian river, where the boundary of the cession to the Seminole Nation defined in the first article of the treaty between the United States of America and the Creek and Seminole Nations, of August seventh, in the year of our Lord one thousand eight hundred and fifty-six, first strikes said Cherokee line; thence down said North Fork to where the eastern boundary line of the said cession to the Seminole Nation strikes the same; thence with that line due south to the Canadian river, at the mouth of the Ok-hai-ap-po, or Pond creek; and thence down said Canadian river to the place of beginning.

Assent of the Creek nation to act May 21, 1861, for the protection of certain Indian tribes. ARTICLE IV. The Creek Nation hereby gives its full, free and unqualified assent to those provisions of the act of Congress of the Confederate States of America entitled "An act for the protection of certain Indian tribes," approved the twenty-first day of May, in the year of our Lord one thousand eight hundred and sixty-one, whereby it was declared that all reversionary and other interest, right, title and proprietorship of the United States in, unto and over the Indian country in which that of said nation is included should pass to, and vest in, the Confederate States; and whereby the President of the Confederate States was authorized to take military possession of all said country; and whereby all the laws of the United States, with the exception hereinafter made applicable to, and in force in, said country and not inconsistent with the letter or spirit of any treaty stipulations entered into with the Creek Nation among others were re-enacted, continued in force, and declared to be in force in said country, as laws and statutes of the

Proviso. Confederate States: *Provided, however,* And it is hereby agreed between the said parties that whatever in the said laws of the United States contained, is or may be contrary to, or inconsistent with, any article or provision of this treaty, is to be of none effect henceforward, and shall, upon the ratification hereof, be deemed and taken to have been repealed and annulled as of the present date, and this assent as thus qualified and conditioned, shall relate to, and be taken to have been given upon the said day of the approval of the said act of Congress.

ARTICLE V. The Confederate States of America do hereby guarantee to the Creek Nation, to be held by it to its own use and behoof in fee simple forever, the lands included within the boundaries defined in the preceding article of this treaty; to be held by the people of the said nation in common as they have heretofore been held, so long as grass shall grow and water run, if the said nation shall so please, but with power of making partition thereof and disposition of parcels of the same by virtue of laws of the nation duly enacted; by which partition or sale, title in fee simple, absolute, shall vest in parceners and purchasers, whenever it shall please the nation of its own free will and accord and without solicitation from any quarter to do so; which solicitation the Confederate States hereby solemnly agree never to use, and the title and tenure hereby guaranteed to the said nation, is and shall be subject to no other conditions, reservations or restrictions whatever than such as are hereinafter specially expressed. *Guarantee of lands to the Creek nation; power to dispose of them.*

ARTICLE VI. None of the said lands hereby guaranteed to the Creek Nation, shall be sold, ceded, or otherwise disposed of, to any foreign nation or to any State or government whatever; and in case any such sale, cession or disposition should be made without the consent of the Confederate States, all the said lands shall thereupon revert to the Confederate States. *Lands not to be sold to any foreign nation, or to any State or government whatever. Penalty.*

ARTICLE VII. The Confederate States hereby agree and bind themselves that in guaranteeing to the Seminole Nation of Indians the country granted, ceded and conveyed to it by the Creek Nation, by the treaty of the seventh day of August, in the year of our Lord one thousand eight hundred and fifty-six, it shall be provided as it was in that treaty, that no part thereof shall ever be sold, or otherwise disposed of, by the said Seminole Nation without the consent of the Creek Nation formally and explicitly given. *Lands granted to Seminoles by Creeks not to be sold by former without consent of latter.*

ARTICLE VIII. The Confederate States of America do hereby solemnly agree and bind themselves that no State or Territory shall ever pass laws for the government of the Creek Nation; and that no portion of the country hereby guaranteed to it shall ever be embraced or included within or annexed to any Territory or Province; nor shall any attempt ever be made, except upon the free, voluntary and unsolicited application of the said nation, to erect the said country, by itself or with any other, into a State or any other territorial or political organization, or to incorporate it into any State previously created. *No State or Territory to pass laws for government of Creeks. Creeks not to be incorporated into any other territorial or political organization without their full consent.*

ARTICLE IX. So far as may be compatible with the Constitution of the Confederate States and with the laws made, enacted or adopted in conformity thereto, regulating trade and intercourse with the Indian tribes, as the same are limited and modified by this treaty, the Creek Nation shall possess the otherwise unrestricted right of self-government, and full jurisdiction, judicial and otherwise, over persons and property within their limits; excepting only such white persons as are not, by birth, adoption or otherwise members of either the Creek or Seminole Nation; and that there may be no doubt as to the meaning of this exception, it is hereby declared that every white person who, having married a Creek or Seminole woman, resides in the said Creek country, or who, without intermarrying, is permanently domiciled therein with the consent of the authorities of the nation, and votes at elections, is to be deemed and taken to be a member of the said nation, within the true intent and meaning of this article; and that the exception contained in the laws for the punishment of offences committed in the Indian country, to the effect that they shall not extend or apply to offences committed by one Indian against the person or property of another Indian, shall be so extended and enlarged by virtue of this article when ratified, and with- *Government. Restrictions. Membership. Punishment of offences.*

out further legislation, as that none of said laws shall extend or apply to any offence committed by any Indian, or negro, or mulatto, or by any such white person, so by birth, adoption or otherwise a member of such Creek or Seminole Nation, against the person or property of any Indian, negro, mulatto, or any such white person, when the same shall be committed within the limits of the said Creek Nation as hereinbefore defined; but all such persons shall be subject to the laws of the Creek Nation, and to prosecution and trial before its tribunals, and to punishment according to such laws, in all respects like native members of the said Creek Nation.

Intruders to be kept out of the Creek country. ARTICLE X. All persons who are not members of either the Creek or Seminole Nation, found in the Creek country, as hereinbefore limited, shall be considered as intruders, and be removed and kept out of the same, either by the civil officers of the nation under the direction of the Executive or the General Council, or by the agent of the Confederate States for the nation, who shall be authorized to demand, if necessary, the aid of the military for that purpose; with the following exceptions only, that is to say : Such individuals, with their families as may be in the employment of the government of the Confederate States; all persons peaceably travelling, or temporarily sojourning in the country, or trading therein under license from the proper authority; and such persons as may be permitted by the Creeks or Seminoles with the assent of the agent of the Confederate States, to reside within their respective limits without becoming members of either of said tribes. .

Reservation of lands for Indian agency. ARTICLE XI. The tract of two sections of land, selected by the President of the United States, under the treaty with the Creek Nation, concluded on the twenty-fourth day of January, in the year of our Lord, one thousand eight hundred and twenty-six, at which the Creek Agency is now maintained, and whereon the public buildings of that agency have been erected is hereby reserved to the Confederate States in the same manner as the same was, by that treaty, reserved to the United States, and is not included in the guarantee of lands aforesaid, but shall be within the sole and exclusive jurisdiction of the Confederate States, except as to members of the Creek or Seminole Nation as above defined, all offences committed by whom thereon shall be punished by the laws and courts of the said nation whenever they would be so punished if **Proviso.** committed elsewhere in the nation : *Provided,* That whenever the agency for the said nation shall be discontinued by the Confederate States, and an agent no longer appointed, the said tract of two sections of land shall pass to and vest absolutely in the Creek Nation in the same manner as its other lands with all the buildings that may be thereupon.

Reservation of lands for forts, military posts and post roads. ARTICLE XII. The Confederate States shall have the right to build, establish and maintain such forts and military posts, temporary or permanent, and to make and maintain such military and post-roads as the President may deem necessary, within the Creek country; and the quantity of one mile square of land, including each fort or post, shall be reserved to the Confederate States, and within their sole and exclusive **Restrictions.** jurisdiction, so long as such fort or post is occupied; but no greater quantity of land beyond one mile square shall be used or occupied, nor any greater quantity of timber felled than of each is actually requisite; and if in the establishment of such fort, post, or roads, or of the agency, the property of any individual member of the Creek Nation, or any property of the nation itself, other than land, timber, stone and earth, be taken, destroyed or injured, just and adequate compensation shall be made by the Confederate States.

Right of way for railroads or telegraph lines. ARTICLE XIII. The Confederate States or any company incorporated by them, or any one of them, shall have the right of way for railroads or telegraph lines through the Creek country; but in case of any incorporated company, it shall have such right of way only upon such terms and payment of such amount to the Creek Nation as may be agreed upon between it and the national council thereof; or, in case of disagreement, by making full compensation, not only to individual parties injured, but also to the nation for the right of way; all damage and injury done to be ascertained and determined in such manner as the President of the Confederate States shall direct. And the right of way granted by said nation for any railroad, shall be perpetual, or for such shorter term as the same may be granted, in the same manner as if no reversion of their lands to the Confederate States were provided for, in case of abandonment by them, or of extinction of their tribe.

ARTICLE XIV. No person shall settle, farm, or raise stock within the limits of any post or fort, or of the agency, except such as are, or may be. [in] the employment of the Confederate States in some civil or military capacity, or such as, being subject to the jurisdiction and laws of the Creek Nation, are permitted by the commanding officer of the fort or post to do so thereat, or by the agent to do so upon the agency reserve. *Farming within the limits of any post, or fort, or the agency prohibited.*

ARTICLE XV. The Confederate States shall protect the Creeks from domestic strife, from hostile invasion, and from aggression by other Indians and white persons not subject to the jurisdiction and laws of the Creek Nation, and for all injuries resulting from such invasion or aggression, full indemnity is hereby guaranteed to the party or parties injured, out of the Treasury of the Confederate States, upon the same principle and according to the same rules upon which white persons are entitled to indemnity for injuries or aggressions upon them committed by Indians. *Creeks to be protected from domestic strife, hostile invasion, and aggression by other Indians, &c.*

ARTICLE XVI. No person shall hereafter be licensed to trade with the Creeks, except by the agent, and with only the exceptions hereinafter mentioned, with the advice and consent of the national council. Every such trader shall execute bond to the Confederate States in such form and manner as was required by the United States, or as may be required by the bureau of Indian affairs; and hereafter it shall be in the power of the general council of the Creek Nation to levy and collect of all licensed traders a tax not exceeding one and one fourth per cent. on the first cost of all goods, wares and merchandise hereafter brought by them into the nation for sale; which first cost shall, in all cases, be ascertained from the invoices, copies whereof are required to be furnished to the agent. Such tax shall be payable immediately upon and after the importation into the nation of each stock of goods, but shall in no case be levied twice on the same stock or part of the same : *Provided*, That no tax shall be levied for the present year, upon the stocks of goods now held by licensed traders; but only upon such as they shall hereafter receive, and upon so much of their present stock as shall remain on hand on the first day of January next. No appeal shall hereafter lie to any officer whatever from the decision of the agent refusing to license any applicant. *License to trade with the Indians. Conditions imposed. Proviso.*

ARTICLE XVII. Immediately upon the signing of this treaty, the agent of the Confederate States shall notify each licensed trader in the Creek Nation that he is required to apply for a license under the laws of the Confederate States within thirty days after the date of such notice; and any one failing to do so shall be considered as an intruder, and be immediately removed from the country. Upon each such application the agent shall decide and grant or refuse the same at his discretion, as heretofore, and his decision shall be final. Every license so granted by him shall be for the term of twelve months in addition to the unexpired portion of the year 1861; and if, at the expiration of the year 1862, a renewal of license should not be granted to any such trader, he shall *Traders to apply for license under laws C. S. within 30 days after signing of treaty.*

nevertheless be entitled to remain in the country such reasonable length of time as may, in the opinion of the agent, be necessary, under the protection of the laws of the Confederate States, as a person peaceably sojourning therein, for the purpose of collecting such debts as may be due him : *Provided*, That no such license shall be granted by the agent, unless the party applying shall have paid the whole amount of compensation for land and timber assessed for the year 1861, by the council with the assent of the agent ; and that any license hereafter granted shall be revoked on failure or refusal to pay in due time the tax that may be legally assessed in any year. When a second license is applied for by any such party, or hereafter when any new party applies for license, it shall be granted with the advice and consent of the national council : *And provided also,* That if the general council has any well founded objection to the present renewal of any license to any person now licensed as a trader, for which such renewal ought not, under the law, to be granted, it may present such objection to the agent, who shall refuse to renew the license in that case if he finds such objection to be well founded and sufficient ; and if he do not so refuse, the general council may carry the matter before the superintendent, whose decision shall be final.

Proviso.

Further proviso.

Removal of certain restrictions in reference to the sale of personal property.

ARTICLE XVIII. All restrictions and limitations heretofore imposed or existing by treaty, law or regulation, upon the right of any member of the Creek Nation freely to sell and dispose of to any person whatever, any chattel or article of personal property whatever, are hereby removed and annulled, except such as the laws of the nation itself may have created.

Appointment of agent and interpreter.

ARTICLE XIX. An agent of the Confederate States and an interpreter shall be continued to be appointed for the Creek Nation, both of whom shall reside at the agency ; and whenever a vacancy shall occur in either of the said offices, the authorities of the nation shall be consulted as to the person to be appointed to fill the same, and no one shall be appointed against whom they in good faith protest ; and the agent may be removed on petition and formal charges preferred by the constituted authorities of the nation, the President being satisfied, upon full investigation, that there is sufficient cause shown for such removal.

What Indians may reside in the Creek country.

ARTICLE XX. The Creek Nation may, by act of its legislative authorities, receive and incorporate in itself as members of the nation, or permit to settle and reside upon the national lands, such Indians of any other tribe as to it may seem good ; and may sell such Indians portions of land, in fee, or by less estate, or lease them portions thereof for years or otherwise, and receive to its own use the price of such sales or leases ; and it alone shall determine who are members and citizens of the nation entitled to vote at elections, hold office or share in annuities, or in the common lands : *Provided,* That when persons of another tribe shall once have been received as members of the Creek Nation they shall not be disfranchised or subjected to any other restrictions upon the right of voting than such as shall apply to the Creeks themselves. But no Indians other than Creeks and Seminoles, not now settled in the Creek country, shall be permitted to come therein to reside, without the consent and permission of the legislative authority of the nation.

Who shall be entitled to vote, hold office, share in annuities or the common lands.

Proviso.

Penalty for settling upon lands of Creek nation without permission.

ARTICLE XXI. If any citizen of the Confederate States or any other person not being permitted to do so by the authorities of said nation, or authorized by the terms of this treaty, shall attempt to settle upon any lands of the Creek Nation, he shall forfeit the protection of the Confederate States, and such punishment may be inflicted upon him, not being cruel, unusual or excessive, as may have been previously prescribed by law of the nation.

ARTICLE XXII. No citizen or inhabitant of the Confederate States shall pasture stock on the lands of the Creek Nation, under the penalty of one dollar per head for all so pastured, to be collected by the authorities of the nation; but their citizens shall be at liberty at all times, and whether for business or pleasure, peaceably to travel the Creek country; and to drive their stock to market or otherwise through the same, and to halt such reasonable time on the way as may be necessary to recruit their stock, such delay being in good faith for that purpose. *Citizens of the C. S. may not pasture stock on Creek lands, but may, at all time, travel the Creek country.*

ARTICLE XXIII. It is also further agreed that the members of the Creek Nation shall have the same right of travelling, driving stock and halting to recruit the same in any of the Confederate States as is given citizens of the Confederate States by the preceding article. *Creeks to have the same right to travel in any of the C. S.*

ARTICLE XXIV. The officers and people of the Creek and Seminole Nations respectively, shall at all times have the right of safe conduct and free passage through the lands of each other; and the members of each nation shall have the right, freely, and without seeking license or permission, to settle within the country of the other, and shall thereupon be entitled to all the rights, privileges and immunities of members thereof, including the right of voting at elections, and of being deemed qualified to hold office, and excepting only that no member of either nation shall be entitled to participate in any funds belonging to the other nation. Members of each nation shall have the right to institute and prosecute suits in the courts of the other, under such regulations as may, from time to time be prescribed by their respective legislatures. *Personal and political rights, privileges and immunities of the Creeks and Seminoles.*

ARTICLE XXV. Any person duly charged with a criminal offence against the laws of either the Creek or Seminole Nation, and escaping into the jurisdiction of the other, shall be promptly surrendered upon the demand of the proper authority of the nation within whose jurisdiction the offence shall be alleged to have been committed. *Fugitives from justice to be surrendered.*

ARTICLE XXVI. The Creek Nation shall promptly apprehend and deliver up all persons accused of any crime against the laws of the Confederate States, or any State thereof, who may be found within its limits, on demand of any proper officer of a State or the Confederate States. *Persons accused of any crime against the C. S. to be delivered up.*

ARTICLE XXVII. In addition to so much and such parts of the act of Congress of the United States, enacted to regulate trade and intercourse with Indian tribes, and to preserve peace on the frontiers as have been re-enacted and continued in force by the Confederate States, and as are not inconsistent with the provisions of this treaty, so much of the laws of the Confederate States as provides for the punishment of crimes amounting to felony at common law or by statute against the laws, authority or treaties of the Confederate States, and over which the courts of the Confederate States have jurisdiction, including the counterfeiting the coin or securities of the Confederate States, or uttering counterfeit coin or securities, and so much of such laws as provides for punishing violators of the neutrality laws, and resistance to the process of the Confederate States, and all the acts of the provisional Congress, providing for the common defence and welfare, so far as the same are not locally inapplicable, shall hereafter be in force in the Creek country. *Laws in force in the Creek country defined.*

ARTICLE XXVIII. Whenever any person who is a member of the Creek Nation shall be indicted for any offence in any court of the Confederate States or in a State court, he shall be entitled as of common right to subpoena, and if necessary compulsory process for all such witnesses in his behalf as his counsel may think necessary for his defence, and the costs of process for such witnesses, and of service thereof, and the fees and mileage of such witnesses shall be paid by the Confederate States, being afterwards made, if practicable, in case of conviction of the property of the accused. And whenever the accused is not able to *Any member of the Creek nation, shall, when indicted by a Confederate or State court, have right to subpoena witnesses.*

Wh nnotable to employ counsel, the court shall assign him one experienced counsel for employ, the court his defence, who shall be paid by the Confederate States a reasonable sh'l assign him compensation for his services, to be fixed by the court, and paid upon the cou..sel. certificate of the judge.

All laws in re-   ARTICLE XXIX. The provisions of all such acts of Congress of the gard to the return of fugitive slaves, Confederate States as may now be in force, or may hereafter be enacted, or fugitives from for the purpose of carrying into effect the provision of the constitution labor or justice in regard to the re-delivery or return of fugitive slaves, or fugitives from extended to the labour and service, shall extend to, and be in full force within the said Creek nation. Creek Nation; and shall also apply to all cases of escape of fugitive slaves from the said Creek Nation into any other Indian nation or into one of the Confederate States, the obligation upon each such nation or State to re-deliver such slaves being in every case as complete as if they had escaped from another State, and the mode of proc dure the same.

Members of Creek   ARTICLE XXX. Persons belonging to the Creek Nation shall hereafter nation . competent witnesses in C. S. be competent as witnesses in all cases, civil and criminal, in the courts courts. of the Confederate States. unless rendered incompetent from some other cause than their Indian blood or descent.

Official acts of   ARTICLE XXXI. The official acts of all judicial officers in the said judicial officers in nation shall have the same effect, and be entitled to the like faith and said nation to have same effec as like credit everywhere, as the like acts of judicial officers of the same grade acts of officers of and jurisdiction in any of the Confederate States; and the proceedings same grade, &c, in of the courts and tribunals of the said nation, and copies of the laws C. S. and judicial and other records of the said nation shall be authenticated like similar proceedings of the courts of the Confederate States, and the laws and office records of the same, and be entitled to like faith and credit.

Existing laws in   ARTICLE XXXII. It is hereby declared and agreed that the institution reference to slavery declared binding. of slavery in the said nation is legal and has existed from time immemorial; that slaves are taken and deemed to be personal property; that the title to slaves and other property having its origin in the said nation, shall be determined by the laws and customs thereof; and that the slaves and other personal property of every person domiciled in said nation shall pass and be distributed at his or her death, in accordance with the laws, usages and customs of the said nation, which may be proved like foreign laws, usages and customs, and shall everywhere be held valid and binding within the scope of their operation.

No ex post fac'o   ARTICLE XXXIII. No ex post facto law or law impairing the obligation of laws impairing the contracts shall ever be enacted by the legislative authority of the Creek obligation of con-tracts. passed by Nation, to effect any other persons than its own people; nor shall any the Creek legisla-citizen of the Confederate States or member of any other Indian nation ture to effect any or tribe be deprived of his property or deprived or restrained of his lib-other than mem-bers of said nation, erty, or fine, penalty or forfeiture be imposed on him in the said country, &c. except by the law of the land, nor without due process of law; nor shall any such citizen be in any way deprived of any of the rights guaranteed to all citizens by the constitution of the Confederate States; and it shall be within the province of the agent to prevent any infringement of such rights and of this article, if it should in any case be necessary.

Post-offices and   ARTICLE XXXIV. That the Congress of the Confederate States shall mails. establish and maintain post-offices at the most important places in the Creek Nation, and cause the mails to be regularly carried at reasonable intervals to and.from the same, at the same rates of postage, and in the same man-ner as in the Confederate States.

Right of ferriage.   ARTICLE XXXV. Whenever any stream, over which may it be desirable to establish ferries, forms the boundary of the Creek country, members of the Creek Nation shall have the right of ferriage from their own land to the opposite shore; and no more onerous terms shall be imposed by the State or nation opposite than such as it imposes upon its own citizens having ferries on the same stream.

ARTICLE XXXVI. In consideration of the common interests of the Creek Nation and the Confederate States, and of the protection and rights guaranteed to the said nation by this treaty, the Creek Nation hereby agrees that it will, either by itself or in conjunction with the Seminole Nation, raise and furnish a regiment of ten companies of mounted men to serve in the armies of the Confederate States for twelve months, the company officers whereof shall be elected by the members of the company, and the field officers by a majority of the votes of the members of the regiment. The men shall be armed by the Confederate States, receive the same pay and allowances as other mounted troops in the service, and not be moved beyond the limits of the Indian country west of Arkansas without their consent. *A regiment of mounted men to be raised to serve in the armies of the C. S.*

ARTICLE XXXVII. The Creek Nation hereby agrees and binds itself at any future time to raise and furnish, upon the requisition of the President, such number of troops for the defence of the Indian country, and of the frontier of the Confederate States as he may fix, not out of fair proportion to the number of its population, to be employed for such terms of service as the President may fix ; and such troops shall always receive the same pay and allowances as other troops of the same class in the service of the Confederate States. *Troops for the defence of the Indian country and the frontier.*

ARTICLE XXXVIII. It is further agreed by the said Confederate States that the said Creek Nation shall never be required or called upon to pay, in land or otherwise, any part of the expenses of the present war, or of any war waged by or against the Confederate States. *Creeks not to pay expenses of present or any future wars.*

ARTICLE XXXIX. It is further agreed that, after the restoration of peace, the Government of the Confederate States will defend the frontiers of the Indian country, of which the Creek country is a part, and hold the forts and posts therein, with native troops, recruited among the several Indian Nations included therein, under the command of officers of the army of the Confederate States, in preference to other troops. *C. S., after peace, to defend Indian frontier with native troops.*

ARTICLE XL. In order to enable the Creek and Seminole Nations to claim their rights and secure their interests without the intervention of counsel or agents, and as they were originally one and the same people and are now entitled to reside in the country of each other, they shall be jointly entitled to a delegate to the House of Representatives of the Confederate States of America, who shall serve for the term of two years, and be a member of one of the said nations, over twenty-one years of age, and labouring under no legal disability by the law of either nation ; and each delegate shall be entitled to the same rights and privileges as may be enjoyed by delegates from any territories of the Confederate States to the said House of Representatives. Each shall receive such pay and mileage as shall be fixed by the Congress of the Confederate States. The first election for delegate shall be held at such time and places, and be conducted in such manner as shall be prescribed by the agent of the Confederate States, to whom returns of such election shall be made, and he shall declare the person having the greatest number of votes to be duly elected, and give him a certificate of election accordingly, which shall entitle him to his seat. For all subsequent elections, the times, places, and manner of holding them and ascertaining and certifying the result, shall be prescribed by law of the Confederate States. *Representation in Congress.* *Election of delegate.*

ARTICLE XLI. It is further ascertained and agreed between the parties to this treaty, that the United States of America, of which the Confederate States of America were heretofore a part, were, before the separation, indebted, and still continue to be indebted to the Creek Nation, and bound *Annuities and interest thereon.*

to the punctual payment to them of the following sums annually, on the first day of July of each year, that is to say:

Perpetual annuities, amounting in the aggregate to twenty-four thousand five hundred dollars, under the fourth article of the treaty of the seventh day of August, A. D., one thousand seven hundred and ninety; the second article of the treaty of the sixteenth day of June, A. D., one thousand eight hundred and two; and the fourth article of the treaty of the twenty-fourth day of January, A. D., one thousand eight hundred and twenty-six.

Interest at the rate of five per cent. per annum on two hundred thousand dollars, which, by the sixth article of the treaty of the seventh day of August, A. D., one thousand eight hundred and *forty* [fifty]-six, the United St tes agreed to invest in some safe stock, paying not less than that rate of interest, and to pay the interest regularly and faithfully, to be applied to purposes of education among the Creeks, but which they never invested; being ten thousand dollars per annum, or more, payable perpetually.

The sum of one thousand seven hundred and ten dollars perpetually, the agreed cost of the wheelwright, blacksmith and assistant, blacksmith, shop and tools, and iron and steel, annually, under the eighth article of the treaty of the twenty-fourth day of January, A. D., one thousand eight hundred and twenty-six.

The sum of eight thousand two hundred and twenty dollars payable annually, until and upon, and ending upon the first day of July, A. D., one thousand eight hundred and sixty-four, being for the sums of six thousand dollars per annum, for education for seven years from and after the fiscal year ending 30th June, A. D., one thousand eight hundred and fifty-seven, under the fourth article of the treaty of the fourth day of January, A. D., one thousand eight hundred and forty-five, as the same is recited in the fifth article of the treaty of the seventh day of August, A. D., one thousand eight hundred and fifty-six; and of two thousand two hundred and twenty dollars, being the estimated annual cost of the provision for two blacksmiths and assistants, shops and tools, iron and steel, under the thirteenth article of the treaty, made the twenty-fourth day of March, A. D., one thousand eight hundred and thirty-two, and which was continued for seven years from and after that fiscal year by the treaty of the seventh day of August, A. D, one thousand eight hundred and fifty-six.

The sum of four thousand seven hundred and ten dollars which was payable during the pleasure of the President of the United States, as follows, to-wit: two thousand dollars per annum for assistance in agricultural operations under the eighth article of the treaty of the twenty-fourth day of January, A. D., one thousand eight hundred and twenty-six; one thousand dollars per annum for education under the fifth article of the treaty of the fourteenth day of February, A. D., one thousand eight hundred and thirty-three; and one thousand seven hundred and ten dollars per annum, the estimated annual cost of the wagon-maker, blacksmith and assistant, shop and tools, iron and steel, under the same fifth article of the same treaty last aforssaid; indefinite continuance of the payment of which three sums was provided for by the treaty of the seventh day of August, A. D., one thousand eight hundred and fifty-six.

And it is also hereby ascertained and agreed between the parties to this treaty that there was due to the Creek Nation, on the first day of July, in the year of our Lord, one thousand eight hundred and sixty-one, for and on account of these annuities, interest and annual instalments, and of arrearages thereof, the sum of seventy-one thousand nine hundred and sixty dollars, as follows, that is to say:

For the perpetual annuities then due, twenty-four thousand five hundred dollars.

For interest and arrearages on the said sum of two hundred thousand dollars, provided to be invested for purposes of education by the sixth article of the treaty of the seventh day of August, A. D., one thousand eight hundred and fifty-six, which has never been invested, and the five instalments of interest whereon at the rate of five per cent. per annum, due up to and upon the first day of July, A. D., one thousand eight hundred and sixty-one, amount to the sum of fifty thousand dollars, whereof twenty-one thousand dollars only has been paid, the sum of twenty-nine thousand dollars.

For the two sums aforesaid due for educational purposes, seven thousand dollars.

For sums due for wagon-makers, blacksmiths, shops, iron and steel, and agricultural purposes, seven thousand six hundred and forty dollars, and for arrearages of same, being one-half of the annual sum due on the first day of July, A. D., one thousand eight hundred and sixty, and unpaid, three thousand eight hundred and twenty dollars, or together eleven thousand four hundred and sixty dollars. And it not being desired by the Confederate States that the Creek Nation should continue to receive these annual sums from the government of the United States, or otherwise have any further connection or communication with that government and its Superintendents and agents; therefore, the said Confederate States of America do hereby assume the payment, for the future, of all the above recited annuities and annual payments, and agree and bind themselves regularly and punctually to pay the same; and do also agree and bind themselves to pay immediately upon the complete ratification of this treaty, the said sum of seventy-one thousand nine hundred and sixty dollars for such annuities and annual payments, due on the first day of July, A. D. one thousand eight hundred and sixty-one, and for arrearages as above stated.

ARTICLE XLII. It is also further agreed between the said parties to this treaty, that the United States of America, while the said several Confederate States were States of the said United States, held and do still continue to hold in their hands, invested in bonds and stocks of certain States, part or all of which are now members of the said Confederacy of States, the sum of two hundred thousand seven hundred and forty-two dollars and sixty cents, bearing an annual interest of eleven thousand six hundred and ninety-four dollars and fifty-four cents, and also arrearages of interest on the same in money, which amounted, on the first day of July, A. D., one thousand eight hundred and sixty-one, to so much as to make, with the principal, the sum of two hundred and forty-nine thousand nine hundred and thirty-seven dollars and fourteen cents, in bonds, stocks and money, in the hands of the United States, and belonging to those persons surviving, and the legal representatives of those persons deceased, who were orphan children of the Creeks, on the twenty-fourth day of March, A. D., one thousand eight hundred and thirty-two, the same being the proceeds of the twenty sections of land selected under the direction of the President of the United States, for such orphan children of the Creeks under and by virtue of the second article of the treaty of that date, and which were sold and the proceeds invested in such stocks as aforesaid, under the direction of the President of the United States, in conformity to the provision of that article that said twenty sections should be divided and retained, or sold, for the benefit of such children as the President might direct.

And it is further agreed that in addition to this sum, and to the sum of two hundred thousand dollars which should have been invested under the sixth article of the treaty of the seventh day of August, A. D., one thousand eight hundred and fifty-six, there has also long been and still

Amount due orphan children of the Creek nation.

Amount due certain claimants.

is due and owing from the said United States to certain individuals in the Creek Nation, from claims allowed by William Armstrong, as Commissioner, in their favour on account of depredations by the Osages, as provided by treaty, the sum of nine thousand seven hundred and fifty-seven dollars and fifty cents, to pay which, and other like claims, there has long remained in the treasury of the United States the sum of sixteen thousand dollars, remainder of the sum óf thirty thousand dollars allowed by treaty with the Osages, made the eleventh day of January, A. D., one thousand eight hundred and thirty-nine, for the purpose of

Payment of orphan children and claims assumed b the Confederate States. paying what should be adjudged for such depredations; and the said Confederate States of America do hereby assume the duty and obligation of collecting and paying over as trustees to the said Creek Nation, for the said orphans and legal representatives of orphan children of the Creeks, all sums of money accruing, whether from interest or capital of the bonds of the several States of the Confederacy now held by the government of the United States as trustee for the said orphans and legal representatives of orphan children of the Creeks, or for the Creek Nation; and the said interest and capital, as collected, shall be paid over to the said orphans or legal representatives of orphans of the Creeks

States not to pay capital or interest of its bonds to U. S. but to C. S. in trust for said orphans. or to the Creek Nation for them. And the said Confederate States will request the several States whose bonds are so held, to provide by legislation or otherwise, that the capital and interest of such bonds shall not be paid to the government of the United States, but to the government of the Confederate States, in trust for the said orphans and legal representatives of orphans.

Final settlement and full payment to be made after the restoration of peace. And the said Confederate States hereby guarantee to the said Creek Nation the final settlement and full payment upon and after the restoration of peace, and the establishment and recognition of their independence, as of debts in good faith and conscience, as well as in law due and owing, on good and valuable consideration, by the said Confederate States and other of the United States, jointly, before the secession of any of the States, of all the said sums of money so due and owing by the late United States, and of any sums received by that government, and now held by it, by way of interest on a capital of said bonds of the States; and do also guarantee to it the full and final settlement and payment, at the same period of the capital and interest of any and all bonds or stocks of any Northern State, in which any of the Creek funds may have been invested.

All other sums due by this treaty to be paid upon the restoration of peace. ARTICLE LXIII. It is also further agreed that whatever sums of money are by this treaty provided to be settled and paid by the Confederate States to the Creek Nation, for itself, upon the restoration of peace, not including those belonging to the said orphans, shall be paid over to the authorities of the nation, to be held by them invested in stocks, or shall be by the government of the Confederate States so invested, in stocks bearing the best rate of interest, and at the market rate of such stocks as the authorities of the nation may require, so that the nation may in either mode, have all the advantages of the investment; and that, if paid over to the authorities of the nation, the government of the Confederate States shall have no further control over the same in any wise, nor be in any wise responsible for its proper investment or disposition.

Treaties with the U. S. not inconsistent with this treaty to be binding. ARTICLE LXIV. It is further agreed between the parties that all provisions of the treaties of the Creek Nation with the United States which secure or guarantee to the Creek Nation, or individuals thereof, any rights or privileges whatever, and the place whereof is not supplied by, and which are not contrary to, the provisions of this treaty, and so far as the same are not obsolete and unnecessary, or repealed, annulled, changed or modified by subsequent treaties, or laws, or by this treaty, are and shall be continued in force, as if made with the Confederate States.

ARTICLE LXV. It is hereby further agreed by the Confederate States *Creeks entitled* that all the members of the Creek Nation as hereinbefore defined, shall *to own land, and* be henceforward competent to take, hold and pass, by purchase or descent, *sue in the courts of any of the States of* lands in any of the Confederate States heretofore or hereafter acquired by *the C. S.* them, and to sue and implead in any of the courts of each of the States, in the same manner and as fully, and under the same terms and restrictions and the same conditions only as citizens of another of the Confederate States can do.

ARTICLE LXVI. A general amnesty of all past offences against the laws *Amnesty.* of the United States, and of the Confederate States, committed in the Indian country before the signing of this treaty, by any member of the Creek Nation, as such membership is defined by this treaty, is hereby declared; and all such persons, if any, whether convicted or not, imprisoned or at large, charged with any such offence, shall receive from the President full and free pardon and be discharged.

ARTICLE LXVII. It is also further agreed that the sum of sev n hundred *Payment of ex-* and fifty dollars shall be appropriated, upon the ratification of this treaty, *penses of Creek commissioners.* by the Congress of the Confederate States, to pay the expenses of the Commissioners of the Creek Nation who have negotiated the same, and that the same shall be paid to the Principal Chief, Motey Kinnaird, who shall distribute the same among the Commissioners as they shall agree and direct.

ARTICLE LXVIII. This treaty shall take effect and be obligatory upon *When to take* the contracting parties, from the tenth day of July, in the year of our *effect.* Lord one thousand eight hundred and sixty-one, whenever it shall be ratified by the General Council of the Creek Nation, and by the Provisional President and Congress, or the President and Senate of the Confederate States.

In perpetual testimony whereof, the said Albert Pike, as Commissioner, with plenary powers, on the part of the Confederate States, doth now hereunto set his hand and affix the seal of his arms, and the undersigned, the Commissioners appointed in this behalf by the General Council of the Creek Nation, do hereunto set their hands and affix their seals.

{ SEAL. }

Done in duplicate, at the place, and upon the day, in the year first aforesaid.

ALBERT PIKE,
Commissioner of the Confederate States to the Indians west of Arkansas.

MOTY KINNIARD,
   Principal Chief.
ICHO HACHO,
   Principal Chief Upper Creeks.
CHILLY McINTOSH,
LOUIS McINTOSH,
JAMES M. C. SMITH,
G. W. STIDHAM,
THOS. C. CARR,

JOHN L. SMITH,
TIM BARNETT,
W. F. McINTOSH,
GEO. W. BRINTON,
OK-CHUN HACHO,
CO-AS-SAT-TI FIX-I-KO,
JOSEPH CORNELLS,
GEO. W. WALKER,
SAMUEL CHECOTE.

Signed in duplicate in our presence.

M. H. GARRETT,
   C. S. Agent.
G. W. STIDHAM,
   C. S. Interpreter.
W. WARREN JOHNSON,
WM. QUESENBERRY,
   Secretary to Commissioner.
H. S. BUCKNER,
W. L. PIKE.

Ratification by the Creek nation. WHEREAS, a treaty of alliance and friendship was made and concluded, subject to the ratification of the general council of the Creek Nation, on the tenth day of July, in the year of our Lord, one thousand eight hundred and sixty-one, by and between Albert Pike, Commissioner with plenary powers, of the Confederate States of America, on the part and behalf of the Confederate States, and Motey Kinnaird, Principal Chief, Icho Hacho, First Chief of the Upper Creeks, Chilly McIntosh, Louis McIntosh, James M C. Smith, Geo. W. Stidham, Thomas C. Carr, John L. Smith, Timothy Barnett, William F. McIntosh, George W. Brinton, Ok-Chun Hacho, Co-as-sa-ti Fixico, Joseph Cornells, George W. Walker, Samuel Chicote and Daniel N. McIntosh, a Committee appointed by the General Council of Mus-ko-ki Nation, at the North Fork Village, on the North Fork of the Canadian River, in the said Creek Nation; and whereas by the forty-ninth article thereof, it is provided in these words, that "This Treaty shall take effect and be obligatory upon the contracting parties, from the tenth day of July, in the year of our Lord, one thousand eight hundred and sixty-one, whenever it shall be ratified by the General Council of the Creek Nation, and by the Provisional President and Congress, or the President and Senate of the Confederate States;"

Now therefore be it known, That the Creek or Mus-ko-ki Nation, in General Council assembled, on this, the twentieth day of July, in the year of our Lord, one thousand eight hundred and sixty-one, at the Council Ground of the said nation, having maturely considered the said treaty, and every article and clause thereof, and being satisfied therewith, doth upon its part, assent to, ratify and confirm the same, as its solemn act and compact, as is therein stipulated, and doth direct that a copy of this ratification signed by the Principal Chief and National Clerk be annexed to each part of the said treaty for authentication thereof.

Thus done and approved, the day and year aforesaid.

A true copy of the original act of ratification, as adopted by the General Council.

MOTEY KINNAIRD,
Principal Chief.

Attest:

   D. N. McINTOSH,
     National Clerk.

Signed and attested in our presence.

W. H. GARRETT,
C. S. Agent for the Creeks.
G. W. STIDHAM,
C. S. Interpreter for the Creeks.

Names of the Chiefs who signed the treaty concluded on the 10th day of July, 1861, and approved by the General Council of the Creek Nation on the 29th July, 1861, between the Confederate States of America and the Creek Nation of Indians:

Echur Harjo,	He-ne-matheo-che,	Ya-ha Harjo,
Cowassart Harjo,	Tullisse Fixico,	Fixico Harjo,
Nocus Emathla,	Tallof Harjo,	Ok-chun Harjo,
Us-so-na Harjo,	No-cus-illy,	Ne-ha Ya-ho-la,
In-suk-ko,	Cha-low Harjo,	Tallise Fixico,
Tustunnuk Kee,	Ok-ta-ha-hassee Harjo,	Jimmy Larney,
Ar-chu-le Harjo,	Ho-siche Boatswain,	Halputter Mikko,
Oh-sa Ya-ho-la,	Thear-ke-ta,	Samuel Lasley,

Ya-ha Tustunnukke,	It-chin Ya-ho-la,	Pow-has-e Marthla,
Ne-ha Ya-ho-la,	Nocus Fixico,	Ok-cus-ca Fixico,
Co-we Harjo,	Mikko Hutke,	Ar-hul Le-mathla,
Wm. Bruner,	Napoche Fixico,	Tul-wa Mikko,
Jacob Derrysaw,	Cotchar Fixico,	Ar-ha-luk Fixico,
E-ne-ha,	James McHenry,	Lou-cher Harjo,
Car-pit-char Ya-ho-la,	Cully Mikko,	Carpechar Fixico.

Attest:

National Clerk.

To the Indian names are subjoined marks.

ARTICLE SUPPLEMENTARY

To the treaty concluded between the Confederate States of America and   July 10, 1861.
*the Creek Nation of Indians, at the North Fork Village, in the Creek
Nation, on the tenth day of July, in the year of our Lord, one
thousand eight hundred and sixty-one.*

ARTICLE. The survivors now residing in the Creek Nation, of the Apala-   Preamble.
chicola Band of Indians, have earnestly represented to the commissioner
of the Confederate States the facts following, that is to say:

That the Apalachicola Band of Indians, being by origin a part of the
Creek Nation, long resided on the Apalachicola river, in what is now the
State of Florida, and were parties to the treaty concluded at camp Moultrie,
with the Florida tribes of Indians, on the eighteenth day of September, A. D.,
one thousand eight hundred and twenty-three.

That by two treaties, made and concluded with the United States on the
eighteenth day of June, A. D., one thousand eight hundred and twenty-
three, by different portions of the said Apalachicola Band, the chiefs and
warriors of that band relinquished all the privileges to which they were
entitled as parties to the treaty aforesaid, concluded at camp Moultrie, and
all their right and title to certain reservations by it secured to them; and
in consideration of that cession, the United States agreed to grant, and to
convey within three years, by patent, to certain named chiefs, for the benefit
of themselves and of the sub-chiefs and warriors of the said Apalachicola
Band, the quantity, in all, of six sections of land, to be laid off under the
direction of the President, after the lands should have been surveyed.

That it was provided by the same two treaties that the said six sections
of land might be disposed of by the chiefs, with the consent and advice of
the Governor of Florida, at any time before the expiration of said term of
three years, and that the said band might thereupon migrate to a country of
their choice. And it was further thereby provided, that if, at any future
time, the chiefs and warriors of the Apalachicola Band should feel disposed
to migrate from Florida to the Creek and Seminole country west, they
might either sell the grants of land made by those treaties, and in that
case must, themselves, bear the whole expense of their migration, subsistence, &c.; or they might surrender to the United States all the rights and
privileges acquired under said two treaties, in which case, they should
become parties to the obligations, provisions, and stipulations of the treaty
of Payne's Landing, made with the Seminoles on the ninth day of May, A.

D., one thousand eight hundred and thirty-two, as a constituent part of that tribe, and re-unite with that tribe in their abode west, in which case the United States would pay six thousand dollars for the reservations in that case relinquished by the first article of the said two treaties.

That in the hostilities that afterwards took place between the Creeks and Seminoles and the United States, the said Apalachicola Band remained loyal to the United States, and maintained their peace and friendship unbroken; but, in the year 1837, they were induced by the urgent solicitation of the emigrating agent of the United States, to remove from the country occupied by them in Florida, to the Indian country west of Arkansas, leaving the lands so granted them as aforesaid, and a large number of horses, mules, cattle, hogs, wagons, and other articles which they could not collect together and carry with them, and which the said emigrating agent persuaded them to leave in his charge, on his promise that the owners should be paid the value of all such property, in money, by the agent of the United States, on their arrival in the country provided for them on the west side of the Mississippi; a schedule of all of which property so abandoned, and of its value, and of the improvements on lands abandoned by them, and the value of each, is annexed to this article, and forms a part of it.

That, by the treaty of Payne's Landing, made on the ninth day of May, A. D., one thousand eight hundred and thirty-two, the United States agreed to pay the Seminole Indians, in full compensation for all their claim to lands in the Territory of Florida, and for all improvements on the lands so ceded, the sum of fifteen thousand four hundred dollars, to be divided among the chiefs and warriors of the several towns in a ratio proportioned to their population; and they further agreed to take the cattle belonging to the Seminoles, at the valuation of some person to be appointed by the President, and to pay the valuation, in money, to the respective owners, or give them other cattle; and the expenses of removal were to be paid by the United States, and subsistence for twelve months, to all emigrants, furnished by them;

And that no compensation has ever been made any of the said Apalachicola Band, for the lands or improvements so abandoned by them, or for the horses, mules, cattle and other property abandoned by them; nor have they ever received any part of the annuities paid the Seminole or Creek Nation since their removal west, or been recognized as an integral part of the Seminole Nation, as it was provided they should be;

And, inasmuch as the forced emigration of the said band, and their surrender and abandonment of their lands, improvements, horses, cattle and other property in consequence thereof, was equivalent, as against the United States, to an election, by them, to surrender the rights, privileges secured by the treaties of the 18th June, 1833, and to claim the rights and privileges thereby vesting in them, as parties to the treaty of Payne's Landing, of the 9th of May, 1832;

C. S., upon res- Therefore, it is hereby agreed by the Confederate States of America, by
toration of peace Albert Pike, its Commissioner, with full powers, with the members and
to investigate and
pay certain claims survivors of the Apalachicola Band of Florida Indians, that upon and after
of Apalachicola the restoration of peace, the said claims of the members of that Band, to
Indians. compensation for the loss of the lands, improvements, horses, cattle, mules and other property, shall be fairly investigated, in a generous and liberal spirit, by an officer or commissioners, to whom that duty shall be assigned by the Confederate States; and that whatever shall appear, upon such investigation, to be justly or equitable owing to members of the said band, on account of such losses as aforesaid, shall be paid to the persons originally entitled to the same, or to the legal representatives of such of them as may be deceased.

And it is also further agreed, that the foregoing provisions of this article shall extend to, and include the claims for losses of the same kind, by members of Black Dirt's Band of friendly Seminoles, who lost property in like manner, in consequence of their hurried removal west, as the same is contained in the schedule thereof, marked B, annexed to this article. *Also, claims of Black Dirt's Band of Seminoles.*

And it is also agreed that the claims to money, in lieu of bounty land warrants, of the persons whose names and those of their heirs are contained in the schedule marked C, annexed to this article, shall in like manner, and at the same period, be investigated, and so far as they shall be found to be well founded, shall be paid by the Confederate States. *Also, claims to money in lieu of land warrants.*

In perpetual testimony whereof, the said Albert Pike, Commissioner, with full powers, of the Confederate States of America, doth hereunto set his hand and affix the seal of his arms.

{ SEAL. } Thus done, signed and sealed, at the North Fork Village, on the North Fork of the Canadian river, this tenth day of July, in the year of our Lord, one thousand eight hundred and sixty-one.

ALBERT PIKE,

Commissioner of the Confederate States to the Indian Nations west of Arkansas.

20

Schedule A.

SCHEDULE A.

Claims of Apalachicola Indians.

NAMES.	Horses. Number.	Value.	Mules. Number.	Value.	Cattle. Number.	Value.	Goats and Hogs. Number.	Value.	Sheep, Oxen. Number.	Value.	Corn, Rice, etc. No. Bu.	Value.	Wagons. Number.	Value.	Improvement on land. Value of.
Charley Walker	6	$180	2	$200	16	$96	19	$76	1	$36				$50	$40
Jemmy Walker					18	176	15	45							35
Watley	3	45			6	48	12	36							20
Betsey Walker	6	180			16	112	25	75							150
Esther Walker	8	240			23	138	24	72							
Tom-l Hacho	5	150			9	54	18	54							200
Dinah Walker	3	120			21	144	30	90							160
Jenkins	8	320			14	98	16	48							25
Tal-si Fic-si-co	3	105			19	152	14	42							20
Ni-ha Thlac-co-chi	2	60					20	60							20
Il-li-cha					17	119	26	78							20
A-lic	3	60			12	72	15	45							30
O-chi Hacho	2	80			8	48	13	39							25
Su-na Co-chi					4	24	8	24							35
Fos I-ma-thla	3	90					15	45							20
	2	60			6	36	14	42							25
Ni-ha	1	40			10	60	16	48							25
I-ma-thla-chi	4	160			7	42	30	90							20
Pa-his Hacho	3	120			7	42	24	72							15
Sally Hacho	3	120			6	36	16	48							40
Pa-no-si-ka	6	240			7	42	8	24							50
To-hii-pi	3	140			28	147	14	42							50
Milly Walker	2	80			23	128	19	57							45
Micco Ya-ho-la	6	180			18	122	16	48							90
John Milly					15	90	14	42							25
Betsey	1	40			5	30	6	18							30
Polly Walker	5	150			12	84	26	78							30
Ti-fa Chi-i-yi	3	120			4	24	6	18							15
Ki-nat Ho-ho-yi	3	90			5	20	8	24							20
So-ni Thlac-co	3	120			5	33	10	30							20
Davy Thlac-co	2	80			11	77	15	45							30
Letty	4	160			8	56	11	33							25
Fi-ho-ki	3	120			30	210	24	72							40
Old Sampson	6	300			18	126	5	15							25
Ya-ha Fic-si-co	3	120			14	98	12	36							15
Cho-il-li	6	240			4	28	5	15							25
Ta-co-si Ya-ho-la	3	120			7	49	11	33							40
Co-a-co-chi	21	840			34	238	5	15							40
Madison	3	120			5	35	14	42							100
No-co-si Ya-ha-lo-chi	3	120			11	77	7	21							
Hii-ya-ya-ka	1	40			4	28	8	24							
Co-si Ya-ho-la	6	240			14	98	15	45							40
A-ha-loc Hacho	6	240			14	98	20	60							28
Cho-ni	6	240			18	126									14
Ok-chai-yi	2	80			21	147	8	24							20
Co-ni	4	160			6	42	14	42							10
Mi-ca-leh	2	80			4	28	6	18							18
Mary	4	160			7	42	12	36							60
Ni-ce	5	200			4	24	8	24							38
Ro-sa-na	3	120			10	60	18	54							27
Capt. Billy or Isa-fa Hacho.	4	160			18	108	20	60						Gun, $30,	90
Lindy	2	80			7	42	13	39							15
Sa-chi-ni-chi	4	120			10	70									20
Co-cho-co-ni	1	30			5	30	7	21							20
Tom Farby	3	120					11	33							20
I-con-cha-ta Micco	6	180			23	138	12	24	13	39					
							32	114							300
I-fa-la Hacho	2	80			12	72	27	51							115
Jo Riley	6	180			36	216	45	135							40
Simon	3	90					25	75							25
Imathla Johnson	4	120			38	228	18	54							40
Fos Hutchi	2	60			7	42	8	24							25
George	2	80			9	54	13	39							20
So-ho llth-li	3	120					18	54							30
Si-hi-chi	2	90					15	45							25
Ok-tuul-ki	4	120			7	42	16	48							30
John Lewis	5	200			11	66	20	60							35
Thlo-po-ti	3	90			8	48	19	57							15
Woc-si Hacho	2	80			10	60	35	105							25

SCHEDULE A.—CONTINUED.

NAMES.	Horses.		Mules.		Cattle.		Goats and Hogs.		Sheep, Oxen.		Corn, Rice, etc.		Wagons.		Improvement on land. Value of.
	Number.	Value.	Number.	Value.	Number.	Value.	Number.	Value.	Number.	Value.	No. Bu.	Value.	Number.	Value.	
Kat-cha Hacho............	3	$105			8	$56	15	$90							$25
Ya-ha Hacho............ ...	1	30			7	42	4	12							20
Susy....................	2	50			6	36	5	15							20
Sim-ma-lii-chi							20	80							30
Tha-thlo Fic-si-co........	5	150			9	54	15	45							
Ha-a-thlum Hacho........	6	180			15	90	13	39							80
Co-cho-co-ni Hacho.......	3	90			8	54	13	39							60
Ya-da-wa Hacho	3	90			6	36	16	48						Gun, $50,	35
So-cos-ki..............	2	60			4	24	8	24							40
Il-li Kat-chi............					6	36	10	40							30
Stim-ma-la-chi..........	5	200			5	30	45	135							50
Wil-yam ca............	6	240			35	245	25	75							250
A-sun-wa..............	2	80			3	18	6	18							40
Wa-hi	4	100			8	56	6	18							30
Co-ha Thlacco........ ...	3	120			15	90	38	114	60	$180	50	$50			150
Charly Imathla............					2	12	140	420			150	150		Gun, $10,	
											40	60			100
Micco Yahola............					25	150	60	180			50	50			
											50	25			125
Susy....					50	300					30	30			
											30	15			75
Towko...................					7	42	20	60			30	30			50
Cho-wus tii Hacho......											40	40			40
Micco Mo-cha-sa..........							13	39			50	50			80
Ok-lii-chi..............											83	83			140
Hillis Hacho-chi.											67	67			85
Chos-ka..............											74	74			84
Sai-yi Ho-ho-ka..											84	84			84
Ta-na-hi-chi.......... ...											55	55			65
Pai-chis-chi............											74	74			74
Cho-co-yii-chi..........											84	84			84
Ti-wa-chi......											160	160			100
Un-dolla Hacho..........											104	104			85
Thli-chi-ca..............											84	84			83
It-sa Fic-sico............											200	200			150
Con-ta I-math-la.....															100
Sti-bi-hai-chi.....											203	203			100
Wol-has-ti											100	100			103
Micco Hacho............											70	70			160
Hok-ti Thlacco............											74	74			84
Shok-ho-ka.											150	150			100
Jenny....................											50	50			150
Hillis Hacho....											70	70			50
Kat-chas Hacho..........											100	100			80
No-cos I-math-la.........											85	85			82
Oc-tai-a-che Ya-ho-la.....											73	73			64
Woc-si Hacho.....											82	82			72
Ikey											55	53			45
Sim-ma-va-hi............							10	30			43	43			54
Chi-pa-ni Thlac-co........	2	105			7	42	21	63			60	60			85
Co-o-sa Micco............											60	60			79
Klaofa Po-o-ka............	2	70					45	13			50	50			84

I certify that the foregoing three folios constitute Schedule A, of the article supplementary to the Creek Treaty, to which are they attached, and so form a part thereof.

ALBERT PIKE,
Commissioner of the Confederate States to the Indian Nations west of Arkansas

Schedule B.

SCHEDULE B.

Claims of Persons of Black Dirt's Band.

	Horses		Mules		Cattle		Hogs		Oxen		Corn, Rice, &c.		Value of Improvements.
	Number	Value.	Number	Value.	Number	Value.	Number	Value.	Number	Value.	Number	Value.	
Fos-hui-chi Tas-te-nug-ge..	2	$90			6	$36	150	$450			56	$56	94
Micco Hacche							50	150					
A-ha-loc Ya-ro-la							2	60					
Cho-wus-tai-yi Ima-thla...	2	100			2	12	14	42					
Hillis Hacho					4	24	17	51					
Sa-ya-ho-la							13	39					
Cosah Micco							10	30					
Hepsy	3	18			13	78	53	159			80	$80	Sugar cane. 120 100
So-wi-ki					14	84	48	144			90	10	20
Fo-kau-pi					3	18	40	120			24	25	50
Ho-po-illi-se	1	55									63	63	87
No-cos Nacho	1	60											
Chul Hacho													
Cho-wus-a-yi Hacho					21	144	90	270					
Fai-i-chi-che							14	42					
Pa-hos Ima-thla	15	525			60	360	60	180			80	80	100
So-ko-i-ki	3	158											
Ok-tar-ar-chi Hacho							150	450					
Ok-ta-a-chi Ya-ho-la					6	36	100	300					
To-wa-chi					10	60	5	15					
Pa-lut Hacho							20	60					
Ok-ta-chi							12	36					
O-sun-i-ha							20	120					
Tai-ya-ki							9	27					
O-thlai-chi							6	18					
Hilis Hacho-chi					2	12	60	180					
Hillis Wacho					4	24	10	30					
I cho Fic-si co	5	90											
Fi-yi-ki-cha	3	120											
Wo-li-cha					41	246							
Co-at-chas Hacho							18	54					
O-sun I-ma-thla	2	90											
Fos Hacho	1	60					100	600					
Ya-ha Hacho					49	210							
Con-tol Hacho							5	15					
Tus-ta-nuk Hacho							13	39			56	56	80
La-ni							18	54					
Lo-ni-si							43	129			20	20	36
Tus-te-nuk-ki	2	90					19	57			33	33	76
Eliza											33	33	110
Chus-si							25	75			40	40	80

I certify that the last foregoing two folios are schedule B. of the article supplementary to the Creek treaty, to which they are attached, and that they form a part thereof.

ALBERT PIKE,
Commissioner of the Confederate States to the Indian nations west of Arkansas.

SCHEDULE C.

Persons of Tus-ti-nuk-o-chi's people entitled to money in lieu of Land Warrants.

Kon-tol Hacho, of I-con-hut-ki town.
Wal-ho-chi, widow of Ya-ha Fic-si-co.
Ok-fus-ki, heir of Api-co-chi I-ma-thla.
Fai-chi-chi, heir of Tul-ma-chi Hacho.
Sa-la-ko-ki, heir of Kon-hut-ki Micco.
Si-ma-thli, heir of Ta-lap I-ma-thla.
Yi-ak-chi, widow of Octai I-ma-thla.
A. W. Fuller, heir of Ho-poi-ilth-thli, of Fos Hutchi town.
Ho-poi-ilth-thli, heir of Ima-thla, of Fos Hutchi town.
I-poi-yi, heir of Imathla Thlacco, of Fos Hutchi town.
So-in-ki-cho-cho, heir of Octai-i-achi Ya-ho-la.
Sa-na, heir of Fos Ha-cho.
Si-a-ka-li, heir of Ya-ho-lo-chi.
Chi-pa-ni Thlacco, heir of Tus-ti-nuk Hache.
La-ni, heir of Pa-hos Ya-ho-la.
Pa-mos-ka, heir of Tus-ti-nuk I-ma-thla.
Si-ma-mai-chi, heir of Us-sun I-math-la.
A-po-lo-ti-ki, heir of Si-i-ya Pus-ka.
Mii-hai-yi, heir of A-tus Ya-ho-la.
Pa-chii-yi-si, heir of In-thla-nis I-ma-thla.
Ca-la-ni, heir of Po-ilth Hacho.
Mun-tul-ka, heir of Ho-poi-yi Hacho.
Mo-lit-tai-ki, heir of Co-o-sa Hacho.
Ma-lit-cha, heir of Ho-pa-ni Hut-ki.
Lo-li, heir of A-tus Micco.
A-pi-la-ni, heir of Micco Hacho.
Sa-lit-hot-chi, heir of Con-tol I-mathla.
Ko-nit Yahola, heir of Pa-kat-cha.
Ot-los-si, heir of Fai-ya-hola.
Pa-ma-chul-li, heir of Hillis Hacho.
Mi-i-ak-ka, heir of Achul-li Hacho.
Sa-nun-ka, heir of Illis Hacho-chi.
Thla-ma-yi, heir of Co-sis Ima-thla.
Si-a-will-i, heir of Ho-o-pa.
Louisa, heir of Cho-co-te Ima-thla.
Sa-hoi-yi, heir of Ni-ha Thlac-co-chi.
Ho-poi-yi, heir of Ho-tul-li I-ma-thla.
Si-li-it-ka, heir of Sa-mo-chi.
Sa-pi-it-ka, heir of Tul-ma Fic-si-co.
Ta-lo-pi, heir of Kat-cha Ya-ho-la.
Sa-mi, heir of Ho-tul-ki Ya-ho-la.
Co-o-sa Micco.

I hereby certify that the foregoing two pages constitute Schedule C, of the article to which they are attached, supplementary to the Creek Treaty, and so are a part of that article.

ALBERT PIKE,
Commissioner of the Confederate States to the Indian Nations West of Arkansas.

RATIFICATION BY THE CONGRESS.

Resolved, (two-thirds of the Congress concuring,) That the Congress of the Confederate States of America, do advise and consent to the ratification of the articles of treaty, including the Secret Article and Supplementary Article, made by Albert Pike, Commissioner of the Confederate States to the Indian Nations west of Arkansas, in behalf of the Confederate States, of the one part, and the Creek Nation of Indians, by its chiefs, headmen and warriors, in general council assembled, of the other part, concluded at the North Fork Village, on the North Fork of the Canadian River, in the Creek Nation, on the tenth day of July, in the year of our Lord, one thousand eight hundred and sixty-one, with the following

AMENDMENTS:

Amendments.

I. Strike out from article xxviii., the following words; "or in a State court," and insert, in lieu thereof, the following words: "or in a State court, subject to the laws of the State."

II. Add at the end of article xxx. the following words: "and the Confederate States will request the several States of the Confederacy to adopt and enact the provisions of this article, in respect to suits and proceedings in their respective courts."

III. Strike out from article xi. the following words: "the same rights and privileges as may be enjoyed by delegates from any Territories of the Confederate States, in the said House of Representatives," and insert, in lieu thereof, the following words: "a seat in the hall of the House of Representatives to propose and introduce measures for the benefit of said nations, and to be heard in regard thereto, and on other questions in which either of said nations is particularly interested, with such other rights and privileges as may be determined by the House of Representatives."

NOTE.—The foregoing amendments were subsequently ratified by General Council of the Creek Nation.

TREATY WITH CHOCTAWS AND CHICKASAWS.

JULY 12, 1861.

A TREATY OF FRIENDSHIP AND ALLIANCE,

Made and concluded at the North Fork Village on the North Fork of the Canadian river, in the Creek Nation, west of Arkansas, on the twelfth day of July, in the year of our Lord, one thousand eight hundred and sixty-one, between the Confederate States of America, by Albert Pike, Commissioner, with plenary powers, of the Confederate States of the one part, and the Choctaw Nation of Indians by Robert M. Jones, Sampson Folsom, Forbis Leflose, George W. Harkins, Allen Wright, Alfred Wade, Coleman Cole, James Riley, Rufus Folsom, William Pitchlynn, McGee King, Wm. King, John Turnbull, and Wm. Bryant, Commissioners appointed by the Principal Chief of the said Choctaw Nation, in pursuance of an act of the Legislature thereof, and the Chickasaw Nation of Indians, by Edmund Pickens, Holmes Colbert, James Gamble, Joel Kemp, William Kemp, Winchester Colbert, Henry C. Colbert, James N. McLish, Martin W. Allen, John M. Johnson, Samuel Colbert, Archibald Alexander, Wilson Frazier, Christopher Columbus, A-sha-lah Tubbi, and John E. Anderson, Commissioners elected by the Legislature of the said Chickasaw Nation of the other part: July 12, 1861.

The Congress of the Confederate States of America, having by "An act for the protection of certain Indian tribes," approved the twenty-first day of May, in the year of our Lord, one thousand eight hundred and sixty-one, offered to assume and accept the protectorate of the several nations and tribes of Indians occupying the country west of Arkansas and Missouri, and to recognize them as their wards, subject to all the rights, privileges and immunities, titles and guarantees with each of said nations and tribes under treaties made with them by the United States of America; and the Choctaw and Chickasaw Nations of Indians having each assented thereto, upon certain terms and conditions; Preamble.

Now therefore, The said Confederate States of America, by Albert Pike, their Commissioner, constituted by the President, under authority of the act of Congress in their behalf, with plenary powers for these purposes, and the Choctaw and Chickasaw nations by their respective Commissioners aforenamed, have agreed to the following Articles, that is to say:

ARTICLE I. There shall be perpetual peace and friendship, and an alliance offensive and defensive, between the Confederate States of America and all of their States and people, and the Choctaw and Chickasaw Nations and all the people thereof. Perpetual peace and friendship.

Protectio of the
C. S.
ARTICLE II. The Choctaw and Chickasaw Nations of Indians acknowledge themselves to be under the protection of the Confederate States of America, and of no other power or sovereign whatever; and do hereby stipulate and agree with them that they will not hereafter, No alliance with any foreign power. nor shall any one of their people contract any alliance, or enter into any compact, treaty or agreement with any individual State or with a foreign power, and the said Confederate States do hereby assume and accept the said protectorate, and recognize the said Choctaw and Chickasaw Nations as their wards; and by the consent of the said Choctaw and Chickasaw Nations, now here freely given, the country whereof Annexation of territory. they are proprietors in fee, as the same is hereinafter described, is annexed to the Confederate States in the same manner and to the same extent as it was annexed to the United States of America before that government was dissolved, with such modifications, however, of the terms of annexation, and upon such conditions as are hereinafter expressed, in addition to all the rights, privileges, immunities, titles and guarantees with or in favor of the said nations, under treaties made with them, and under the statutes of the United States of America.

Acceptance of the protectorate by the C. S.
ARTICLE III. The Confederate States of America, having accepted the said protectorate, hereby solemnly promise the said Choctaw and Chickasaw Nations never to desert or abandon them, and that under no circumstances will they permit the Northern States or any other enemy to overcome them and sever the Choctaws and Chickasaws from the Confederacy; but that they will, at any cost and all hazards, protect and defend them and maintain unbroken the ties created by identity of interests and institutions, and strengthened and made perpetual by this treaty.

Boundaries of the Choctaw and Chickasaw country.
ARTICLE IV. The following shall constitute and remain the boundaries of the Choctaw and Chickasaw country, that is to say: Beginning at a point on the Arkansas river one hundred paces east of old Fort Smith, where the western boundary line of the State of Arkansas crosses that river, and running thence to Red river by the line between the State of Arkansas and the Choctaw and Chickasaw country, as the same was resurveyed and marked under the authority of the United States, in the year of our Lord, one thousand eight hundred and fifty-five; thence up Red river to the point where the meridian of one hundred degrees west longitude crosses the same; thence north along said meridian to the main Canadian river; thence down said river to its junction with the Arkansas river; thence down said river to the place of beginning. The boundaries of the said country, on the north and on the south, between the said east and west lines being the same in all respects, with all riparian and other rights and privileges, as they were fixed, created and continued by the treaties of the eighteenth day of October, A. D, one thousand eight hundred and twenty, and of the twenty-seventh day of September, A. D., one thousand eight hundred and thirty.

Boundaries of the Chickasaw country.
ARTICLE V. It is hereby agreed by and between the Choctaw and Chickasaw Nations that the boundaries of the Chickasaw country shall hereafter continue to be as follows, that is to say: beginning on the north bank of Red river, at the mouth of Island bayou, where it empties into Red river, about twenty-six miles on a straight line, below the mouth of False Wachita; thence running a northwesterly course along the main channel of said bayou to the junction of the three prongs of said bayou, nearest the dividing ridge between the Wachita and Low Blue rivers, as laid down on Captain R. L. Hunter's map; thence northerly along the eastern prong of Island Bayou to its source; thence due north to the Canadian river; thence west along the main

Canadian to the ninety-eighth degree of west longitude; thence south to Red river; and thence down Red river to the beginning: *Provided,* *however,* If the line running due north, from the eastern source of Island bayou, to the main Canadian, shall not include Allen's or Wa-pa-nacka academy. within the Chickasaw district, then an offset shall be made from same line so as to leave said academy two miles within the Chickasaw district, north, west, and south from the lines of boundary. Proviso.

ARTICLE VI. The remainder of the country held in common by the Choctaws and Chickasaws, including the leased district, shall constitute the Choctaw district, and their officers and people shall at all times have the right of safe conduct and free passage through the Chickasaw district. Choctaw district.

ARTICLE VII. The Choctaw and Chickasaw Nations hereby give their full. free and unqualified assent to those provisions of the act of Congress of the Confederate States of America, entitled "An act for the protection of certain Indian tribes," approved the twenty-first day of May, in the year of our Lord, one thousand eight hundred and sixty-one, whereby it was declared that all reversionary and other interest, right. title. and proprietorship of the United States in, unto, and over the Indian country in which that of the said nations is included, should pass to, and vest in the Confederate States; and whereby the President of the Confederate States was authorized to take military possession and occupation of all said country; and whereby all the laws of the United States, with the exception thereinafter made applicable to, and in force in said country. and not inconsistent with the letter or spirit of any treaty stipulations entered into with the Choctaw and Chickasaw Nations among others were re-enacted, continued in force, and declared to be in force in said country, as laws and statutes of the said Confederate States: *Provided, however,* And it is hereby agreed between the said parties that whatever in the said laws of the United States contained, is or may be contrary to, or inconsistent with any article or provision of this treaty, is to be of none effect henceforward, and shall, upon the ratification hereof, be deemed and taken to have been repealed and annulled as of the present date, and this assent. as thus qualified and conditioned, shall relate to, and be taken to have been given upon the said day of the approval of the said act of Congress. A sent given to
act of May 21,
1861, vesting terri-
tory in the C. S.

Laws of the U.
S d clared to be
in force.

Provi o.

ARTICLE VIII. The Confederate States of America do hereby solemnly guarantee to the Choctaw and Chickasaw nations to be held by them to their own use and behoof in fee simple forever, the lands included within the boundaries defined in article IV of this treaty; to be held by the people of both the said nations in common, as they have heretofore been held, so long as grass shall grow and water run, if the said nations shall so please, but with power to survey the same, and divide it into sections and other legal sub-divisions when it shall be so voted by a majority of the legal voters of each nation respectively; and of making partition thereof and disposition of parcels of the same by virtue of the laws of both said nations, duly enacted: by which partition or sale title in fee simple absolute shall vest in parceners and purchasers whenever it shall please both nations of their own free will and accord, and without solicitation from any quarter to do so; which solicitation the Confederate States hereby solemnly agree never to use; and the title and tenure hereby guaranteed to the said nations is and shall be subject to no other conditions, reservations, or restrictions whatever than such as are hereinafter specially expressed. Lands included
with in certain
bounda ies guar-
ant d to the Choc-
taw and Chickasaw
Nations.

Partition and
s le of such lands.

ARTICLE IX. None of the lands hereby guaranteed to the Choctaw and Chickasaw Nations shall be sold, ceded or otherwise disposed of to any foreign nation or to any State or government whatever; and in case Sale, &c., of
lands to any for-
eign nation, inhib-
ited.

any such sale, cession or disposition should be made without the consent of the Confederate States, all the said lands shall thereupon revert to the Confederate States.

No State or Territory to pass laws for said nations. ARTICLE X. The Confederate States of America do hereby solemnly agree and bind themselves that no State or Territory shall ever pass laws for the government of the Choctaw and Chickasaw Nations; and that no portion of the country guaranteed to them shall ever be embraced or **Not to be incorporated into any other political organization without their free consent.** included within or annexed to any Territory or Province; nor shall any attempt ever be made, except upon the free, voluntary, and unsolicited application of both said nations to erect their said country, by itself or with any other, into a State, or any other Territorial or political organization, or to incorporate it into any State previously created.

Lease made to the U. S. of certain territory by the treaty of June 22, 1855, renewed to the C. S. ARTICLE XI. The lease made to the United States by the treaty of the twenty-second day of June, A. D., one thousand eight hundred and fifty-five, by the Choctaw and Chickasaw Nations of all that portion of their common territory which lies west of the ninety-eighth parallel of west longitude, is hereby renewed to the Confederate States, but for the **C. S. may settle and maintain certain bands of Indians therein.** term of ninety-nine years only, from the date of this treaty; and it is agreed that the Confederate States may settle and maintain therein, upon reserves with definite limits, but of sufficient extent, all the bands of the Wichitas or Fa-wai-hash, Huecos, Caddos, Fa-hua-cu-ros, Ana-dagh-cos, Kichais, Fon-ca-was, Ionais, Comanches, Delawares, Kickapoos and Shawnees, and any other bands whose permanent ranges are south of the Canadian, or between it and the Arkansas, and which are now therein, or that they may desire, hereafter, to place therein, but not including any of the Indians in New Mexico, nor any other bands than those included in the above specification and description, without the consent **Proviso.** of both the Choctaw and Chickasaw Nations: *Provided,* And it is hereby further agreed that whenever the said Choctaw and Chickasaw Nations become a State, the reserves so apportioned to the said several bands shall belong to them in fee, not exceeding, however, for each band, the same quantity of good land as would belong, upon a partition of the lands of the two nations to an equal number of Choctaws and Chickasaws in the whole country; and when the said bands consent to a partition among themselves, each individual shall have and receive in fee, within the said leased country, as large a quantity of good land as shall or would be apportioned to each Choctaw or Chickasaw in partition of all the national lands, with the right, however, now and in all future time, to the said several bands so settled or to be settled in said leased district to hunt upon all the vacant and unoccupied parts of the same without let or molestation.

Indians settled upon reserves in the country so leased, subject to the laws of the C. S. ARTICLE XII. It is hereby further agreed between the parties to this treaty that the Indians so settled upon reserves in the country so leased shall be until they are capable of self-government, or until they shall be with their own consent incorporated among the Choctaws and Chickasaws, subject to the laws of the Confederate States, and to their exclusive control, under such rules and regulations, not inconsistent with the rights and interests of the Choctaws and Chickasaws, or with the Con- **Proviso.** stitution and laws of the Confederate States, as may from time to time be prescribed by the President for their government: *Provided, however,* That the country so leased shall continue open to settlement by the Choctaws or Chickasaws as heretofore; and all members of each nation settled therein shall be subject to the jurisdiction and laws of the Choctaw Nation, except as hereinafter provided; for which purpose the said leased district may be a district of that nation; but no interference with or trespass upon the settlements or improvements of the reserve Indians shall be permitted, under any pretext whatever; nor shall any of the laws of either the Choctaw or Chickasaw Nations be in force in said leased country, except so far as those of the Choctaw Nation can, without infraction of this treaty, apply to the members of either nation residing in the district in question.

ARTICLE XIII. All navigable streams of the Confederate States and of the Indian country shall be free to the people of the Choctaw and Chickasaw Nations, who shall pay no higher toll or tonnage duty or other duty than the citizens of the Confederate States; and the citizens of those nations living upon Red river, shall have, possess, and enjoy upon that river, the same ferry privileges, to the same extent, in all respects, as citizens of the Confederate States on the opposite side thereof, subject to no other or a different tax or charge than they.

Free navigation.

Ferry privileges to citizens living upon Red river.

ARTICLE XIV. So far as may be compatible with the Constitution of the Confederate States and with the laws made, enacted, or adopted in conformity thereto, regulating trade and intercourse with the Indian tribes, as the same are limited and modified by this treaty, the Choctaw and Chickasaw Nations shall possess the otherwise unrestricted right of self-government, and full jurisdiction, judicial and otherwise, over persons and property within their respective limits; excepting only such white persons as are not, by birth, adoption or otherwise, members of either the Choctaw or Chickasaw Nation; and that there may be no doubt as to the meaning of this exception, it is hereby declared that every white person who, having married a Choctaw or Chickasaw woman, resides in the said Choctaw or Chickasaw country, or who, without intermarrying, is permanently domiciled therein with the consent of the authorities of the nation, and votes at elections, is to be deemed and taken to be a member of the said nation within the true intent and meaning of this article; and that the exception contained in the laws for the punishment of offences committed in the Indian country, to the effect that they shall not extend or apply to offences committed by one Indian against the person or property of another Indian shall be so extended and enlarged by virtue of this article when ratified, and without further legislation, as that none of said laws shall extend and apply to any offence committed by any Indian, or negro, or mulatto, or by any white person so by birth, adoption or otherwise a member of such Choctaw or Chickasaw Nation against the person or property of any Indian, negro, mulatto, or any such white person, when the same shall be committed within the limits of the said Choctaw or Chickasaw Nation as hereinbefore defined; but all such persons shall be subject to the laws of the Choctaw and Chickasaw Nations respectively, and to prosecution and trial before their tribunals, and to punishment according to such laws, in all respects like native members of the said nations respectively.

Rights of self-government, and full jurisdiction, judicial and otherwise, over persons and property.

ARTICLE XV. All persons, not members of the Choctaw or Chickasaw Nation, who may be found in the Choctaw and Chickasaw country, as hereinbefore limited, shall be considered as intruders, and be removed and kept out of the same, either by the civil officers of the Nation, under the direction of the Executive or Legislature, or by the agent of the Confederate States for the Nation, who shall be authorized to demand, if necessary, the aid of the military for that purpose; with the following exceptions only, that is to say: Such individuals, with their families, as may be in the emplyment of the government of the Confederate States; all persons peaceably travelling, or temporarily sojourning in the country, or trading therein under license from the proper authority; and such persons as may be permitted by the Choctaws or Chickasaws with the assent of the agent of the Confederate States, to reside within their respective limits without becoming members of either of said nations.

Who considered as intruders; how they may be removed.

ARTICLE XVI. A tract of two sections of land in each of said nations,

Cession of land to the C. S.

to be selected by the President of the Confederate States, at such points as he may deem most proper, including, if he pleases, the present site of the agency in each nation, is hereby ceded to the Confederate States; and when selected shall be within their sole and exclusive jurisdiction:

Proviso.

Provided, That whenever the agency for either nation shall be discontinued, the tract so selected therein shall revert to the said Choctaw and Chicka-

Further proviso.

saw Nations, with all the buildings that may then be thereon: And provided, also, That the President may, at any time, in his discretion, select in lieu of either said reserves, any unoccupied tract of land in the same nation, and in any other part thereof, not greater in extent than two sections, as a site for the agency for such nation, which shall, in such case, constitute the reserve, and that first selected shall thereupon revert to the Choctaw and Chickasaw Nations.

Forts and military posts, and military and post-roads

ARTICLE XVII. The Confederate States shall have the right to build, establish and maintain such forts and military posts, temporary or permanent, and such military and post-roads as the President may deem necessary within the Choctaw and Chickasaw country; and the quantity of one mile square of land, including each fort or post, shall be reserved to the Confederate States, and within their sole and exclusive jurisdiction, so long as such fort or post is occupied; but no greater quantity of land beyond one mile square shall be used or occupied, nor any greater quantity of timber

Compensation for private property taken for public use.

felled than of each is actually requisite; and if, in the establishment of such fort, post or road, or of the agency, the property of any individual member of the Choctaw or Chickasaw Nation, or any property of either nation, other than land, timber, stone and earth, be taken, destroyed or injured, just and adequate compensation shall be made by the Confederate States,

Right of way for railroad is and telegraph

ARTICLE XVIII. The Confederate States, or any company incorporated by them, or any one of them, shall have the right of way, for railroads or telegraph lines, through the Choctaw and Chickasaw country; but in the case of any incorporated company, it shall have such right of way only upon such terms and payment of such amount to the Choctaw and Chickasaw Nations, as may be agreed on between it and the National Councils thereof; or, in case of disagreement, by making full compensation not only to individual parties injured, but also to the nation for the right of way; all damage and injury done to be ascertained and determined in such manner as the President of the Confederate States shall direct. And the right of way granted by said nations for any railroad, shall be perpetual, or for such shorter term as the same may be granted, in the same manner as if no reversion of their lands to the Confederate States were provided for in case of abandonment by them, or extinction of their nation.

No person to settle, farm or raise stock within certain limits.

ARTICLE XIX. No persons shall settle, farm or raise stock within the limits of any post or fort or of either agency, except such as are or may be in the employment of the Confederate States, in some civil or military capacity; or such as, being subject to the jurisdiction and laws of the Choctaw or Chickasaw Nation, are permitted by the commanding officer of the fort or post to do so thereat, or by the agent to do so, upon the agency reserve.

Appointment of agent and interpreters. Where to reside.

Vacancy in said offices, how filled.

ARTICLE XX. An agent of the Confederate States, for the Choctaw and Chickasaw Nations, and an interpreter for each shall continue to be appointed. The interpreters shall reside at their respective agencies; and the agent at one of them or alternately at each And whenever a vacancy shall occur in either of the said offices, the authorities of the nation shall be consulted as to the person to be appointed to fill the same, and no one shall be appointed against whom they protest, and the agent may be removed, on petition and found charges preferred by the constituted authorities of the nation, the President being satisfied, upon full investigation, that there is sufficient cause for such removal.

ARTICLE XXI. The Confederate States shall protect the Choctaws and Chickasaws from domestic strife, from hostile invasion, and from aggression by other Indians and white persons, not subject to the jurisdiction and laws of the Choctaw or Chickasaw Nation; and for all injuries resulting from such invasion or aggression, full indemnity is hereby guaranteed to the party or parties injured, out of the Treasury of the Confederate States, upon the same principle and according to the same rules upon which white persons are entitled to indemnity for injuries or aggressions upon them committed by Indians. · Protection from domestic strife, invasion and aggression.

ARTICLE XXII. It is further agreed between the parties that the agent of the Confederate States upon the application of the authorities of the Choctaw and Chickasaw Nations will not only resort to every proper legal remedy, at the expense of the Confederate States, to prevent intrusion upon the lands of the Choctaws and Chickasaws, and to remove dangerous or improper persons, but he shall call upon the military power, if necessary, and to that end all commanders of military posts in the said country shall be required and directed to afford him, upon his requisition, whatever aid may be necessary to effect the purposes of this article. Prevention of invasion, and removal of dangerous and improper persons.

ARTICLE XXIII If any property of any Choctaws or Chickasaws be taken by citizens of the Confederate States, by stealth or force, the agent, on complaint made to him in due form, by affidavit, shall use all proper legal means and remedies, in any State where the offender may be found, to regain the property or compel a just remuneration, and, on failure to procure redress, payment shall be made for the loss sustained, by the Confederate States, upon the report of the agent, who shall have power to take testimony and examine witnesses in regard to the wrong done and the extent of the injury. Remedy for recovery of property carried off by stealth or force by citizens of the C. S.

ARTICLE XXIV. No person shall be licensed to trade with the Choctaws and Chickasaws, except by the agent, and with the advice and consent of the National Council. Every such trader shall execute bond to the Confederate States, in such form and manner as was required by the United States, or as may be required by the Bureau of Indian Affairs. The authorities of the Choctaw and Chickasaw Nations may, by a general law, duly enacted, levy and collect on all licensed traders in the nation a tax of not more than one-half of one per cent. on all goods, wares and merchandize brought by them into the Choctaw and Chickasaw country for sale, to be collected whenever such goods, wares and merchandize are introduced, and estimated upon the first cost of the same at the place of purchase, as the same shall be shown by the copies of the invoices filed with the agent: *Provided*, That no higher tax shall be levied and collected than is actually levied and collected in the same year of native traders in the nation; nor shall one be taxed at all unless the others are. No appeal shall hereafter lie from the decision of the agent or council, refusing a license, to the Commissioner of Indian Affairs, or elsewhere, except only to the Superintendent, in case of refusal by the agent. And no license shall be required to authorize any member of the Choctaw or Chickasaw Nation, who is by birth and blood an Indian, to trade in the Choctaw and Chickasaw country; nor to authorize any person to sell flour, meat, fruits and other provisions, or stock, wagons, agricultural implements, or arms brought from any of the Confederate States into the country; nor shall any tax be levied upon such articles or the proceeds of sale thereof. And all other goods, wares and merchandize exposed to sale by a person not qualified, without a license, shall be forfeited, and be delivered and given to the authorities of the nation, as also shall all wines and liquors illegally introduced. License to trade with the Choctaws and Chickasaws. Tax on traders. Proviso. Appeal from decision refusing license. When license not required. Goods, &c., sold by a person not qualified, forfeited.

ARTICLE XXV. All restrictions contained in any treaty made with the United States, or created by any law or regulation of the United States, Restrictions on the right to sell and dispose of personal property, removed. upon the unlimited right of any member of the Choctaw or Chickasaw Nation to sell and dispose of, to any person whatever, any chattel or other article of personal property, are hereby removed ; and no such restrictions shall hereafter be imposed, except by their own legislation.

Purchase or descent of lands. ARTICLE XXVI. It is hereby further agreed by the Confederate States, that all the members of the Choctaw and Chickasaw Nations, as hereinbefore defined, shall be henceforward competent to take, hold and pass, by purchase or descent, lands in any of the Confederate States, heretofore or hereafter acquired by them.

Delegate to the House of Representatives of the U. S. How long to serve. ARTICLE XXVII. In order to enable the Choctaw and Chickasaw Nations to claim their rights and secure their interests without intervention of agents or counsel, and as they are now entitled to reside in the country of each other, they shall be jointly entitled to a delegate to the House of Representatives of the Confederate States of America, who shall serve for the term of two years, and be a member, by birth or blood, on either the father's or mother's side, of one of said nations, over twenty-one years of age, and laboring under no legal disability by the laws of either nation ; and such delegate shall be entitled to the same rights and privileges as may be enjoyed by delegate from any Territory of the Confederate States.

First election of delegate. The first election for delegate shall be held at such time and places, and be conducted in such manner as shall be prescribed by the agent of the Confederate States, to whom returns of such election shall be made, and he shall declare the person having the greatest number of votes to be duly elected, and give him a certificate of election accordingly, which shall entitle him to his seat.

Subsequent elections. For all subsequent elections, the times, places and manner of holding them, ascertaining and certifying the result

Delegates to be elected alternately from each nation. shall be prescribed by law of the Confederate States. The delegates shall be elected alternately from each nation, the first being a Choctaw, by blood, on either the father's or mother's side, and resident in the Choctaw country ; and the second a Chickasaw, by blood, on either the father's or mother's side, and resident in the Chickasaw country, and so on alternately.

Who eligible. At the respective elections, such persons only as fulfill the foregoing requisites shall be eligible, and when one is elected to fill a vacancy and serve out an unexpired term, he must belong to, and be resident in, the same nation as the person whose vacancy he fills.

Admission of the Choctaw and Chickasaw country into the Confederacy as one of the C. S. ARTICLE XXVIII. In consideration of the uniform loyalty and good faith, and the tried friendship for the people of the Confederate States, of the Choctaw and Chickasaw people, and of their fitness and capacity for self-government, proven by the establishment and successful maintenance, by each, of a regularly organized republican government, with all the forms and safe-guards to which the people of the Confederate States are accustomed, it is hereby agreed by the Confederate States, that whenever and so soon as the people of each of said nations shall, by ordinance of a convention of delegates, duly elected by majorities of the legal voters, at an election regularly held after due and ample notice, in pursuance of an act of the Legislature of each, respectively, declare its desire to become a State of the Confederacy, the whole Choctaw and Chickasaw country, as above defined, shall be received and admitted into the Confederacy as one of the Confederate States, on equal terms, in all respects, with the original States, without regard to population ; and all the members of the Choctaw and Chickasaw Nations shall thereby become citizens of the Confederate States, not including, however, among such members, the individuals of the bands settled in the leased district aforesaid.

Proviso. Provided, That, as a condition precedent to such admission, the said nations shall provide for the survey of their lands, the holding in severalty of parts thereof by their people, the dedication of at least one section in every thirty-six to purposes of education, and the sale of such portions as are not reserved for these, or other special purposes, to citizens of the Confederate States alone, on such terms as the said nation shall see fit to fix, not intended or calculated to prevent the sale thereof.

ARTICLE XXIX. The proceeds of such sales shall belong entirely to members of the Choctaw and Chickasaw Nations, and be distributed among them or invested for them in proportion to the whole population of each, in such manner as the Legislatures of said nations shall provide; nor shall any other persons ever have any interest in the annuities or funds of either the Choctaw or Chickasaw people, nor any power to legislate in regard thereto. *Proceeds of sale of lands; to whom they belong and how distributed.*

ARTICLE XXX. Whenever the desire of the Creek and Seminole people and the Cherokees to become a part of the said State shall be expressed, in the same manner and with the same formalities, as is above provided for in the case of the Choctaw and Chickasaw people, the country of the Creeks and Seminoles, and that of the Cherokees, respectively, or either by itself, may be annexed to and become an integral part of said State, upon the same conditions and terms, and with the same rights to the people of each, in regard to citizenship and the proceeds of their lands. *Country of the Creeks and Seminoles and the Cherokees may become an integral part of said State.*

ARTICLE XXXI. The Choctaw and Chickasaw Nations may, by joint act of their legislative authorities, receive and incorporate in either nation as members thereof, or permit to settle and reside upon the national lands, such Indians of any other nation or tribe as to them may seem good; and each nation alone shall determine who are members and citizens of the nation entitled to vote at elections and share in annuities: *Provided,* That when persons of another nation or tribe shall once have been received as members of either nation, they shall not be disfranchised or subjected to any other restrictions upon the right of voting than such as shall apply to the Choctaws or Chickasaws themselves. But no Indians, other than Choctaws and Chickasaws, not settled in the Choctaw and Chickasaw country, shall be permitted to come therein to reside, without the consent and permission of the legislative authority of each nation. *Indians of other nations may settle on the lands of the Choctaws and Chickasaws. Who to vote at elections and share in annuities. Proviso.*

ARTICLE XXXII. If any citizen of the Confederate States, or any other person, not being permitted to do so by the authorities of either of said nations, or authorised by the terms of this treaty, shall attempt to settle upon any lands of said nation, he shall forfeit the protection of the Confederate States, and such punishment may be inflicted upon him, not being cruel, unusual or excessive, as may have been previously prescribed by the law of said nation. *Punishment of persons for settling on their lands without authority.*

ARTICLE XXXIII. No citizen or inhabitant of the Confederate States shall pasture stock on the lands of the Choctaw or Chickasaw Nation; but their citizens shall be at liberty at all times, and whether for business or pleasure, peaceably to travel the Choctaw and Chickasaw country, to drive their stock through the same, and to halt such reasonable time, on the way, as may be necessary to recruit their stock, such delay being in good faith for that purpose and for no other; and members of the Choctaw and Chickasaw Nations shall have the same rights and privileges under the same and no other restrictions and limitations in each of the Confederate States. *Who not to pasture stock on their lands. Liberty given to travel in their country, and drive stock through the same.*

ARTICLE XXXIV. If any person hired or employed by the agent, or by any other person whatever, within the agency reserve, or any post or fort, shall violate the laws of the nation in such manner as to become an unfit person to continue in the Choctaw or Chickasaw country, he or she shall be removed by the superintendent, upon the application of the Executive of the nation in which such person is, the superintendent being satisfied of the truth and sufficiency of the charges preferred. *Unfit persons employed within the agency reserve may be removed.*

ARTICLE XXXV. The officers and people of the Choctaw and Chickasaw Nations, respectively, shall, at all times, have the right of safe- *Rights, privileges and immuni-*

ties of the Choc- conduct and free passage through the lands of each other; and the
taws and Chicka- members of each nation shall have the right freely, and without seeking
saws respectively. license or permission, to settle within the country of the other, and
shall, thereupon, be entitled to all the rights, privileges and immunities
of members thereof, including the right of voting at all elections and of
being deemed qualified to hold all offices whatever; except that no
Choctaw shall be eligible in the Chickasaw Nation to the office of Chief
Proviso.   Executive or to the Legislature: *And provided, also*, That no member
of either nation shall be entitled to participate in any funds belonging
to the other.   Members of each nation shall have the right to institute
and prosecute suits in the courts of the other, under such regulations as
may, from time to time, be prescribed by their respective Legislatures.

Surrender of fu-   ARTICLE XXXVI. Any person duly charged with a criminal offence
gitives from jus- against the laws of either the Choctaw or Chickasaw Nation, and escap-
tice.   ing into the jurisdiction of the other, shall be promptly surrendered
upon the demand of the proper authority of the nation within whose
jurisdiction the offence shall be alleged to have been committed.

ARTICLE XXXVII. The Choctaw and Chickasaw Nations shall
promptly deliver up all persons accused of any crime against the laws of
the Confederate States, or any State there f, who may be found within
their limits, on the demand or requisition of the Executive of a State, or
the Executive or other proper officer of the Confederate States; and
each of the Confederate States shall, on the like demand or requisition
of the Executive of the Choctaw and Chickasaw Nation, promptly
deliver up all persons accused of any crime against the laws of such
Nation, who may be found within their limits.

Choctaw and   ARTICLE XXXVIII. In order to secure the due enforcement of so
Chickasaw coun- much of the laws of the Confederate States in regard to criminal
try erected into a offences and misdemeanors as is or may be in force in the said Choctaw
judicial circuit. and Chickasaw country, and to prevent the Choctaws and Chickasaws from being further harassed by judicial proceedings had in
foreign courts and before juries not of the vicinage, the said country is
hereby erected into and constituted a judicial district of the Confederate States to be called the Tush-ca-hom-ma District, for the special
District court purposes and jurisdiction hereinafter provided; and there shall be
for such district, created and semi-annually held, within such district, at Boggy Depot, a
where to be held. district court of the Confederate States, with the powers of a circuit
court, so far as the same shall be necessary to carry out the provisions of
Jurisdiction co- this treaty, and with jurisdiction co-extensive with the limits of such
extensive with district, in such matters, civil and criminal, to such extent and between
limits of the dis- such parties as may be prescribed by law, and in conformity to the terms
trict.   of this treaty.

Laws declared   ARTICLE XXXIX. In addition to so much and such parts of the acts
to be in force. of Congress of the United States enacted to regulate trade and intercourse with Indian tribes, and to preserve peace on the frontiers, as have
been re-enacted and continued in force by the Confederate States, and
as are not inconsistent with the provisions of this treaty, so much of the
laws of the Confederate States, as provides for the punishment of crimes
amounting to felony at common law or by statute, against the laws,
authority or treaties of the Confederate States, and over which the courts
of the Confederate States have jurisdiction, including the counterfeiting
the coin of the United States or of the Confederate States, or the securities of the Confederate States, and so much of said laws as provides
for punishing violators of the neutrality laws, and resistance to the
process of the Confederate States, and all the acts of the Provisional
Congress, providing for the common defence and welfare, so far as the
same are not locally inapplicable, shall hereafter be in force in the Choc-

taw and Chickasaw country, and the said district court shall have
exclusive jurisdiction to try, condemn and punish offenders against any
such laws, to adjudge and pronounce sentence, and cause execution
thereof to be done in the same manner as is done in any other district
courts of the Confederate States.

ARTICLE XL. The said district court of the Confederate States of   Admiralty juris-
America, for the district of Tush-ca-hom-ma shall also have the same diction of the dis-
admiralty jurisdiction as other district courts of the Confederate States; trict court.
and jurisdiction in all civil suits for fines, penalties and forfeitures of
the Confederate States against any person or persons whatever residing
or found within the district; and in all civil suits at law or in equity,   Jurisdiction in
when the matter in controversy is of greater value than five hundred civil cases.
dollars, between a citizen or citizens of any State or States of the Confederate States, or any Territory of the same, or an alien or aliens and a
citizen or citizens of the said district, or person or persons, residing
therein; and the Confederate States will, by suitable enactments, provide for the appointment of a Judge and other proper officers of the   Appointment of
said court, and make all necessary enactments and regulations for the judge and other
complete establishment and organization of the same, and to give full officers of the
effect to its proceedings and jurisdiction.

ARTICLE XLI. The trial of all offences, amounting to felony at com-   Trial of felonies
mon law or by statute, committed by an Indian of any one of the tribes committed by cer-
or bands settled in the leased district aforesaid, against the person or against Choctaws
property of a member of the Choctaw or Chickasaw Nation, or by one or Chickasaws, and
of the latter against the person or property of one of the former, shall be vice versa.
had in the district court of the Confederate States hereby provided for;
and, until such court is established, in the district court of the Confederate States for the district, or for the western district of Arkansas.

ARTICLE XLII. The district court shall have no jurisdiction to try   The court to
and punish any person for any offence committed prior to the day of the have no jurisdic-
signing of this treaty; nor shall any action in law or equity be main- the offence was
tained therein except by the Confederate States or one of them, committed, or the
where the cause of action shall have accrued more than three years be- cause of action ac-
fore the same day of the signing hereof, or before the bringing of the crued prior to the
suit. signing of this
treaty.

ARTICLE XLIII. All persons who are members of the Choctaw or   Choctaws or
Chickasaw Nation, and are not otherwise disqualified or disabled, shall Chickasaws com-
hereafter be competent witnesses, in all civil and criminal suits and pro- petent as witnesses
ceedings in any court in the Confederate States, or any one of the States,
any law to the contrary notwithstanding.

ARTICLE XLIV. Whenever any person, who is a member of the   When indicted
Choctaw or Chickasaw Nation, shall be indicted for any offence in any in any court of the
court of the Confederate States, including the district court of the C. S or State court
Tush-ca-hom-ma district, or in a State court, he shall be entitled, as of for witnesses.
common right, to subpœna, and, if necessary, compulsory process for all
such witnesses in his behalf as his counsel may think material for his
defence; and the costs of process for such witnesses, and of service Costs of process
thereof, and the fees and mileage of such witnesses, shall be paid by the and fees and mile-
Confederate States, being afterwards made, if practicable, in case of age of witnesses.
conviction, out of the property of the accused. And whenever the   When accused
accused is not able to employ counsel, the court shall assign him one may be assigned
experienced counsel for his defence, who shall be paid by the Confede- counsel.
rate States a reasonable compensation for his services, to be fixed by the
court, and paid upon the certificate of the judge.

ARTICLE XLV. The provisions of all such acts of Congress of the   Rendition of fu-
Confederate States as may now be in force or as may hereafter be enacted, gitive slaves.
for the purpose of carrying into effect the provision of the Constitution

in regard to the re-delivery or return of fugitive slaves or fugitives from labor and service, shall extend to and be in full force within the said Choctaw and Chickasaw Nations; and shall also apply to all cases of escape of fugitive slaves from the Choctaw and Chickasaw Nations, into any any other Indian nation, or into one of the Confederate States, the obligation upon each such nation or State to re-deliver such slaves being in every case as complete as if they had escaped from another State, and the mode of procedure the same.

Faith and credit given to official acts of judicial officers. ARTICLE XLVI. The official acts of all judicial officers in the said nations shall have the same effect and be entitled to like faith and credit everywhere, as like acts of judicial officers of the same grade and juris **Authentication of records, laws, &c.** diction in any one of the Confederate States; and the proceedings of the courts and tribunals of the said nations, and the copies of the laws and judicial and other records of the said nations shall be authenticated like similar proceedings of the courts of the Confederate States, and the laws and office records of the same, and be entitled to the like faith and credit.

Existing laws, usages and customs in regard to slavery, declared binding. ARTICLE XLVII. It is hereby declared and agreed that the institution of slavery in the said nations is legal and has existed from time immemorial; that slaves are taken and deemed to be personal property; that the title to slaves and other property having its origin in the said nations shall be determined by the laws and customs thereof; and that the slaves and other personal property of every person domiciled in said nations shall pass and be distributed at his or her death in accordance with the laws, usages and customs of the said nations, which may be proved like foreign laws, usages and customs, and shall everywhere be held valid and binding within the scope of their operation.

Post-offices. ARTICLE XLVIII. It is further agreed that the Congress of the Confederate States shall establish and maintain post-offices at the most important places in the Choctaw and Chickasaw Nations, and cause the mails to be regularly carried, at reasonable intervals, to and from the same, at the sames rate of postage and in the same manner as in the Confederate States.

Choctaws and Chickasaws to furnish a regiment to serve in the army of the C. S. ARTICLE XLIX. In consideration of the common interests of the Choctaw and Chickasaw Nations and the Confederate States, and of the protection and rights guaranteed to the said nations by this treaty, the said nations hereby agree that they will raise and furnish a regiment of ten companies of mounted men to serve in the armies of the Confederate States for twelve months. The company officers of the regiment shall be elected by the members of each company, respectively, the Colonel shall be appointed by the President, and the Lieutenant Colonel and Major be elected by the members of the regiment. The men shall be **Pay and allowances.** armed by the Confederate States, receive the same pay and allowances as other mounted troops in the service, and not be marched beyond the limits of the Indian country west of Arkansas against their consent.

To pay no part of expenses of the present or any future war. ARTICLE L. It is further agreed by the Confederate States, that neither the Choctaw nor Chickasaw Nation shall ever be called on or required to pay, in land or otherwise, any part of the expenses of the present war, or of any war waged by or against the Confederate States.

Troops for the defence of the Indian country and frontier of the C. S. ARTICLE LI. The Choctaw and Chickasaw Nations hereby agree and bind themselves at any future time to raise and furnish, upon the requisition of the President, such number of troops for the defence of the Indian country and of the frontier of the Confederate States, as he may fix, not out of fair proportion to the number of their inhabitants, to be employed for such terms of service as the President may fix; and **Pay and allowances.** such troops shall always receive the same pay and allowances as other troops of the same class in the service of the Confederate States.

ARTICLE LII. It is further agreed, that after the restoration of peace, the government of the Confederate States will defend the frontiers of the Indian country of which the Choctaw and Chickasaw country is a part, and hold the forts and posts therein with native troops, recruited among the several Indian Nations included, under the command of officers of the army of the Confederate States in preference to other troops. *C. S. to defend the frontiers of the Indian country, and hold the fort's and posts.*

ARTICLE LIII. It is hereby ascertained and agreed by and between the Confederate States and the Choctaw Nation, that the United States of America, of which the Confederate States were heretofore a part, were, before the separation, indebted, and still continue to be indebted, to the Choctaw Nation, and bound to the punctual payment thereof in the following sums annually, on the first day of July of each year, that is to say: *Debts due by the U. S. to the Choctaw Nation:*

Perpetual annuities amounting to nine thousand dollars; under the second article of the treaty of the sixteenth day of November, A. D , one thousand eight hundred and five, and the second article of the treaty of the twentieth day of January, A. D., one thousand eight hundred and twenty-five. *for perpetual annuities;*

The sum of six hundred dollars per annum for the support of light horsemen, under the thirteenth article of the treaty of the eighteenth day of October, A. D., one thousand eight hundr d and twenty. *for the support of light horsemen;*

The sum of six hundred dollars per annum in lieu of the permanent provision for the support of a blacksmith, and the sum of three hundred and twenty dollars, in lieu of permanent provision for iron and steel, under the sixth article of the said treaty of the eighteenth day of October, A. D., one thousand eight hundred and twenty, and the ninth article of the said treaty of the twentieth day of January, A. D., one thousand eight hundred and twenty-five. *for the support of a blacksmith, and in lieu of provision for iron and steel;*

The annual interest on the sum of five hundred thousand dollars, held in trust for the Choctaw Nation by the United States, under the thirteenth article of the treaty of the twenty-second day of June, A. D , one thousand eight hundred and fifty-five; which by that article was to be held in trust for the said nation, and to constitute part of a general Choctaw fund, yielding an annual interest of not less than five per cent, per annum; and no part thereof has been invested in stocks or bonds of any kind, but remains in the hands of the United States. *for annual interest on $500,000 held in trust.*

And it is hereby ascertained and agreed between the said Confederate States and the Choctaw Nation that there was due to the said nation, on the first day of July, A. D., one thousand eight hundred and sixty-one, for, and on account of these annuities, annual payments and interests, the sum of thirty-five thousand five hundred and twenty dollars, that is to say: *Sum due the Choctaw Nation on account of these annuities, annual payments and interests.*

For the permanent annuities and other annual payments and allowances then due, ten thousand five hundred and twenty dollars.

For interest on the said sum of five hundred thousand dollars, for the year which ended on the thirtieth day of June, A. D., one thousand eight hundred and sixty-one, twenty-five thousand dollars.

And it not being desired by the Confederate States that the Choctaw Nation should continue to receive these annual sums from the government of the United States, or otherwise have any further connection or communication with that government and its superintendent and agents; therefore, the Confederate States of America do hereby assume the payment for the future of all the above recited annuities, annual payments and interest, and do agree and bind themselves regularly and punctually to pay the same to the treasurer of the said nation, or to such other person or persons as shall be appointed by the general council of the Choctaw Nation to receive the same; and they do also agree and bind *The C. S. assume the payment of the above recited annuities, annual payments and interests.*

themselves to pay to the treasurer of the said nation, immediately upon the ratification by all parties of this treaty, the said sum of thirty-five thousand five hundred and twenty dollars due on the first day of July of the present year, as aforesaid.

General Choctaw fun l held in trust by the U. S.

ARTICLE LIV. And it is further ascertained and agreed, between the Confederate States and the Choctaw Nation, that the United States of America, while the said several Confederate States were included in the said Union held, and do continue to hold, in their hands the sum of five hundred thousand dollars, paid by the Chickasaw Nation to the United States, for the Choctaw Nation, under the treaty of the seventeenth day of January, A. D., one thousand eight hundred and thirty-seven, and which it was agreed by that treaty should be invested in some safe and secure stocks under the direction of the government of the United States, redeemable within a period of not less than twenty years, and the interest thereon be annually paid to the Choctaw Nation, and be subject to the entire control of the general council; and which sum having been invested in bonds or stocks of certain States, part or all whereof are now members of the Confederate States, it was agreed by the United States, by the thirteenth article of the treaty of the twenty-second day of June, A. D., one thousand eight hundred and fifty-five, that the same should continue to be held in trust by the United States, and constitute with certain other sums, a general Choctaw fund, yielding an annual interest of not less than five per cent.

Other moneys due and owing from the U. S. to Choctaw Nation.

And it being further agreed that, in addition to the sums of money above mentioned, other moneys were justly due and owing from the United States of America when the Confederate States were parts thereof, and still continue due and owing and unpaid to the said Choctaw Nation, in part appropriated and in part unappropriated, by the Congress of the United States, under existing treaties;

The C. S. assume the duty a d obligation of collecting and paying over. to the several States of the Confederacy held in trust by the U. S. for the said nation.

Therefore the Confederate States do hereby assume the duty and obligation of collecting and paying over as trustees, to the said Choctaw Nation all sums of money accruing, whether from interest or capital of the bonds of the several States of the Confederacy, or of any bonds or stocks guaranteed by either of them, now held by the government of the United States in trust for the Choctaw Nation, and will pay over to the said nation the said interest and capital as the same shall be collected. And the said Confederate States will request the several States of the Confederacy whose bonds or stocks, or any bonds or stocks guaranteed by them are so held, to provide by legislation or otherwise, that the capital and interest of such bonds or stocks shall not be paid to the government of the United States, but to the government of the Confederate States in trust for the Choctaw Nation.

Full payment of all d bts due by the late U. S. to the Choctaw Nation, guaranteed by the C. S. to the said nation, after the restoration of peace.

And the said Confederate States do hereby guarantee to the Choctaw Nation, the final settlement and full payment upon and after the restoration of peace, and the establishment and recognition of their independence, as of debts, in good faith and conscience as well as in law, due and owing, on good and valuable consideration by the said Confederate States, and the other of the United States, jointly, before the secession of any of the States, of all sums of money that are so as aforesaid justly due and owing, by the late United States under existing treaties, to the Choctaw Nation or people, for itself, or in trust for individuals, and of any sums received by that government and now held by it by way of interest on or as part of the capital of any of the bonds or stocks of any of the States wherein any funds of the Choctaws had been invested; and do also guarantee to it the final settlement and full payment at the same period, of the capital and interest of all bonds or stocks of any of

Also of all bonds or stocks of any of the Northern States in which the

the Northern States, in which any of the said Choctaw funds may have been invested.

ARTICLE LV. All the said annuities, annual payments, and interest and the arrearages thereof, shall be applied, under the exclusive direction of the general council of the Choctaw Nation, to the support of their government, to the purposes of education, and to such other objects, for the promotion and advancement of the improvement, welfare, and happiness of the Choctaw people and their descendants, as shall to the general council seem good; and the capital sums of five hundred thousand dollars each shall be invested or re-invested, after the restoration of peace, in stocks of the States, at their market price, and in such as bear the highest rate of interest, or be paid over to the Choctaw Nation, to be invested by its authorities or otherwise used, applied and appropriated, as its legislature may direct; and the other moneys due and owing to the said nation, and payment whereof is hereby guaranteed, shall be used, applied and appropriated by the Choctaw Nation in accordance with treaty stipulations, and so as to maintain, unimpaired, the good faith of the Choctaw Nation to those for whom it will thus become trustee. And no department or office of the government of the Confederate States shall have power to impose any conditions, limitations or restrictions, on the payment to the said nation of any of said annual sums or arrearages of the said capital sums of five hundred thousand dollars each, or in any wise to control or direct the mode in which such moneys, when received by the authorities of the nation, shall be disposed of or expended. Nor shall any appeal lie to any department, bureau or officer of the Confederate States from the decision of the general council of the Choctaw Nation or of any committee, court or tribunal to which it may commit the adjudication, by any person or persons from any decision that may be rendered under the twelfth article of the treaty of the twenty-second day of June, A. D., one thousand eight hundred and fifty-five, adverse to the justice and equity of any claim presented as one of those which, under that article, the Choctaw Nation became liable and bound to pay; but the adjudication and decision of the Legislature, or of any committee, court, or tribunal, to which it may entrust the investigation or decision, against any such claim shall be absolutely final.

ARTICLE LVI. It is hereby ascertained and agreed by and between the Confederate States and the Chickasaw Nation, that the United States of America, of which the Confederate States were heretofore a part, were before the separation, indebted and still continue to be indebted to the Chickasaw Nation, and bound to the punctual payment thereof in the following amounts annually on the first day of July, in each year, that is to say: Permanent annuity of three thousand dollars, under the act of Congress of the United States, approved on the —— day of —— A. D., one thousand seven hundred and ninety.

The annual interest, at six per cent., on the sum of two hundred and seventy-six thousand seven hundred and eighty-one dollars and fifty-seven cents, the amount of so much of the United States six per cent. loans in which the funds of the Chickasaw Nation were invested, under the third and eleventh articles of the treaty of the 24th day of May, A. D., one thousand eight hundred and thirty-four.

And the annual interest, at six per cent., on the further sum of one hundred thousand dollars, the principal of that amount of Ohio six per cent. stock, in which part of the Chickasaw fund had been invested, under the same articles of the same treaties, and which was paid into the treasury of the United States, on the ninth day of January, A. D., one thousand eight hundred and fifty-seven, to the credit of the treasurer of the United

S'ates, and having been duly covered into the treasury on the fourteenth day of January in that year, there still remains.

And it is also hereby ascertained and agreed, between the said Confederate States and the Chickasaw Nation, that there was due to the said nation, on the first day of July, one thousand eight hundred and sixty-one, for and on account of the said annuity and interest, the sum of twenty-five thousand six hundred and six dollars and eighty-nine cents.

The payment of annuities and interest assumed by the C. S. And it not being desired by the Confederate States that the Chickasaw Nation should continue to receive these annual sums from the Government of the United States, or otherwise have any communication or connection with that Government, its superintendent and agents, therefore, the Confederate States of America do hereby assume the payment, for the future, of the above recited annuity and interest, and do agree and bind themselves regularly and punctually to pay the same to the treasurer of the said nation, or to such other person or persons as shall be appointed by the Legislature of the Chickasaw Nation to receive the same; and they do also agree and bind themselves to pay to the treasurer of the said nation, immediately upon ratification by all parties of this treaty, the sum of twenty-five thousand six hundred and six dollars and eighty nine cents, due on the first day of July of the present year, as aforesaid.

Moneys arising from the sales of lands ceded to the U. S. by the Chickasaw Nation. ARTICLE LVII. Whereas, it was agreed between the United States and the Chickasaw Nation, by the third article of the treaty made between them on the twentieth day of October, A. D., one thousand eight hundred and thirty-two, that as a full compensation to the Chickasaw Nation for the country ceded to the United States by that treaty, the United States would pay over to the said nation all the moneys arising from the sales of lands so ceded, after deducting therefrom the whole cost and expenses of surveying and selling the lands, including every expense attending the same;

Investment of funds resulting from entries and sales of lands, in stocks. And, whereas, by the eleventh article of the treaty of the twenty-fourth day of May, A. D., one thousand eight hundred and thirty-four, between the United States and the Chickasaw Nation, it was agreed that all funds resulting from all entries and sales of such lands, after deduction of the expenses of surveying and selling, and other advances made by the United States, should, from time to time, be invested in some secure stocks, redeemable within a period of not more than twenty years the interest whereon the United States should cause to be annually paid to the Chickasaws;

National fund of the Chickasaws held in trust by the U. S. And, whereas, by the fifth article of the treaty of the twenty-second day of June, A. D., one thousand eight hundred and fifty-two, it was agreed between the United States and the Chickasaw Nation, that the United States should continue to hold in trust the national fund of the Chickasaws, and constantly keep the sum invested in safe and profitable stocks, the interest of which should be annually paid to the Chickasaw Nation;

Sums arising from the sales of their lands that were invested by the U. S. in funds and stocks of certain of the States. And, whereas, it is now, by the Confederate States and the Chickasaw Nation, ascertained and agreed that the following sums, part of the said fund of the Chickasaws arising from the sales of their lands were invested by the United States, while the Confederate States were part thereof, in bonds and stocks of certain of the States, in manner following that is to say:

In the five per cent. stock of the State of Indiana, two hundred and ten thousand dollars;

In six per cent. stock of the State of Maryland, fourteen thousand four hundred and ninety-n ne dollars and seventy-five cents;

In six per cent stock of the State of Tennessee, one hundred and seventy thousand six hundred and sixty-six dollars and sixty-six cents;

In six per cent. stock of the State of Arkansas, ninety thousand dollars, on which no interest has been paid since the first day of July, A. D., one thousand eight hundred and forty-two;

In six per cent. stock of the State of Illinois, seventeen thousand dollars;

In six per cent. stock of the Richmond and Danville Railroad, guaranteed by the State of Virginia, one hundred thousand dollars;

And in six per cent. stock of the Nashville and Chattanooga Railroad, guaranteed by the State of Tennessee, five hundred and twelve thousand dollars.

And it being claimed by the Chickasaws that all the moneys received by the United States from the sales of their lands, after deduction of proper disbursements out thereof, have not been invested, that they have been charged with losses and expenses which should properly have been borne by the United States, and that in many cases moneys held in trust by the United States for the benefit of the orphan and incompetent Chickasaws, had been wrongfully paid out to persons having no right to receive the same; in consequence of which complaints, then as now made, it was agreed by the fourth article of the treaty between the same parties, of the twenty-second day of June, A. D., one thousand eight hundred and fifty-two, that an account should be stated as soon thereafter as practicable, under the direction of the Secretary of the Interior, exhibiting in detail all the moneys that had, from time to time, been placed in the Treasury to the credit of the Chickasaw Nation, resulting from the said treaties of the years, one thousand eight hundred and thirty-two, and one thousand eight hundred and thirty-four, and all the disbursements made therefrom; and that to the account so stated, the Chickasaws should be entitled to take exceptions which should be referred to the Secretary of the Interior, who should adjudicate the same according to the principles of law and equity, and his decision should be final; and it was also, by the same article, agreed that the cases of wrongfully made payments should be investigated by the Congress of the United States, under the direction of the Secretary of the Interior, and if any person had been defrauded by such payments, the United States should account for the amounts so misapplied, as if no such payment had been made;

Stating of account between the U. S. and the Chickasaws, of all moneys placed in the Treasury to the credit of the Chickasaw Nation, and all disbursements made therefrom.

Exceptions to account.

The U. S. to account for sums misapplied.

Therefore, the Confederate States do hereby assume the duty and obligation of collecting and paying over, as trustees, to the said Chickasaw Nation, at par, and dollar for dollar, all sums of money accruing, whether from interest or capital, of the said bonds or stocks of the said States of the Confederacy, or of stocks guaranteed by them, so held by the Government of the United States in trust for the Chickasaw Nation, and will pay over to the said nation the said interest and capital, as the same shall be collected. And the said Confederate States shall request those States to provide, by legislation or otherwise, that the capital and interest of such bonds or stocks shall not be paid to the Government of the United States; but to the Government of the Confederate States, in trust for the Chickasaw Nation.

The C. S. assume the obligation of collecting paying over as trustees, to the Chickasaw Nation, all sums of money held by the U. S. in trust for the said nation.

And the said Confederate States do hereby guarantee to the said Chickasaw Nation, the final settlement and full payment, upon, and after the restoration of peace, and the establishment of their independence, as of debts of good faith and conscience, as in law due and owing, on good and valuable consideration, by the said Confederate States and the other of the United States, jointly, before the secession of any of the States, of all sums of money received by that Government from the sales of the Chickasaw lands, or otherwise, however, in trust for the Chickasaw Nation or individuals thereof, and which remain uninvested, or which it expended in unwarranted disbursements, or in the payment of charges or expenses not properly chargeable to the Chickasaws; for the ascertainment whereof such account shall be taken, after the restoration of peace, by or under the direction of the Commissioner of Indian Affairs, as was directed by

Final settlement and full payment of all sums of money received by the U. S. from the sales of the Chickasaw lands or otherwise, guaranteed by the C. S. to the Chickasaw Nation, after the restoration of peace.

Account to be taken under the direction of the

Commissioner of Indian Affairs. the fourth article of the treaty of the twenty second day of June, A. D., one thousand eight hund ed a d fifty-two, and in accordance with th legal rules of stating accounts of trust funds and investments.

Final settlement and full payment, also guaranteed, of moneys belonging to orphans or incompetent persons; And the Confederate States also hereby guarantee to the Chickasaw Nation, the final settlement and full payment, at the same period, of all moneys belonging to orphans or incompetent persons, or to other Chickasaws, and wrongfully paid by the United States to persons unauthorized to receive them, and for that reason, or for any other not yet paid to the proper persons, under the same fourth article of the treaty last mentioned, as qualified and limited by the *proviso* added thereto by way of amendment, or under article ten of the said treaty; which cases shall be investigated by the Commissioner of Indian Affairs or by the agent under his direction;

also of sums invested in U. S. stocks, and of any other sums received by that government; And they also guarantee to it the final settlement and full payment, after the same period, of the said sums invested in United States stocks, and the said sum of one hundred thousand dollars, so covered into the Treasury on the fourteenth day of January, A. D., one thousand eight hundred and fifty-seven; and of any other sums received by that Government, and now held by it, by way of interest on, or as part of the capital of any of the bonds or stocks of any of the States wherein any funds of the Chickasaws had been invested; and they do also guarantee to it the

and of all bonds or stocks of any of Northern States. final settlement and full payment, at the same period, of the capital and interest of all bonds or stocks of any of the Northern States, in which any of said Chickasaw funds have been invested.

Annuities, interest and arrearages assumed by the C. S., how to be applied. ARTICLE LVIII. It is further hereby agreed, that the said annuity, interest and arrearages hereby assumed and agreed to be paid by the Confederate States, shall be applied, under the exclusive direction of the Legislature of the Chickasaw Nation, to the support of their Government, to purposes of education, and to such other objects, for the promotion and advancement of the improvement, welfare and happiness of the Chickasaw

Re-investment of the capital of the bonds and stocks of States, &c., and the principal of moneys due by the U. S. people and their descendants, as shall to the Legislature seem good; and the capital, in full, of all the said bonds and stocks of States, corporations, and the principal of moneys due by the United States shall be invested or re-invested, after the restoration of peace, in stocks of the States, at their market price, and in such as bear the highest rate of interest, or be paid over to the Chickasaw Nation, to be invested by its authorities, or otherwise used, applied, and appropriated, as its Legislature may direct; without any control or interference on the part of any department, bureau, or officer of the Confederate States.

When the C. S. may pay claims out of the Chickasaw funds. ARTICLE LIX. It is hereby further agreed, that no claim or account shall hereafter be paid by the Government of the Confederate States out of the Chickasaw funds, unless the same shall have first been considered and allowed by the Chickasaw Legislature.

Boundary line between the Choctaw and Chickasaw country and the State of Arkansas. ARTICLE LX. Whereas, by the first article of the treaty between the United States of America and the Choctaw and Chickasaw Nations, on the twenty-second day of June, A. D., one thousand eight hundred and fifty-five, it was provided that the boundary of the Choctaw and Chickasaw country should begin " at a point on the Arkansas river, one hundred paces east of old Fort Smith, where the western boundary of the State of Arkansas crosses the said river," and run thence " due south to Red river," which also was the line of boundary fixed by the treaties of the twentieth day of January, A. D., one thousand eight hundred and twenty five, and the twenty-seventh day of September, A. D., one thousand eight hundred and thirty; *and, whereas*, when the said line was originally run between the State of Arkansas and the Choctaw Nation it was erroneously run to the westward of a due south line from that point of beginning on the Arkansas river; *and, whereas*, when the said line was again run, by the

United States, after the making of the said treaty of the twenty-second day of June, A. D., one thousand eight hundred and fifty-five, it was arbitrarily ordered by the Secretary of the Interior, in violation of the said treaties, that the said line should not be run due south, in accordance therewith, but that the old erroneous line should in lieu thereof be retraced, and the same was accordingly done, thus leaving within the limits of the State of Arkansas a strip of country belonging to the Choctaw and Chickasaw Nations, in the shape of a triangle having Red river for its base; *and, whereas*, all the lands contained therein that are of any value, were sold or granted by the United States, and are chiefly, held and have been improved by private individuals; it is therefore agreed by the Confederate States and the said Choctaw and Chickasaw Nations that the said line so run and retraced shall be perpetuated as the line between the Choctaw and Chickasaw country and the State of Arkansas, and that the said triangular tract of land shall belong to, and continue to form an integral part of that State; and all titles to lands therein, from and under the United States, be confirmed; and it is further agreed, that in consideration therefor, the said Choctaw and Chickasaw Nations shall, upon the restoration of peace, and the establishment and recognition of the independence of the Confederate States, be paid by them the fair value of the lands included in said tract, in their natural state and condition, and unimproved, and of all the salt springs therein, at the date of the said treaty of the year of our Lord, one thousand eight hundred and fifty-five, and without interest; which fair actual value shall be ascertained by a commission of four persons, two of whom shall be appointed by the President of the Confederate States, one by the Choctaw Legislature, and one by the Chickasaw Legislature, and the expenses of which commission shall be borne by the Confederate States. *(Payment to be made to the Choctaw and Chickasaw Nati ns for their lands in the State of Arkansas, and the salt springs therein.)* *(The value thereof, how ascertained.)*

Article LXI. It is further agreed, that if the present war continues, the Confederate States will, upon the request of the Executive of the Choctaw and Chickasaw Nations respectively, advance to the Choctaw Nation the sum of fifty thousand dollars, and to the Chickasaw Nation two thousand dollars, in discharge of so much of the moneys due to each respectively, by the United States, and will invest each sum in the purchase for each nation respectively, of such arms and ammunition as shall be specified by the Executive. *(Advancement by the C. S. to the said nations.)* *(Investment of sums advanced in arms and ammunition.)*

Article LXII. All provisions of the treaties made by the Choctaws and Chickasaws, or either, with the United States, under which any rights or privileges were secured or guaranteed to the Choctaw or Chickasaw Nation, or to individuals of either, and the place whereof is not supplied by any provision of this treaty, and the same not being obsolete or no longer necessary, and so far as they are not repealed, annulled, changed, or modified, by subsequent treaties or statutes, or by this treaty, are continued in force as if the same had been made with the Confederate States. *(Certain provisions of the treaties of the Choctaws and Chickasaws with the U.S. continued in force as if made with the C. S.)*

Article LXIII. It is further agreed that the sum of two thousand dollars shall be appropriated and paid by the Confederate States, immediately upon the ratification of this treaty, to defray the expenses of the delegations of Choctaws and Chickasaws by whom this treaty has been negotiated, and that the same shall be paid over to R. M. Jones, and by him equally divided among the members of the said delegations. *($2,000 to be paid by the C. S., upon the ratification of this treaty.)*

Article LXIV. A general amnesty of all past offences against the laws of the United States or of the Confederate States, committed before the signing of this treaty, by any member of the Choctaw or Chickasaw Nation, as such membership is defined in this treaty, is hereby declared; and all such persons, if any, charged with any such offence shall receive from the President full and free pardon, and if imprisoned or held to bail, before or after conviction, be discharged; and the Confederate States will espe- *(General amnesty declared.)*

States of Arkan- cially request the States of Arkansas and Texas to grant the like amnesty
sas and Texas to as to all offences committed by Choctaw or Chickasaw against the laws of
be requested to
grant like amnesty. those States respectively, and the Governor of each to reprieve or pardon
the same, if necessary.

In perpetual testimony whereof, the said Albert Pike, as Commissioner,
with plenary powers, on the part of the Confederate States, doth
{ SEAL. } now hereunto set his hand and affix the seal of his arms, and
the undersigned Commissioners, with full powers of the Choctaw and Chickasaw Nations, do hereunto set their hands and affix their
seals.

Done in triplicate, at the place and upon the day, in the year, first aforesaid.

ALBERT PIKE,
Commissioner of the Confederate States.

R. M. Jones,	Alfred Wade,	McKee King,
Sampson Folsom,	Coleman Cole,	William King,
Forbis Leflore,	James Riley,	John P. Turnbull,
Geo. W. Harkins, jr.,	Rufus Folsom,	William Bryant.
Allen Wright,	William B. Pitchlynn,	

Commissioners of the Choctaw Nation.

Edmund Pickens,	Henry C. Colbert,	A. Alexander,
Holmes Colbert,	James McM. Lish,	Wilson Frazier,
James Gamble,	Martin W. Allen,	C. Columbus,
Joel Kemp,	John M. Johnson,	Ashalatobbe,
William Kemp,	Samuel Colbert,	John E Anderson.
Winchester Colbert,		

Commissioner of the Chickasaw Nation.

Signed, sealed and copies exchanged in our presence, July 12, 1861.

Wm. Quesenbury,   W. L. Pike,
    Secretary to the Com'r,   Wm. H. Faulkner.
W. Warren Johnson,

Dec. 20, 1861.

RATIFICATION.

Resolved, (two-thirds of the Congress concurring,) That the Congress
Ratification by of the Confederate States of America, do advise and consent to the ratifica-
Congress of treaty
with the Choctaw tion of the articles of a treaty, made by Albert Pike, Commissioner of the
and Chickasaw Confederate States to the Indian nations west of Arkansas, in behalf of the
Nations. Confederate States, of the one part, and by the Choctaw and Chickasaw
Nations of Indians, by their respective Commissioners thereunto appointed
and elected, of the other part, concluded at the North Fork Village, on the
north fork of the Canadian river, in the Creek Nation, on the twelfth day
of July, in the year of our Lord, one thousand eight hundred and sixty-
one, with the following

Amendments.

AMENDMENTS:

I. Strike out from article xxvii. the words, "to the same rights and
privileges as may be enjoyed by delegates from any Territory of the Confederate States," and insert in lieu thereof, the following words: "to a seat
in the Hall of the House of Representatives, to propose and introduce
measures for the benefit of said nations, and to be heard in regard thereto,
and on other questions in which either of said nations is particularly
interested, with such other rights and privileges as may be determined by
the House of Representatives."

II. Strike out from artic'e xxviii. the following words: "the whole Choctaw and Chickasaw country, as above defined. shall be received and admitted into the Confederacy as one of the Confederate States, on equal terms, in all respects, with the original States, without regard to population, an!—" and insert in lieu thereof, the following words: "the application of the said nations to be admitted as a State into the Confederacy, on equal terms, in all repects, with the original States, shall be referred to and considered by the Congress of the Confederate States, by whose act alone, under the Constitution, new States can be admitted, and whose consent it is not in the power of the President of the present Congress to guarantee in advance, and, if the Congress shall assent to such admission, the whole Choctaw and Chickasaw country, as above herein defined, shall constitute the State so admitted, and in case of such admission."

III. Strike out from article xliii. the following words: "or of any one of the States," and add at the end of this article the following words: "and the Confederate States will request the several States of the Confederacy to adopt and enact the provisions of this article, in respect to suits and proceedings in their several courts."

IV. Strike out from article xliv. the following words: "or in a State court," and insert in lieu thereof, the following words: "or in a State court subject to the laws of the State."

V. Strike out from the fourth paragraph of article lvii. in the phrase "two hundred and ten thousand dollars," the word "ten," and insert in lieu thereof. the word "two."

Note.—The foregoing treaty, together with the amendments, was duly ratified by the Choctaw and Chickasaw Nations, respectively.

TREATY WITH THE SEMINOLE NATION.

AUGUST 1ST, 1861.

A TREATY OF FRIENDSHIP,

Aug. 1, 1861.

Made and concluded at the Seminole Council House in the Seminole Nation, west of Arkansas, on the first day of August, in the year of our Lord, one thousand eight hundred and sixty-one, between the Confederate States of America, by Albert Pike, Commissioner, with plenary powers, of the Confederate States, of the one part, and the Seminole Nation of Red men, by its Chiefs, head men and warriors, in General Council assembled, of the other part:

Preamble.

The Congress of the Confederate States of America, having, by "An act for the protection of certain Indian tribes," approved the twenty-first day of May, in the year of our Lord, one thousand eight hundred and sixty, offered to assume and accept the protectorate of the several nations and tribes of Indians occupying the country west of Arkansas and Missouri, and to recognize them as their wards, subject to all the rights, privileges and immunities, titles and guarantees with each of the said nations and tribes under treaties made with them by the United States of America; and the Seminole Nation of Red men having assented thereto upon certain terms and conditions;

Now, therefore, the said Confederate States of America, by Albert Pike, their Commissioner, appointed by the President, under authority of the act of Congress in their behalf, with plenary powers for these purposes, and the Seminole Nation, in General Council assembled, have agreed to the following articles, that is to say:

Perpetual peace and friendship.

ARTICLE I. There shall be perpetual peace and friendship between the Confederate States of America and the people and the Seminole Nation of Red men and all its towns and individuals.

The Seminole Nation acknow-lodges itself to be under the protec-tion of the C. S.

ARTICLE II. The Seminole Nation of Red men acknowledges itself to be under the protection of the Confederate States of America, and of no other power or sovereign whatever, and doth hereby stipulate and agree with them that it will not hereafter, nor shall any of its towns or individuals, contract any alliance, or enter into any compact, treaty or agreement with any individual State, or with a foreign power:

Proviso.

Provided, That it may make such compacts and agreements with neighboring nations and tribes of Indians, for their mutual welfare and the prevention of difficulties as may not be contrary to this treaty or inconsistent with

The C. S. as-sume the protec-torate of said na-tion.

its obligations to the Confederate States; and the said Confederate States do hereby assume and accept the said protectorate, and recognize the said Seminole Nation as their ward; and by the consent of the said Seminole Nation now here freely given, the country whereof it is proprietor in fee, as the same is hereinafter defined, is annexed to the Confederate States, in the same manner and to the same extent as if it was annexed to the United Stetes of America before that Government was dissolved, with such modifications, however, of the terms of annexation, and upon such conditions as are hereinafter expressed, in addition to all the rights, privileges, immunities, titles and guarantees with or in favor of the said nation, under treaties made with it, and under statutes of the United States of America.

The Semino's country annexed to the C. S.

ARTICLE III. The following shall constitute and remain the boundries of the Seminole country, viz:' beginning on the Canadian river, a few miles east of the ninety-seventh parallel of west longitude where Okhai-ap-po or Pond creek empties into the same; thence due north to the north fork of the Canadian; thence up the said north fork of the Canadian to the southern line of the Cherokee country; thence with that line, west, to the one hundredth parallel of west longitude, thence south along said parallel of longitude to the Canadian river; and thence down and with that river to the place of beginning.

Boundaries.

ARTICLE IV. The Seminole Nation hereby gives its full, free and unqualified assent to those provisions of the act of Congress of the Confederate States of America, entitled "An act for the protection of certain Indian tribes," approved the twenty-first day of May, in the year of our Lord, one thousand eight hundred and sixty-one, whereby it was declared that all the reversionary and other interest, right, title and proprietorship of the United States in, unto and over the Indian country in which that of the said nation is included, should pass to and vest in the Confederate States; and whereby the President of the Confederate States was authorized to take military possession of all said country; and whereby all the laws of the United States, with the exception thereinafter made, applicable to, and in force in said country, and not inconsistent with the letter or spirit of any treaty stipulations entered into with the Seminole Nation, among others were re-enacted, continued in force, and declared to be in force in said country, as laws and statutes of the said Confederate States: *Provided, however*, And it is hereby agreed between the said parties that whatever in the said laws of the United States contained, is or may be contrary to or inconsistent with any article or provision of this treaty, is to be of none effect henceforward, and shall, upon the ratification hereof, be deemed and taken to have been repealed and annulled as of the present date, and this assent thus qualified and conditioned, shall relate to, and be taken to have been given upon the said day of the approval of the said act of Congress.

Assent of the Seminole Nation to the act of May 21, 1861, for the protection of certain Indian tribes.

Proviso.

ARTICLE V. The Confederate States of America do hereby solemnly guarantee to the Seminole Nation, to be held by it to its own use and behoof in fee simple forever, the lands included within the boundries defined in the preceding article of this treaty; to be held by the people of the said nation in common, as they have heretofore been held so long as grass shall grow and water run, if the said nation shall so please, but with power of making partition thereof and disposition of the same by laws of the nation duly enacted; by which partition or sale, title in fee simple absolute shall vest in parceners and purchasers whenever it shall please the nation of its own free will and accord and without solicitation from any quarter to do so; which solicitation the Confederate States hereby solemnly agree never to use; and the title and tenure hereby guaranteed to the said nation is and shall be subject to no other conditions, reservations or restrictions whatever, than such as are hereinafter specially expressed.

Guarantee of lands to the Seminole Nation included within the boundaries defined

Power to dispose of said lands or make partition thereof.

Lands not to be disposed of to any foreign power, State or Government. ARTICLE VI. None of the said lands hereby guaranteed to the Seminole Nation shall be sold, ceded, or otherwise disposed of to any foreign power, or to any State or government whatever; and in case any such sale, cession or disposition should be made without the consent of the Confederate States, all the said lands shall thereupon revert to the Confederate States.

Country ceded to the Seminole Nation by the treaty of Aug. 7, 1856, not to be disposed of without the consent of both the Creek and Seminole Nations. ARTICLE VII. It is further hereby agreed and stipulated, that no part of the tract of country hereinbefore guaranteed to the Seminole Nation, being the same that was ceded to it by the treaty of the seventh day of August, A. D., one thousand eight hundred and fifty-six, between the United States of America and the Creek and Seminole Nations of Indians, shall ever be sold or otherwise disposed of without the consent of both of said nations being legally given.

No State or Territory to pass laws for the Government of the Seminole Nation. ARTICLE VIII. The Confederate States of America do hereby solemnly agree and bind themselves, that no State or Territory shall ever pass laws for the Government of the Seminole Nation; and that no portion of the country hereby guaranteed to it shall ever be embraced or included within

Seminoles not to be incorporated into any other territorial or political organization. or annexed to any Territory or Province; nor shall any attempt ever be made, except upon the free, voluntary and unsolicited application of the said nation, to erect the said country, by itself or with any other, into a State, or any other territorial or political organization, or to incorporate it into any State previously created.

Unrestricted right of self-government and full jurisdiction over persons and property, guaranteed. ARTICLE IX. So far as may be compatible with the Constitution of the Confederate States, and with the laws made, enacted or adopted in conformity thereto, regulating trade and intercourse with the Indian tribes, as the same are limited and modified by this treaty, the Seminole Nation shall possess the otherwise unrestricted right of self government, and full jurisdiction, judicial and otherwise, over persons and property within its

Exception. limits, excepting only such white persons as are not, by birth, adoption or otherwise, members of either the Seminole or Creek Nation; and that

Membership defined. there may be no doubt as to the meaning of this exception, it is hereby declared that every white person who, having married a Seminole or Creek woman, resides in the said Seminole country, or who, without intermarrying, is permanently domiciled therein with the consent of the authorities of the nation, and votes at elections, is to be deemed and taken as a member of the said nation, within the true intent and meaning of

Punishment of offences. this article; and that the exception contained in the laws for the punishment of offences committed in the Indian country, to the effect that they shall not extend or apply to offences committed by one Indian against the person and property of another Indian shall be so extended and enlarged by virtue of this article when ratified, and without further legislation, as that none of said laws shall extend or apply to any offence committed by any Indian, or negro, or mulatto, or by any such white person, so by birth, adoption, or otherwise, a member of the Seminole or Creek Nation against the person or property of any Indian, negro, or mulatto, or any such white person, when the same shall be committed within the limits of the said Seminole Nation as hereinbefore defined; but all such persons shall be subject to the laws of the Seminole Nation, and to prosecution and trial before its tribunals, and to punishment according to such laws in all respects like native members of the said Nation.

Intruders to be kept out of the country. ARTICLE X. All persons who are not members of either the Seminole or Creek Nation found in the Seminole country as hereinbefore limited, shall be considered as intruders, and be removed and kept out of the same, either by the civil officers of the nation under the direction of the Executive, or the General Council, or by the agent of the Confederate States for the nation, who shall be authorized to demand, if necessary, the aid of the

Exceptions. military for that purpose; with the following exceptions only, that is to say: such individuals with their families as may be in the employment of the Government of the Confederate States; all persons peaceably travelling, or temporarily sojourning in the country, or trading therein under license from the proper authority; and such persons as may be permitted by the Seminoles or Creeks with the assent of the agent of the Confederate States to reside within their respective limits without becoming members of either of said tribes.

ARTICLE XI. A tract of two sections of land, to be laid off under the direction of the President of the Confederate States, and to include the site of the present Seminole agency, whereon the public buildings of that agency have been erected, is hereby reserved to the Confederate States and not included in the guarantee of lands aforesaid, but shall be within the sole and exclusive jurisdiction of the Confederate States, except as to members of the Seminole or Creek Nation as above defined, all offences committed by whom thereon shall be punished by the laws and courts of the Seminole Nation whenever they would be so punished if committed elsewhere in the nation: *Provided*, That whenever the agency for the said nation shall be discontinued by the Confederate States, and an agent no longer appointed, the said tract of two sections of land shall pass to and vest absolutely in the Seminole Nation in the same manner as its other lands with all the buildings that may be thereupon. *Reservation of lands for Indian agency.* *Proviso.*

ARTICLE XII. The Confederate States shall have the right to build, establish, and maintain such forts and military posts, temporary or permanent, and to make and maintain such military and post-roads as the President may deem necessary in the Seminole country; and the quantity of one mile square of land, including each fort or post, shall be reserved to the Confederate States, and within their sole and exclusive jurisdiction, so long as such fort or post is occupied; but no greater quantity of land beyond one mile square shall be used or occupied, nor any greater quantity of timber felled than of each is actually requisite; and if in the establishment of such fort, post or road, or of the agency, the property of any individual member of the Seminole Nation, or any property of the nation itself, other than land, timber, stone and earth, be taken, destroyed or injured, just and adequate compensation shall be made by the Confederate States. *Reservation of lands for forts, military posts and post-roads.*

ARTICLE XIII. The Confederate States, or any company incorporated by them, or any one of them, shall have the right of way for railroads or telegraph lines through the Seminole country; but in the case of any incorporated company, it shall have such right of way only upon such terms and payment of such amount to the Seminole Nation as may be agreed upon between it and the National Council thereof; or, in case of disagreement, by making full compensation, not only to individual parties injured, but also to the nation for the right of way; all damage and injury done to be ascertained and determined in such manner as the President of the Confederate States shall direct. And the right of way granted by said nation for any railroad, shall be perpetual, or for such shorter term as the same may be granted, in the same manner as if no reversion of their lands to the Confederate States were provided for, in case of abandonment by them, or of extinction of their tribe. *Right of way for railroads or telegraph lines.*

ARTICLE XIV. No person shall settle, farm or raise stock within the limits of any post or fort, or of the agency, except such as are or maying be in the employment of the Confederate States, in some civil or military capacity; or such as being subject to the jurisdiction and laws of the Seminole Nation are permitted by the commanding officer of the post or fort, or by the agent to do so upon the reserve. *Settling, farming, or raising stock within certain limits, prohibited.*

ARTICLE XV. The Confederate States shall protect the Seminoles from domestic strife, from hostile invasion, and from aggression by other *Protection from domestic strife.*

hostile invasion or Indians and white persons, not subject to the jurisdiction and laws of
aggression. the Seminole Nation; and from all inquiries resulting from such invasion or aggression, full indemnity is hereby guaranteed to the party or
parties injured out of the Treasury of the Confederate States upon the
same principle, and according to the same rules upon which white persons are entitled to indemnity for injuries or aggressions committed upon
them by Indians.

License to trade   ARTICLE XVI. No person shall hereafter be licensed to trade with
with the Indians. the Seminoles, except by the agent, and with the advice and consent of
the National Council, which advice and consent, however, shall not be
necessary, in the case of traders now trading under license, until the
expiration of the year one thousand eight hundred and sixty-two.
Trader to exe- Every licensed trader shall execute bond to the Confederate States in
cute bond. such form and manner as was required by the United States, or as may
No appeal from be required by the Bureau of Indian Affairs; and no appeal shall heredecision refusing after lie to any officer whatever, from the decision of the agent refusing
license. license to any applicant.

Licensed traders   ARTICLE XVII. All persons licensed by the Confederate States to
to pay annual com. trade with the Seminoles shall be required to pay to the authorities of
pensation for land the Seminole Nation a moderate annual compensation for the land and
and timber used timber used by them, the amount of such compensation in each case to
by them. be assessed by the proper authorities of the said Seminole Nation,
subject to the approval of the Confederate States agent therefor.

No license to be   ARTICLE XVIII. It is further hereby agreed, that no license
granted to trader shall hereafter be granted to any trader who is in arrear on account of any
who is in arrear. amount legally assessed to be paid by him as compensation for land and
When license timber used, and that any license hereafter granted shall be revoked on
may be revoked. failure or refusal to pay, in due time, the amount that may be therefore
How long trader legally assessed in any years. And when a renewal of license is refused
to whom renewal any trader, he shall nevertheless be entitled, if he be not a dangerous or
of license has been improper person, to remain in the Seminole country such reasonable
refused, to remain length of time as may, in the opinion of the agent, be necessary for the
in the country. purpose of collecting such debts as may be due him, being during such
time under the protection of the laws of the Confederate States, as a
person peaceably sojourning in the country.

Removal of re-   ARTICLE XIX. All restrictions or limitations heretofore imposed or
strictions upon the existing by treaty, law or regulation upon the right of any member of
right to sell per- the Seminole Nation freely to sell and dispose of to any person whatsonal property. ever, any chattel or article of personal property whatever are hereby
removed and annulled, except such as the laws of the nation itself may
have created.

Appointment of   ARTICLE XX. An agent of the Confederate States and an interpreter
agent and inter- shall continue to be appointed for the Seminole Nation, both of whom
preter shall reside at the agency; and whenever a vacancy shall occur in either
Where to reside. of the said offices, the authorities of the nation shall be consulted as to
Vacancy in said the person to be appointed to fill the same, and no one shall be appointed
offices, how filled against whom they in good faith protest; and the agent may be removed
How agent may on petition and formal charges preferred by the constituted authorities
be removed. of the nation, the President being satisfied, upon investigation, that
there is sufficient cause for such removal.

What Indians   ARTICLE XXI. The Seminole Nation may, by act of its legislative
may reside in the authorities, receive and incorporate in itself as members of the nation,
Seminole country. or permit to settle and reside upon the national lands such Indians of
Sale or lease of any other tribe as to it may seem good; and may sell to such Indians porlands to such In- tions of land, in fee or by less estate, or lease them portions thereof for
dians. years or otherwise, and receive to its own use the price of such sales or
leases; and it alone shall determine who are members and citizens of the

nation, entitled to vote at elections, hold office or share in annuities, or in the common lands: *Provided*, That when persons of another tribe shall once have been received as members of the Seminole Nation, they shall not be disfranchised or subjected to any other restrictions upon the right of voting than such as shall apply to the Seminoles themselves. But no Indians other than Seminoles and Creeks, not now settled in the Seminole country, shall be permitted to come therein to reside, without the consent or permission of the legislative authority of the nation.

The Seminole Nation alone to determine who are members and citizens of the nation entitled to vote, hold office, &c. Proviso.

ARTICLE XXII. If any citizen of the Confederate States, or any other persons, not being permitted to do so by the authorities of said nation, or authorized by the terms of this treaty, shall attempt to settle upon any lands of the Seminole Nation, he shall forfeit the protection of the Confederate States, and such punishment shall be inflicted upon him, not being cruel, unusual or excessive, as may have been previously prescribed by law of the nation.

Penalty for settling upon lands of the Seminole Nation without permission.

ARTICLE XXIII. No citizen or inhabitant of the Confederate States shall pasture stock on the lands of the Seminole Nation under the penalty of one dollar per head, for all so pastured, to be collected by the authorities of the nation; but their citizens shall be at liberty at all times, and whether for business or pleasure, peaceably to travel the Seminole country; and to drive their stock to market or otherwise, through the same, and to halt such reasonable time on the way as may be necessary to recruit their stock, such delay being in good faith for that purpose. It is also further agreed, that the members of the Seminole Nation shall have the same right of travelling, driving stock, and halting to recruit the same in any of the Confederate States.

Citizens of the C. S. not to pasture stock on Seminole lands. Right of travelling, driving stock and halting to recruit the same.

ARTICLE XXIV. The officers and people of the Seminole and Creek Nations respectively, shall have, at all times, the right of safe conduct through the lands of each other; and the members of each nation shall have the right, freely and without seeking license or permission, to settle within the country of the other, and shall thereupon be entitled to all the rights, privileges and immunities of members thereof, including the right of voting at all elections, and being deemed qualified to hold office, and excepting only that no member of either nation shall be entitled to participate in any funds belonging to the other nation. Members of either nation shall have the right to institute and prosecute suits in the courts of the other, under such regulations as may, from time to time, be prescribed by their respective legislatures.

Personal and political rights, privileges and immunities of the Seminoles and Creeks.

ARTICLE XXV. Any person duly charged with a criminal offence against the laws of either the Seminole or Creek Nation, and escaping into the jurisdiction of the other, shall be promptly surrendered upon the demand of the proper authority of the nation within whose jurisdiction the offence shall be alleged to have been committed.

Fugitives from justice to be surrendered.

ARTICLE XXVI. The Seminole Nation shall promptly apprehend and deliver up all persons accused of any crime against the laws of the Confederate States or any State thereof, who may be found within its limits, on demand of any proper officer of a State of the Confederate States; and the authorities of each of said States shall in like manner deliver up, on demand of the Executive authority of the Seminole Nation, any person subject to the jurisdiction of the tribunals of such nation, and accused of any crime against its laws.

Apprehension and surrender of persons accused of crime.

ARTICLE XXVII. In addition to so much and such parts of the acts of Congress of the United States, enacted to regulate trade and intercourse with Indian tribes, and to preserve peace on the frontiers, as may have been re-enacted and continued in force by the Confederate States, and as are not inconsistent with the provisions of this treaty, so much of the law of the Confederate States as provide for the punishment of

Laws in force in the Seminole country defined.

22

crimes amounting to felony at common law, or by statute, against the laws, authority or treaties of the Confederate States, and over which the courts of the Confederate States have jurisdiction, including the counterfeiting the coin of the Confederate States or of the United States, or the securities of the Confederate States, or in uttering counterfeit coin or securities, and so much of such laws as provides for the punishment of violators of neutrality laws and resistance to the process of the Confederate States and all the acts of the Provisional Congress providing for the common defence and welfare, so far as the same are not locally inapplicable, shall hereafter be in force in the Seminole country.

Any member of the Seminole Nation indicted in any court of the C. S. entitled to process for witnesses.

ARTICLE XXVIII. Whenever any person who is a member of the Seminole Nation shall be indicted for any offence in any court in the Confederate States, or in a State court, he shall be entitled as of common right to subpœna, and if necessary, compulsory process for all such witnesses in his behalf as his council may think material for his defence; and the costs of process for such witnesses and of service thereof, and the fees and mileage of such witnesses shall be paid by the Confederate States, being afterwards made, if practicable, in the case of conviction, of the property of the accused. And whenever the accused is not able to employ counsel, the court shall assign him one experienced counsel for his defence, who shall be paid by the Confederate States a reasonable compensation for his services, to be fixed by the court, and paid upon the certificate of the judge.

Costs of process and fees and mileage of witnesses paid by the C. S.

When accused may be assigned counsel.

Law in regard to the rendition of fugitive slaves or fugitives from labor, extended to the Seminole Nation.

ARTICLE XXIX. The provisions of all such acts of the Congress of the Confederate States as may now be in force, or as may hereafter be enacted for the purpose of carrying into effect the provisions of the Constitution in regard to the re-delivery of fugitive slaves or fugitives from labor and service, shall extend to, and be in full force within the said Seminole Nation; and shall also apply to all cases of escape of fugitive slaves from the said Seminole Nation into any other Indian nation or into one of the Confederate States; the obligation upon each such nation or State to re-deliver such slaves being in every case as complete as if they had escaped from another State, and the mode of procedure the same.

Persons of the Seminole Nation made competent witnesses in cases in the C. S. courts.

ARTICLE XXX. Persons belonging to the Seminole Nation shall hereafter be competent witnesses in all cases, civil and criminal, in the courts of the Confederate States, unless rendered incompetent from some other cause than their Indian blood or descent.

May take hold and pass lands by purchase or descent, and sue and implead in any of the courts of the C. S.

ARTICLE XXXI. It is hereby further agreed by the Confederate States, that all the members of the Seminole Nation as hereinbefore defined, shall be henceforward competent to take, hold and pass by purchase or descent, lands in any of the Confederate States heretofore or hereafter acquired by them, and to sue and implead in any of the courts of each of the States, in the same manner, and as fully, and under the same terms and restrictions, and on the same conditions only as citizens of another of the Confederate States can do.

Effect of official acts of judicial officers in said nation.

ARTICLE XXXII. Whenever regular courts of justice shall be established in the Seminole Nation, the official acts of all its judicial officers shall have the same effect, and be entitled to the like faith and credit everywhere as the like acts of judicial officers of the same grade and jurisdiction in any one of the Confederate States; and the proceedings of the courts and tribunals of the said nation and copies of its laws and judicial and other records shall be authenticated like similar proceedings of the courts of the Confederate States and the laws and office records of the same, and be entitled to the like faith and credit.

Authentication of records and laws.

Existing laws, usages and cus-

ARTICLE XXXIII. It is hereby declared and agreed, that the institution of slavery in the Seminole Nation is legal and has existed from

time immemorial; that slaves are taken and deemed to be personal
property; that the title to slaves and other property having its origin in
the said nation shall be determined by the laws and customs thereof;
and that the slaves and other personal property of every person domiciled
in said nation shall pass and be distributed at his or her death in accordance with the laws, usages and customs of the said nation, which may
be proved like foreign laws, usages and customs, and shall everywhere
be held valid and binding within the scope of their operation.

Toms, in respect to slavery, declared binding.

ARTICLE XXXIV. No *ex post facto* law or law impairing the obligation of contracts shall ever be enacted by the legislative authority of
the Seminole Nation to affect any other persons than its own people;
nor shall any citizen of the Confederate States or member of any other
Indian nation or tribe be deprived of his property, or deprived or restrained of his liberty, or fine, penalty or forfeiture be imposed on him in
the said country, except by the law of the land, nor without due process
of the law; nor shall any such citizen be in any way deprived of any of
the rights guaranteed to all citizens by the Constitution of the Confederate States; and it shall be within the province of the agent to prevent
any infringement of such rights and of this article, if it should in any
case be necessary.

No ex post facto law, or law impairing the obligation of contracts, affect any other than its own people. Rights of person and property secured to citizens of the C. S. and members of other Indian Nations.

ARTICLE XXXV. It is hereby further agreed, that the Congress of
the Confederate States shall establish and maintain post-offices at the
most important places in the Seminole Nation, and cause the mails to be
regularly carried, at reasonable intervals, to and from the same, at the
same rates of postage and in the same manner as in the Confederate
States.

Post-offices and mails.

ARTICLE XXXVI. It is further agreed by the said Confederate
States, that the said Seminole Nation shall never be required or called
upon to pay, in land or otherwise, any part of the expenses of the
present war, or of any war waged by or against the Confederate States.

Seminoles not to pay expenses of present or any future war.

ARTICLE XXXVII. In order to enable the Creek and Seminole
Nations to claim their rights and secure their interests without the
intervention of counsel or agents, and as they were originally one and
the same people and are now entitled to reside in the country of each
other, they shall be jointly entitled to a delegate to the House of Representatives of the Confederate States of America, who shall serve for
the term of two years, and be a member of one of said nations, over
twenty-one years of age, and laboring under no legal disability by the
law of either nation; and each delegate shall be entitled to the same
rights and privileges as may be enjoyed by the delegate from any Territory of the Confederate States to the said House of Representatives.
Each shall receive such pay and mileage as shall be fixed by the Congress of the Confederate States. The first election for delegate shall be
held at such time and places, and be conducted in such manner as shall
be prescribed by the agent of the Confederate States for the Creeks, to
whom returns of such election shall be made, and he shall declare the
person having the greatest number of votes to be duly elected, and give
him a certificate of election accordingly, which shall entitle him to his
seat. For all subsequent elections, the times, places and manner of holding them and ascertaining and certifying the result shall be prescribed
by law of the Confederate States.

Representatives in Congress.

Election of dele-gate.

ARTICLE XXXVIII. It is hereby ascertained and agreed by and between
the Confederate States and the Seminole Nation, that the United States of
America, of which the Confederate States were heretofore a part, were,
before the separation, indebted, and still continue to be indebted, to the
Seminole Nation in the following sums, annually, and bound to the punc-

Annuities, inter-est and annual in-stalments and ar-rearages there o f due by the U. S. to the Seminole Na-tion.

tual payment thereof to them, on the thirteenth day of December, in each year, that is to say:

Perpetual annuities, amounting to the sum of twenty-five thousand dollars, being the annual interest at the rate of five per cent. per annum on the two sums of two hundred and fifty thousand dollars each, which were, by the eighth article of the treaty of the seventh day of August, A. D., one thousand eight hundred and fifty-six, to be invested by the United States at that rate of interest, and the interest to be regularly paid over to the nation *per capita* as annuity; no part of which was ever invested.

And the sums of three thousand dollars, for the support of schools, two thousand dollars, for agricultural assistance, and two thousand two hundred dollars, for the support of smiths and smith-shops among the Seminoles, which were, by the same treaty, to be paid annually for ten years from and after the making of the said treaty.

And it is hereby further ascertained and agreed, that there was due to the Seminole Nation from the United States of America, on the thirtieth day of December, in the year of our Lord, one thousand eight hundred and sixty, on account of said annual payments, and the arrearages thereof, the sums following, that is to say:

For arrearages of the said sum of three thousand dollars, annually, for the support of schools, from the seventh day of August, A. D., one thousand eight hundred and fifty-six, until, and including the payment for, the thirtieth day of December, A. D., one thousand eight hundred and sixty, thirteen thousand dollars.

The sum of two thousand dollars, for agricultural assistance, and the sum of two thousand two hundred dollars, for the support of smiths and smith-shops, both payable on the day last mentioned.

And it not being desired by the Confederate States that the Seminole Nation should continue to receive these annual sums from the Government of the United States, or otherwise have any further connection or communication with that Government; and they being willing, for the benefit and improvement of the Seminole people, to extend the time during which the said annual sums of three thousand dollars, for the support of schools, and of two thousand two hundred dollars, for the support of smiths and smith-shops, shall be paid; therefore, the said Confederate States of America, do hereby assume the payment, for the future, of the above-recited annuity and annual payments, and do agree and bind themselves regularly and punctually to pay the same in manner following, that is to say:

The C. S. assume the payment of the annuities and annual payments.

The said annuity or annual interest of twenty-five thousand dollars, annually, forever, commencing with the thirtieth day of December next, five thousand dollars thereof, annually, to the treasurer of the nation, to be used and disbursed as the General Council shall direct for governmental and other purposes, and the residue of twenty thousand dollars, annually, *per capita*, to all the individuals of the Seminole Nation, equally and share and share alike: *Provided*, That after the restoration of peace, and the establishment and recognition of the independence of the Confederate States, and if it be required by the General Council of the Seminole Nation, the capital sum of five hundred thousand dollars, on which the said annual interest is hereby provided to be paid, shall be invested by the President in safe stocks, at their market value, bearing an annual interest of at least six per cent., so that the most advantageous investment possible shall be made for the Seminole Nation; which stocks shall be thereafter held in trust for the Seminole people, and the interest thereon collected by the Confederate States, and by them paid annually to the Seminoles, five thousand dollars in each year to the treasurer of the nation, to be applied to such governmental and other purposes as the General Council shall direct, and the whole residue, *per capita*, to all the individuals of the nation. The said sum of three thousand dollars, for the support of schools, annually, for twenty years from and after the making of this treaty, beginning with the present year of our Lord, one thousand eight hundred and sixty-one, and payable on the thirtieth day of December in each year; to be expended and applied under the direction of the President of the Confederate States by the agent of the Seminoles.

The said sum of two thousand two hundred dollars, for the support of smiths and smith-shops, annually, for ten years from and after the making of this treaty, beginning with the present year of our Lord, one thousand eight hundred and sixty-one, and payable on the thirtieth day of December in each year, to be expended and applied by, or under the direction of, the General Council for the support of smiths and smith-shops in the said nation.

The said sum of two thousand dollars, for agricultural assistance, annually, for five years, from and after the making of this treaty, beginning with the present year of our Lord, one thousand eight hundred and sixty-one, and payable on the thirtieth day of December in each year, to be expended and applied, under the direction of the President, in the way of agricultural assistance, by the agent of the Confederate States for the said nation.

And the said Confederate States do also agree and bind themselves to appropriate and pay immediately after the complete ratification of this treaty, the sum of seventeen thousand two hundred dollars, the aggregate of the sums which were so due and payable as aforesaid, on the thirtieth day of December, A. D., one thousand eight hundred and sixty; the sums of thirteen thousand and two thousand dollars, part thereof, to be expended and disbursed by the agent, under the direction of the President, the former for the support of schools, and the latter in the way of agricultural assistance; and the sum of two thousand two hundred dollars, the residue thereof, to be paid to the treasurer of the nation, and applied by the General Council to the support of smiths and smith-shops: *Provided*, That the President shall not be required to expend the whole of said sum of thirteen thousand dollars at once; but shall apply the same judiciously, from time to time, and at such times and in such sums, as shall seem to him best calculated to diffuse the benefits of education and knowledge among the children of the Seminoles. And it is further agreed by the Confederate States that they will also add to the said sum the further sum of one thousand dollars, to be applied by the agent to the erection of two additional school houses, at suitable points in the Seminole country.

ARTICLE XXXIX. It being alleged by the Seminole people that certain persons among them are entitled to compensation for the loss sustained by them by being dispossessed of a large number of slaves about the year one thousand eight hundred and forty-seven, by an illegal order of General Thomas S. Jesup, and which were protected against the claims of the owners by order of that General, at Fort Gibson or elsewhere, for a long time, and until they were delivered up to the United States sub-agent, for the Seminoles, about the first of January, A. D., one thousand eight hundred and forty-nine, by virtue of an order from the President, promulgated by the Secretary of War, in an order dated fifth of August, one thousand eight hundred and forty-eight, to be by the sub-agent delivered to the Chiefs of the Seminoles, who were to decide the right of property in and to said slaves; and that this was done by a decree of the General Council, of the fifteenth day of May, one thousand eight hundred and forty-nine, by which decree all the slaves, and their increase, having formerly belonged

Claim for compensation for loss sustained by the Seminole people by being dispossessed of a large number of their slaves.

to King Payne, were decided to belong to and to be under the control of Mieco Mut-cha-sa or Jem Jumper, the Principal Chief of the nation.

And it being also alleged by the Seminoles that the claims of the various owners of said slaves, so dispossessed of their property and deprived of the use of the same for three years or more, were made out before, and filed with, Marcellus Du Val, the sub-agent for the Seminoles, prior to the fifth of September, one thousand eight hundred and fifty-four;

And it being alleged by them, that fifty of said negroes belonged to Car-pit-cha Micco, now deceased, seven to Chilto, forty to Nelly Factor, and thirty to Eliza Chopco, daughter of Billy Bowlegs;

And it being also alleged by the Seminoles, that they could never obtain any consideration or hearing of or for these claims from the Government of the United States, not even at the time of making the treaty of the year of our Lord, one thousand eight hundred and fifty-six, on account of the determination of northern members of the Cabinet and of Congress, not to admit any right of property in slaves or pay any claim on account of the seizure or detention of slaves, even to foreign governments;

And the said negroes being alleged to have been illegally seized and detained without warrant of law or color of right, of war or otherwise;

Investigation and adjudication of such claims. Therefore, it is hereby further agreed by and on the part of the Confederate States, that the said claims shall, at the earliest convenient season, be examined and investigated by the Commissioner of Indian Affairs, who shall do so under the direction of the Secretary of War, and subject to an appeal to him and from him to the President, in such manner as shall be just and liberal under the circumstances and after such lapse of time, and

The C. S. assume the payment of the money due for the loss of service of the slaves. shall adjudicate the same upon such principles as shall be just and equitable; and if it be upon such investigation ascertained and determined that the slaves in question were illegally detained, then the Confederate States will pay to the several owners or their heirs, within a reasonable time, such amounts of money as shall be determined to have been justly and equitably due to the said several owners, for the loss of service of said slaves during such times as they shall be found to have been so detained, according to the current value of such service in the Seminole country at the time.

Payment to the heirs of Sally Factor, deceased, for two slaves killed while in the service of the U. S. ARTICLE XL. Whereas, during the war between the United States and the Seminoles, in Florida, in the years from one thousand eight hundred and thirty-six, to one thousand eight hundred and forty ——, inclusive, the United States military authorities, in Florida, compelled July and Murray, two slaves of Sally Factor, now deceased, to serve as interpreters, and retained them in such service and had them in possession for the space of nearly or quite four years, until both of them were killed, one by a soldier of the United States, and the other by the hostile Seminoles, whereby the owner lost both, and their services for four years; but her claim for compensation could never obtain a hearing or consideration at the hands of the United States, because to pay it would have been to admit the legality of property in slaves, and, therefore, even an examination of it was refused at the making of the treaty of the year one thousand eight hundred and fifty-six; therefore, the Confederate States do hereby agree to pay to the heirs of the said Sally Factor, deceased, in full satisfaction for said claim, the sum of five thousand dollars, immediately after the ratification of this treaty.

Payment of John Jumper, the Principal Chief, and others in full of their claims and in view of their loyalty and good faith. ARTICLE XLI. It being urged, with much reason, by the authorities of the Seminole Nation, that the delegates, forty in number, who went with the Superintendent of Indian Affairs to Florida, in the year one thousand eight hundred and fifty-seven, to bring about the removal of the hostile Seminoles, received but an insufficient compensation from the

United States for their time and services, in the payment of the sum of
two hundred dollars each, for four months absence from their homes; and
the said Confederate States being desirous to leave no just and fair claim
of the Seminoles, or any of them, unadjusted, or any of their friends
among the Red Men justly dissatisfied, it is, therefore, hereby agreed on
the part of the Confederate States, that they will pay upon the ratification of this treaty, to the Principal Chief, John Jumper, or Hi-na-ha
Micco, for his services at that time and in consideration of his loyalty
at the present time, the sum of five hundred dollars for himself, and the
sum of twelve hundred and fifty dollars, to be equally divided by him
among five of the principal men among the said delegates; and will also
pay to him for each of the other thirty-four delegates the sum of one
hundred dollars in full of all their claims, and in view of their present
loyalty and good faith.

ARTICLE XLII. It is hereby further agreed by the Confederate States, *Further payment*
that they will pay, upon the complete ratification of this treaty, to the *to the Principal*
Principal Chief of the Seminole Nation, to be equally divided, by him, *Chief, to be divided*
among the commissioners appointed by the General Council, and who *commission'rs who*
have negotiated this treaty, the sum of five hundred dollars, by way of *have negotiated*
compensation for their time and services therein. *this treaty.*

ARTICLE XLIII. To give the Seminoles full and entire assurance of *Letters patent of*
the completeness of their title to their lands, the Confederate States *conveyance of the*
hereby agree that there shall be executed and delivered to the Seminole *noles and assur-*
Nation letters patent of conveyance and assurance of the same, whereby *ance, to be exe-*
the same shall be guaranteed to them in fee simple forever, with *cuted and deliv-*
power of disposition, in the language of article four of this treaty, *to the Seminole*
under the Great Seal of the Confederate States, and signed by the Pres- *Nation.*
dent, upon parchment, so that it may not decay or its letters fade.

ARTICLE XLIV. A general amnesty of all past offences against the *General amnesty*
laws of the United States and of the Confederate States, committed in *declared.*
the Indian country before the signing of this treaty, by any member of
the Seminole Nation, as such membership is defined in this treaty, is
hereby declared, and all such persons, if any, whether convicted or not,
imprisoned or at large, charged with any such offence, shall receive from
the President full and free pardon, and be discharged.

ARTICLE XLV. It is further agreed between the parties that all *Certain provi-*
provisions of the treaties of the Seminole Nation with the United States *ions of the treaties*
which secure or guarantee to the Seminole Nation, or individuals thereof, *of the Seminole*
any rights or privileges whatever, and the place whereof is not supplied *U. S. continued in*
by, and which are not contrary to the provisions of this treaty, and so *force as if made*
far as the same are not obsolete or unnecessary, or repealed, annulled, *with the C. S.*
changed or modified by subsequent treaties or laws, or by this treaty, are
and shall be continued in force, as if made with the Confederate States.

ARTICLE XLVI. This treaty shall take effect and be obligatory upon *When this treaty*
the contracting parties from the first day of August, in the year of our *to take effect.*
Lord, one thousand eight hundred and sixty-one, whenever it shall be
ratified by the provisional President and Congress, or the President and
Senate of the Confederate States.

In perpetual testimony whereof, the said Albert Pike, as Commissioner,
with plenary power, on the part of the Confederate States,
doth now hereunto set his hand and affix the seal of his arms,

{ SEAL. } and the undersigned chiefs, head men and warriors of the
Seminole Nation, and commissioners with plenary powers
thereof, on the part of the Seminole Nation, do hereunto
set their hands and affix their seals.

Done in duplicate, at the place, and upon the day, in the year first aforesaid.

ALBERT PIKE,
Commissioner of the Confederate States of America to the Indian Nations west of Arkansas.

JOHN JUMPER,
Principal Chief of the Seminole Nation.
PAS-CO-FA,
Town Chief.
GEORGE CLOUD,
Town Chief.
FOS-HUT-CHI TUS-TI-NUK-KI,
Town Chief.
TA-CO-SA FIC-SI-CO,
Town Chief.
HAL-PA-TA,
Town Chief.
I-MA-THLA,
Town Chief.

FOS-HUT-CHI HA-CHO-CHI,
Town Chief.
TA-LO-A HA-CHO,
Town Chief.
O-CHI-SI CHO-FO-TO-A,
Town Chief.
CHO-FO-TOP HACHO,
Town Chief.
SU-NUK MICCO,
Town Chief.
TUS-TI-NUK CO-CHO-CO-NI,
Town Chief.

Signed, sealed and mutually delivered in our presence.

WM. QUESENBURY,
Secretary to the Commissioner.
E. RECTOR,
Superintendent of Indian Affairs for the Western Superintendency.
SAMUEL M. RUTHERFORD,
Agent of the Confederate States for the Seminoles.
JAMES M. C. SMITH,
CHARLES B. JOHNSON,
W. WARREN JOHNSON,
W. L. PIKE,
W. H. FAULKNER.

To the Indian names are subjoined marks.

A CONVENTION SUPPLEMENTARY

Aug. 1, 1861.

To the treaty of friendship this day made and concluded at the Council House of the Seminole Nation, on the first day of August, in the year of our Lord, one thousand eight hundred and sixty-one, between the Confederate States of America, by Albert Pike, their Commissioner, with full powers, of the one part, and the Seminole Nation of red men, by their Chiefs, head men and warriors in General Council assembled, of the other part.

The Seminole Nation to furnish five companies of mounted men to serve in the army of the C. S.

In addition to the said treaty, and by way of separate convention and agreement, it is hereby agreed between the said parties, that in consideration of the common interests of the Confederate States and the Seminole Nation, and of the protection and rights secured and guaranteed to the latter by said treaty, the said Seminole Nation will raise and furnish, and the Confederate States will receive into their service not less than two nor more than five companies of mounted men, to serve in the armies of the Confederate States for twelve months. Each company shall be composed of not less than sixty-four nor more than one hundred men in all. The company officers shall be elected by the member of the company; and the major commanding by a majority of the votes of all the members of the battalion. The men shall be armed by the Confederate States, receive the same pay and allowances as other mounted troops in the service, and not be moved beyond the limits of the Indian country, west of Arkansas, without their consent.

In testimony whereof, the said Albert Pike, as such Commissioner of the Confederate States, doth hereunto set his hand and affix the seal of his arms, and Hin-i-ha Micco or John Jumper, Principal Chief of the Seminole Nation, Pas-co-fa, George Cloud, Fos-hut-chi Tas-ti-nuk-ki, Ta-co-sa Fic-si-co, Hal-pa-ta, I-ma-thla, Fos-hut-chi Ha-cho-chi, Sa-to-a Hacho, O-chi-si Cho-fo-to-a, Cho-fo-top Hacho, Su-nuk Micco and Tus-ti-nuk Co-cho-co-ni Town Chiefs, Commissioners, with plenary powers thereof, on the part of the Seminole Nation, do hereunto set their hands and affix their seals.

{ SEAL. }

Done in duplicate at the Seminole agency, in the Seminole Nation, on the second day of August, in the year first aforesaid.

ALBERT PIKE,
Commissioner of the Confederate States of America to the Indian Nations west of Arkansas.

JOHN JUMPER,
Principal Chief of the Seminole Nation.
PAS-CO-FA,
Town Chief.
GEORGE CLOUD,
Town Chief.
FOS-HUT-CHI TUS-TI-NUK-KI,
Town Chief.
TA-CO-SA FIC-SI-CO,
Town Chief.
HAL-PA-TA,
Town Chief.
I-MA-THLA,
Town Chief.

FOS-HUT-CHI HA-CHO-CHI,
Town Chief.
SA-TO-A HACHO,
Town Chief.
O-CHI-SI CHO-FO-TO-A,
Town Chief.
CHO-FO-TOP HACHO,
Town Chief.
SU-NUK MICCO,
Town Chief.
TUS-TI-NUK CO-CHO-CO-NI,
Town Chief.

Signed, sealed and mutually delivered in our presence.

WM. QUESENBURY,
Secretary to the Commissioner.
E. RECTOR,
Superintendent of Indian Affairs for the Western Superintendency.
SAMUEL M. RUTHERFORD,
Agent of the Confederate States for the Seminoles.
JAMES M. C. SMITH,
Special Interpreter.
CHARLES B. JOHNSON,
W. WARREN JOHNSON,
W. L. PIKE,
W. H. FAULKNER.

To the Indian names are subjoined marks.

RATIFICATION.

Dec. 20, 1861.

Resolved, (two-thirds of the Congress concurring,) That the Congress of the Confederate States of America do advise and consent to the ratification of the articles of a treaty made by Albert Pike, Commissioner

Ratification by Congress of treaty with the Seminole Nation.

of the Confederate States to the Indian nations west of Arkansas, in behalf of the Confederate States, of the one part, and by the Seminole Nations of Indians, by its Chiefs, headmen and warriors, in General Council assembled, of the other part, concluded at the Seminole Council House in the Seminole Nation, on the first day of August, in the year of our Lord, one thousand eight hundred and sixty-one, with the following

Amendments.   AMENDMENTS:

I. Add at the end of article xxx. the following words: "and the Confederate States will request the several States of the Confederacy to adopt and enact the provisions of this article, in respect to suits and proceedings in their respective courts."

II. Strike out from article xxxvii. the following words: "the same rights and privileges as may be enjoyed by the delegates from any Territory of the Confederate States to the said House of Representatives," and insert, in lieu thereof, the following words; "a seat in the hall of the House of Representatives to propose and introduce measures for the benefit of said nations, and to be heard in regard thereto, and on other questions in which either of said nations is particularly interested, with such other rights and privileges as may be determined by the House of Representatives."

III. Strike out from article xxxviii. the following words: "or in a State court," and insert, in lieu thereof, the following words: "or in a State court, subject to the laws of the State."

Resolved further, (two thirds of the Congress concurring,) That the Congress do also advise and consent to the ratification of the Convention, supplementary to the aforesaid treaty with the Seminoles, made by the same parties of each part, and concluded at the same time and place with the same.

NOTE.—The foregoing treaty, together with the amendments, was duly ratified by the Seminole Nation.

TREATY WITH THE COMANCHES

AND OTHER TRIBES AND BANDS.

AUGUST 12TH, 1861.

ARTICLES OF A CONVENTION

Entered into and concluded at the Wichita Agency, near the False Washita river, in the country leased from the Choctaws and Chickasaws, on the twelfth day of August, in the year of our Lord, one thousand eight hundred and sixty-one, between the Confederate States of America, by Albert Pike, their Commissioner, with full powers, appointed by the President, by virtue of an act of the Congress in that behalf, of the one part, and the Pen-e-tegh-ca Band of the Ne-un or Comanches, and the tribes and bands of Wichitas, Cado-Ha-da-chos, Hue-cos, Ta-hua-ca-ros, A-na-dagh-cos, Ton-ca-wes, Ai-o-nais, Ki-chais, Shawnees and Delawares, residing in the said leased country, by their respective Chiefs and Head Men, who have signed these articles, of the other part.

ARTICLE I. The Pen-e-tegh-ca Band of the Ne-um or Comanches, and the tribes and bands of the Wich-i-tas, Cado-Ha-da-chos, Hue-cos, Ta-hua-ca-ros, A-na-dagh-cos, Ton-ca-wes, Ai-o-nais, Ki-chais, Shawnees and Delawares, now residing within the country north of Red river and south of the Canadian, and between the ninety-eighth and one hundredths parallels of west longitude, leased for them and other tribes from the Choctaw and Chickasaw Nations, do hereby place themselves under the laws and protection of the Confederate States of America, in peace and war forever. *The Comanches, &c., place themselves under the protection of the C. S.*

ARTICLE II. The Confederate States of America do hereby promise and engage themselves to be, during all time, the friends and protectors of the Pen-e-tegh-ca Band of the Ne-um, and of the Wich-i-tas, Cado-Ha-da-chos, Hue-cos, Ta-hua-ca-ros, An-a-dagh-cos, Ton-ca-wes, Ai-o-nais, Ki-chais, Shawnees and Delawares, residing, or that may hereafter come to reside, in the said leased country; and that they will not allow them henceforward to be in any wise troubled or molested·by any power or people, State or person whatever. *The C. S. assume the protectorates.*

ARTICLE III. The reserves at present occupied by the said several tribes and bands may continue to be occupied by them, if they are satisfied therewith; and if any of them are not, the tribe or tribes, band or bands dissatisfied may select other reserves instead of those now occupied by them, in the same leased country, with the concurrence and assent of the agent of the Confederate States for the reserve Indians, at any time within two years from the day of the signing of these articles. *Occupation of reserves.*

Extent of each reserve.

ARTICLE IV. Each reserve shall be of sufficient extent of good arable and grazing land, amply to supply the needs of the tribe or band that is to occupy it; and each shall have a separate reserve, unless two or more elect to settle and reside together, and hold their reserves in common.

Reserves, how defined.

The reserves shall, as far as practicable, be defined by natural boundaries that may be described, and so far as this is not practicable, by permanent monuments and definite courses and distances; and full and authentic descriptions of the reserves shall be made out and preserved by the Confederate States.

Right of property in reserve secured to each tribe or band.

ARTICLE V. Each tribe or band shall have the right to posses, occupy and use the reserve allotted to it, as long as grass shall grow and water run, and the reserves shall be their own property like their horses and cattle.

Hunting and killing of game.

ARTICLE VI. The members of all the said several bands and tribes of Indians shall have the right, henceforward forever, to hunt and kill game in all the unoccupied part of the said leased country, without let or molestation from any quarter.

Perpetual peace and brotherhood between the tribes and bands.

ARTICLE VII. There shall be perpetual peace and brotherhood between the Pen-e-tegh-ca Band of the Ne-um or Camanches, and the tribes and bands of the Wich-i-tas, Ca-do-Ha-da-chos, Hue-cos, Ta-hua-ca-ros, An-a-dagh-cos, Ton-ca-wes, Ai-o-nais, Ki-chais, Shawnees and Delawares,

Injuries, &c., forgiven.

between each of them and each and all of the others; and every injury or act of hostility which either has heretofore sustained at the hands of the other shall be forgiven and forgotten.

Tribes and bands to be good neighbors to each other.

ARTICLE VIII. The said several tribes and bands shall henceforth be good neighbors to each other, and there shall be a free and friendly intercourse among them. And it is hereby agreed by all, that the horses,

Right of property in horses, cattle and stock.

cattle and other stock and property of each tribe or band and of every person of each, is his or its own, and that no tribe or band nor any person belonging to any tribe or band shall, or will hereafter, kill, take away or injure any such property of another tribe or band or of any member of any other tribe or band, or in any other way do them any harm.

Perpetual peace and brotherhood between the Comanches, &c., and certain other tribes.

ARTICLE IX. There shall be perpetual peace and brotherhood between each and all of said tribes and bands, and the Cherokee, Mus-ko-ki, Seminole, Choctaw and Chickasaw Nations; and the chiefs and head men of each of the said tribes and bands shall do all in their power

Return of stolen property.

Apprehension and delivery of any wrong doer.

to take and return any negroes, horses or other property stolen from white men or from persons who belong to the Cherokee, Mus-ko-ki, Seminole, Choctaw or Chickasaw Nation, and to catch and give up any person among them who may kill or steal or do any other very wrong thing.

Laws of Choctaws and Chickasaws to have no force.

ARTICLE X. None of the laws of the Choctaws and Chickasaws shall ever be in force in the said leased country so as to affect any of the members of the said several tribes and bands, but only as to their own people who may settle therein; and they shall never interfere in any way with the reserves, improvements or property of the reserve Indians.

Hostilities and enmities between the said tribes and bands and State of Texas, forgotten and forgiven.

ARTICLE XI. It is distinctly understood by the said several tribes and bands, that the State of Texas is one of the Confederate States, and joins this Convention, and signs it when the Commissioner signs it, and is bound by it; and that all hostilities and enmities between it and them are now ended and are to be forgotten and forgiven on both sides.

No war to be waged or councils held except with the consent of the agent.

Who may live among them.

ARTICLE XII. None of the braves of the said tribes and bands shall go upon the war-path, against any enemy whatever, except with the consent of the agent, nor hold any councils or talks with any white men or other Indians without his knowledge and consent. And the Confederate States will not permit improper persons to live among them, but only such persons as are employed by the Confederate States and traders licensed by them, who shall sell to the Indians and buy from them at fair prices, under such regulations as the President shall make.

ARTICLE XIII. To steal a horse or other any article of property from an Indian or a white man, shall hereafter be considered disgraceful, and the chiefs will discountenance it by every means in their power. For if they should not, there never could be any permanent peace.

The stealing of property to be considered disgraceful.

ARTICLE XIV. The Confederate States ask nothing of the Pen-e-tegh-cas, Wich-i-tas, Ca-do-Ha-da-chas, Hue-cos, Ta-hua-ca-ros, A-na-dagh-cos, Ton-ca-wes, Ai-o-nais, Ki-chais, Shawnees and Delawares, except that they will settle upon their reserves, become industrious, prepare to support themselves, and live in peace and quietness; and in order to encourage and assist them in their endeavors to become able to support themselves, the Confederate States agree to continue to furnish them rations of provisions in the same manner as they are now doing, to include, also, sugar and coffee, salt, soap and vinegar, for such time as may be necessary to enable them to feed themselves. They agree to furnish each tribe or band with twenty cows and calves for every fifty persons contained in the same, and one bull for every forty cows and calves; and also to furnish to all of said tribes and bands together two hundred and fifty stock hogs, all of which animals shall be distributed by the agent to such persons and families as shall, in his judgment, be most proper to receive them, and most likely to take care of them. And they also agree to furnish, for the use of the said tribes and bands, such number of draught oxen, wagons, carts, ploughs, shovels, hoes, pick-axes, spades, scythes, rakes, axes and seeds as may be necessary, in addition to their present supply, to enable them to farm successfully. They also agree to furnish each tribe or band, annually, with such quantities as the agent shall estimate for and the superintendent require, of all such articles as are mentioned and contained in the schedule hereunto annexed, marked A, to be issued and delivered to them by the agent.

Nothing asked by the C. S. of certain of the tribes, except that they will settle upon their reserves, live peaceably, &c.

The C. S. agree to furnish rations, stock, agricultural implements, &c.

ARTICLE XV. The Confederate States will maintain one agency for the said tribes and bands at the present agency house or some other suitable and convenient location, at which the agent shall continually reside; and they do promise the said tribes and bands that they shall never be abandoned by the agent, and that he shall not be often nor for any long time away from his agency.

Agency for the tribes and bands.

ARTICLE XVI. The Confederate States will also employ and pay an interpreter for each language spoken among the said tribes and bands, and also one blacksmith, who shall also be a gun-smith, one striker and one wagon-maker, for all; all of whom shall reside at the agency; and they will furnish, from time to time, such tools and such supplies of iron, steel and wood as may be needed for the work of the said tribes and bands; and will also furnish all the people of said tribes and bands who may be sick, with medicines and medical service, at the agency, where a physician shall be employed to reside, for their benefit exclusively. They will also employ for five years and as much longer as the President shall please, a farmer for each reserve, to instruct the Indians in cultivating the soil, so that they may soon be able to feed themselves; and will erect such a number of horse-mills, to grind their corn, as the superintendent shall consider to be necessary, in order to accommodate all. And the stock and animals to be given to the tribes and bands shall be in charge of the farmers, that they may not be foolishly killed or let to perish by neglect.

Interpreter, blacksmith, striker and wagon-maker.

Tools and supplies of iron, steel and wood.

Medicines and medical service.

Farmer for each reserve.

Grist mills.

Stock and animals given, to be in charge of the farmers.

ARTICLE XVII. The Confederate States also agree to erect such buildings for the mills, and the blacksmith's shops, and houses for the farmers and interpreters, as have been erected among the other Indian tribes, and also to assist the said Indians in building houses for themselves, and in digging wells for water, and opening their lands.

Erection of buildings.

ARTICLE XVIII. The said bands and tribes agree to remain upon their

Bands and tribes reserves, and not at any time to leave them in order to make crops else-
to remain on their where. And, if they should leave them, the Confederate States shall
reserves. not be bound any longer to feed them or make them presents, or give
them any assistance.

Rifle and ammu- ARTICLE XIX. The Confederate States also agree to furnish each
nition to be fur- warrior of the said tribes and bands who has not a gun, with a flint-
nished each war- lock rifle and ammunition, which he agrees never to sell or give away,
rior. and the Confederate States will punish any trader or other white man
who may purchase one from them.

Promises made ARTICLE XX. The Confederate States invite all the other bands of
by the C. S. to the the Ne-um or Comanches to abandon their wandering life and settle
Comanches, should within the leased country aforesaid; and do promise them, in that case,
they settle within the same protection and care as is hereby promised to said tribes and
the leased country, bands now residing therein; and that there shall be allotted to them
and atone for reserves of good land, of sufficient extent, to be held and owned by them
crimes committed. forever; and that all the other promises made by these articles shall be
considered as made to them also, as well as to the tribes and bands now
residing on reserves; and that the same presents shall be made them,
and assistance given them, in all respects; and the same things in all
respects are also hereby offered the Cai-a-was and agreed to be given
them, if they will settle in said country, atone for the murders and robberies they have lately committed, and show a resolution to lead an
honest life; to which end the Confederate States send the Cai-a-was,
with this talk, the wampum of peace and the bullet of war, for them to
take their choice, now and for all time to come.

Indemnity for ARTICLE XXI. The Confederate States hereby guarantee to the mem-
horses or other bers of the aforesaid tribes and bands, full indemnity for any horses or any
property killed or other property that may be killed or stolen from them by any citizen of
stolen. the Confederate States or by Indians of any other tribe or band:

Proviso. Provided, That the property, if stolen, cannot be recovered and restored,
and that sufficient proof is produced to satisfy the agent, that it was
killed or stolen within the limits of the Confederate States.

Settlement of ARTICLE XXII. If any difficulty should hereafter arise between any
difficulties between of the bands or tribes, in consequence of the killing of any one, of the
any of the bands stealing or killing of horses, cattle or other stock, or of injury in any
or tribes on ac- other way to person or property, the same shall be submitted to the agent
count of injuries of the Confederate States, who shall settle and decide the same equitably
to person or prop- and justly, to which settlement all parties agree to submit, and such
erty. atonement and satisfaction shall be made as he shall direct.

No private re- ARTICLE XXIII. In order that the friendship which now exists
venge or retalia- between the said several tribes and bands of Indians and the people of
tion to be taken the Confederate States, and of the Choctaw and Chickasaw Nations may
for injuries. not be interrupted by the conduct of individuals, it is hereby agreed
that if any white man or any Choctaw or Chickasaw injures an Indian
of any one of said tribes and bands, or if any one of them injures a
white man or a Choctaw or Chickasaw, no private revenge or retaliation
Offenders to be shall take place, nor shall the Choctaws or Chickasaws try the person,
tried and punished who does the wrong, and punish him, in their courts, but he shall
by the C. S. be tried and punished by the Confederate States; and the life of every
Punishment for person belonging to said tribes and bands shall be of the same value as
killing without the life of a white man; and any Indian or white man who kills one of
cause. them without cause, shall be hung by the neck until he is dead.

Texan troops to ARTICLE XXIV. It is further hereby agreed by the Confederate
be withdrawn. States, that all the Texan troops now within the limits of the said
leased country shall be withdrawn across Red river, and that no Texan
troops shall hereafter be stationed in forts or garrisons in the said country
or be sent into the same, except in the service of the Confederate States,

and when on the war-path against the Cai-a-was or other hostile Indians.

ARTICLE XXV. This convention shall be obligatory on the tribes and bands whose Chiefs and headmen sign the same, from the day of its date, and on the Confederate States from and after its ratification by the proper authority.   *When this Convention to take effect.*

In perpetual testimony whereof, the said Albert Pike, as Commissioner, with plenary powers, of the Confederate States of America, to the Indian nations and tribes west of Arkansas, for and on behalf of the said Confederate States, doth now hereunto set his hand and affix the seal of his arms; and the undersigned Chiefs and headmen for and on behalf of their respective tribes and bands, do now hereunto respectively set their hands affix their seals.

{ SEAL. }

Done at the Wichita Agency, aforesaid, on this the twelfth day of August, in the year of our Lord, one thousand eight hundred and sixty-one.

ALBERT PIKE,
Commissioner of the Confederate States to the Indian Nations and Tribes west of Arkansas.

KE-KA-RE-WA,
Principal Chief of the Pen-e-tegh-ca Band of the Ne-um.
TO-SA-WI,
Second Chief of the Pen-e-tegh-ca Band of the Ne-um.
PA-IN-HOT-SA-MA,
War Chief of the Pen-e-tegh-ca Band of the Ne-um.
I-SA-DO-WA,
Principal Chief the Wich-i-tas.
A-WA-HE,
Second Chief the Wich-i-tas.
A-SA-CA-RA,
Chief of the Wich-i-tas.
TA-NAH,
Principal Chief of the Cado-Hadachos.
TAI-O-TUN,
Second Chief of the Cado-Hadachos.
CHA-WIHI-WIN,
Captain of the Cado-Hadachos.
CHA-WAH-UN,
Captain of the Cado-Hadachos.
A-HE-DAT,
Principal Chief of the Hue-cos.
CA-CA-DIA,
Second Chief of the Hue-cos.

TE-ATS,
Sub. Chief of the Hue-cos.
O-CHI-RAS,
Principal Chief of the Ta-hua-ca-ros.
SAM HOUSTON,
Second Chief of the Ta-hua-ca-ros.
CA-SHAO,
Principal Chief of the Ai-o-nais.
JOSE MARIA,
Principal Chief of the An-a-dagh-cos.
CO-SE-MU-SO,
Second Chief of the An-a-dagh-cos.
KE-SE-MIRA,
Captain of the An-a-dagh-cos.
JIM TON-CA-WE,
Captain of the Ton-ca-wes.
KI-IS-QUA,
Second Chief of the Ki-chais.
JOHN LINNY,
Chief of Sha-wa-nos,
KEH-KA-TUS-TUN,
Chief of the Delawares.

Signed, sealed and copies exchanged in presence of us.

WM. QUESENBURY,
Secretary to the Commissioner.
E. RECTOR,
Superintendent of Indian Affairs for the Confederate States.
M. LUPER,
Agent of the Confederate States for the Wich-t-tas and other Bands.
MOTEY KINNARD,
Principal Chief of the Mus-ko-kis.
JOHN JUMPER,
Principal Chief the Seminoles.

CHILLY McINTOSH,
ISRAEL G. VORE,
W. WARREN JOHNSON,
W. L. PIKE,
H. P. JONES,
CHARLES B. JOHNSON,
J. J. STURM,
WM. SHIRLEY,
W. H. FAULKNER,

To the Indian names are subjoined marks.

SCHEDULE A.

Of articles of merchandize, &c., agreed to be furnished annually, under the foregoing convention to the Comanches, Wich-i-tas, Hue-cos, Cado-Hadachos, An-a-dagh-cos, Ta-hua-ca-ros, Ki-chais, Ai-o-nais, Shaw-nees and Delawares, living on reserves in the country leased from the Choctaws and Chickasaws:

Blue drilling, warm coats, calico, plaid check, regatta cotton shirts, socks, hats, woolen shirts, red, white and blue blankets, red and blue list cloth, shawls and handkerchiefs, brown domestic, thread, yarn and twine, shoes, for men and women, white drilling, ribbons, assorted colors, beads, combs, camp kettles, tin cups and buckets, pans, coffee pots and dippers, needles, scissors and shears, butcher knives, large iron spoons, knives and forks, nails, hatchets and hammers, augers, drawing knives, gimlets, chopping axes, fish-hooks, ammunition, including powder, lead, flints and percussion caps, tobacco.

This is schedule A, of the treaty with the Pen-e-tegh-ca Band of Ne-um, and the Wich-i-tas and other bands, to which it is annexed as a part thereof.

{ SEAL. }

ALBERT PIKE, *Commissioner, &c.*

ARTICLE SUPPLEMENTARY

To the Convention between the Confederate States of America and the Pen-e-tegh-ca Band of Ne-um or Comanches, Wich-i-tas, Cado-Ha-du-chos, and other Bands settled upon reserves, made and concluded at the Wich-i-ta Agency, near the False Washita river, on the twelfth day of August, in the year of our Lord, one thousand eight hundred and sixty-one.

ARTICLE. It being well known to all surrounding tribes and univer-sally acknowledged, that, from time immemorial, the Ta-wa-i-hash people of Indians, now called, by white men, the Wich-i-tas, and of whom the Hue-cos and Ta-hua-ca-ros are offshoots, possessed and inhabited, to the exclusion of all other tribes and bands of Indians, the whole country lying between the Red river and the False Washita, from their junc-tion to the west of the Wich-i-ta mountains, and with the aid of the Ta-nei-weh Band of the Ne-um, held all that country against all comers, and had their villages and fields in the vallies of the Wich-i-ta moun-tains and upon the creeks, and there cultivated the soil, raised stock and led an industrious life; all which facts were known to the Commissioner of the Confederate States twenty-nine years ago.

And the United States of America, having, in the year eighteen hundred and twenty, and by subsequent renewals of the grant, ceded, the whole of that country to the Choctaws; and having afterwards, by patent, conveyed and assured the same to them in fee, and they having made the Chickasaws joint and equal owners of the same with them-selves; whereby the same has been wholly lost to the Ta-wa-i-hash, except such small portion thereof as has been assigned to them by way of reserve; and no compensation whatever has been made them therefor, although they respectfully presented their claim on account of the same to the Commissioner of Indian Affairs of the United States, and appealed to that Government for payment of some reasonable price for their said country, to be paid them in such manner as should be most for their benefit and improvement;

And the Commissioner knowing that their claim to compensation is a just one, and seeing how poor and helpless they are, and being willing to save them from the necessity of employing persons to urge their claim, and of dividing with them what they may receive, but not deeming himself authorized to decide what amount shall be allowed them therefor, nor in what manner it shall be paid.

It is, therefore, hereby agreed by the Confederate States, that the claim of the Ta-wa-i-hash or Wich-i-tas to compensation for their country, between the Red river and the False Washita, shall be submitted to the President for his consideration, who, if he also agrees that it is just, shall determine what amount shall be paid or allowed them in satisfaction thereof, and in what manner that amount shall be paid; and that amount shall accordingly be paid them in such manner as he shall direct.

Claim of the Wich-i-tas to compensation for their country between the Red river and False Washita to be determined by the President.

In testimony whereof, the said Albert Pike, Commissioner of the Confederate States of America to the Indian Nations and Tribes west of Arkansas, doth hereunto set his hand, on behalf of the said Confederate States, and affix the seal of his arms.

{ SEAL. }

So done and signed and sealed, at Wich-i-ta Agency, near the False Wash-i-ta river, on the thirteenth day of August, in the year first aforesaid.

ALBERT PIKE,
Commissioner of the Confederate States to the Indian Nations and Tribes west of Arkansas.

WM. QUESENBURY,
Secretary to the Commissioner.

RATIFICATION

Dec. 21, 1861.

Resolved, (two-thirds of the Congress concurring,) That the Congress of the Confederate States of America, do advise and consent to the ratification of the articles of a convention, made by Albert Pike, Commissioner of the Confederate States to the Indian Nations west of Arkansas, in behalf of the Confederate States, of the one part, and the Pen-e-tegh-ca Band of Ne-um or Comanches, and the Tribes and Bands of the Wich-i-tas Cado-Ha-da-chos, Hue-cos, Ta-hau-ca-ros, An a-dagh,cos, Ton-ca-wes, Ai-o-wais, Ki-chais, Shawnees and Delawares, residing in the country leased from the Choctaws and Chickasaws, each by its Chiefs and headmen, who signed the said articles, of the other part; concluded at the Wich-i-ta Agency, near the False Washita river, in the said leased country, on the twelfth day of August, in the year of our Lord, one thousand eight hundred and sixty-one. And that the Congress also advises and consents to the ratification of the supplementary article of the same Convention, made and concluded at the same time and place, by the said Commissioner in behalf the Confederate States, with the Ta-wai-hash or Wich-i-ta Band of Indians, with the amendments adopted, to wit:

Ratification of the foregoing treaty and supplementary article.

1st. Strike out all of article nineteen.
2nd. Strike out all of article twenty-four.

TREATY WITH THE COMANCHES

OF THE PRAIRIES AND STAKED PLAIN.

AUGUST 12, 1861.

ARTICLES OF A CONVENTION,

Aug. 12, 1861. *Entered into and concluded at the Wichita Agency, near the False Washita river, in the country leased from the Choctaws and Chickasaws, on the twelfth day of August, in the year of our Lord one thousand eight hundred and sixty-one, between the Confederate States of America, by Albert Pike, their Commissioner, with full powers, appointed by the President, by virtue of an act of the Congress in that behalf, of the one part, and the Ne-co-ni, Ta-ne-i-we, Co-cho-tih-ca and Ya-pa-rih-ca bands of the Ne-um or Comanches of the Prairies and Staked Plain, by their Chiefs and head men who have signed these articles, on the other part.*

The Comanches make peace with and place themselves under the protection of the C. S.

ARTICLE I. The No-co-ni, Ta-nei-weh, Co-cho-tih-ca and Ya-pa-rih-ca bands of the Ne-um, called by the white men the Comanches of the Prairies and the Staked Plain, do hereby make peace with the Confederate States of America, and do renew and continue the peace heretofore existing between them and the Cherokee, Mus-ko-ki, Seminole, Choctaw and Chickasaw Nations of red men, and do hereby take each and all of them by the hand of friendship, having-smoked with them the pipe of peace, and received the wampum of peace; and do hereby place themselves under the laws and protection of the Confederate States of America, and agree to be true and loyal to them in peace and in war forever, and to hold them by the hand, and have but one heart with them always.

The C S. assume the protectorate.

ARTICLE II. The Confederate States of America do hereby promise and engage themselves to be, during all time, the friends and protectors of the No-co-ni, the Ta-ne-i-weh, Ya-pa-rih-ca and Co-cho-tih-ca bands of the Ne-um, and that they will not allow them to be molested by any power or people, State or person whatever.

Settlement upon reserves.

ARTICLE III. The No-co-ni, Ta-ne-i-we, Ya-pa-rih-ca and Co-cho-tih-ca bands of the Ne-um hereby agree that they will abandon their wandering mode of life and come in from the Prairies and Staked Plain, and settle upon reserves to be allotted to them in that country which lies north of the Red river and south of the Canadian, and between the ninety-eighth and one hundredth parallels of west longitude, and which has been leased for them and other tribes of red men, by the Confederate States from the Choctaws and Chickasaws, and in which the Confederate States have offered all the Ne-um homes.

ARTICLE IV. The No-co ni, Ta-ne-i-weh, Ya-pa-rih-ca and Co-cho-tih-ca *Indians allowed to choose their own homes.* bands of the Ne-um shall be allowed to choose their own homes, in any unoccupied part of the said leased country, on or near the Canadian or False Washita rivers, or near the Wich-i-ta mountains, as may best suit them, with the concurrence and assent of the agent of the Confederate States for the reserve Indians. Each reserve shall be of sufficient extent of *Extent of each reserve.* arable and grazing lands, amply to supply their needs; and the bands may have one reserve together, or four separate reserves, as they may choose. The reserve or reserves shall, as far as practicable, be defined *Reserves, how defined.* by the natural boundaries that may be described; and so far as this is not practicable, by permanent monuments and definite courses and distances; and full and authentic descriptions of the reserves shall be made out and reserved by the Confederate States.

ARTICLE V. The said No-co-ni, Ta-ne-i-weh, Ya-pa-rih-ca and Co-cho-tih-ca bands of the Ne-um shall have the right to possess, occupy and *Right of property in reserve.* use the reserve or reserves allotted to them as long as grass shall grow or water run; and the reserves shall be their own property, like their horses and cattle.

ARTICLE VI. The members of the said No-co-ni, Ta-ne-i-weh, Ya-pa- *Hunting and killing of game.* rih-ca and Co-cho-tih-ca bands of the Ne-um shall have the right, during all time, to hunt and kill game in all the unoccupied part of said leased country without let or molestation from any quarter.

ARTICLE VII. There shall be perpetual peace and brotherhood between *Perpetual peace and brotherhood.* the No-co-ni, Ta-ne-i-weh, Ya-pa-rih-ca and Co-cho-tih-ca bands of the Ne-um, and between each of them and all the other tribes and bands of the Ne-um and of the Wich-i-ta, Ca-do-ha-da-chos, Hue co, An-a-dagh-co, Ki-chai, Ai-o-nai, Ta-hua-ca-ro, Ton-ca-we, Shawnee and Delaware Indians, occupying reserves in the said leased country, and any other bands of the Ne-um that may hereafter settle in said leased country, and every injury or act of hostility which either has heretofore sus- *Injuries, &c, forgiven.* tained at the hands of the other, shall be forgiven and forgotten forever.

ARTICLE VIII. The said several tribes and bands of the Ne-um, and *Tribes and bands to be good neighbors to each other.* the said other tribes and bands, shall henceforth be good neighbors to each other, and there shall be free and friendly intercourse among them. And it is hereby agreed by the said four bands of the Ne-um, that the *Right of property in horses, cattle and stock.* horses, cattle and other stock and property of every tribe or band, and every person of each, is his or its own, and that no one of said four tribes or bands, nor any person belonging to any one of them, shall or will hereafter kill, take away or injure any such property of another tribe or band, or of any member of any other tribe or band, or in any other way do them any harm.

ARTICLE IX. There shall be perpetual peace and brotherhood between *Perpetual peace and brotherhood between certain tribes and bands.* each and all of the No-co-ni, Ta-ne-i-weh, Ya-pa-rih-ca and Co-cho-tih-ca bands of the Ne-um, and the Cherokee, Mus-ko-ki, Seminole, Choctaw and Chickasaw Nations; and the chiefs and head men of each of the said *Return of stolen property.* bands shall do all in their power to take and return any negroes, horses or other property stolen from white men or from persons belonging to the Cherokee, Mus-ko-ki, Seminole, Choctaw or Chickasaw Nations, and to *Apprehension and delivery of wrong doer.* catch and give up any person among them who may kill or steal or do any other very bad thing.

ARTICLE X. It is distinctly understood by the said four bands of the *Hostilities and enmities between the Indians and State of Texas.* Ne-um, that the State of Texas is one of the Confederate States, and joins in this Convention, and signs it when the Commissioner signs it, and is bound by it; and that all hostilities and enmities between it and *forgotten and forgiven.* them are now ended, and are to be forgotten and forgiven forever on both sides.

ARTICLE XI. None of the braves of the said four bands of the Ne-um

No war to be shall go upon the war-path, after they are settled upon reserves, against waged or councils any enemy whatever, or as guides to any war-party, except with the held, except with knowledge and consent of the agent, nor hold any councils or talks with the consent of the agent. any white men or other Indians without his knowledge and consent.

Who may live And the Confederate States will not permit improper persons to live, among them. among them, but only such persons as are employed by the Confederate States and traders licensed by them, who shall sell to the Indians and buy from them at fair prices, under such regulations as the President shall make.

The stealing of ARTICLE XII. To steal a horse or any other article of property from property to be con- another Indian or white man, shall hereafter be considered disgraceful, sidered disgrace- and the chiefs will discountenance it by every means in their power. ful. For if they should not, there never could be any permanent peace.

White prisoners ARTICLE XIII. If there should be among the No-co-nis, Ta-ne-i-wes, to be delivered up. Ya-pa-rih-cas or Co-cho-tih-cas, any white prisoner or prisoners, it is agreed that they shall be delivered up when they come in to settle; and that if they can peaceably procure possession of any that may be held by any other band of the Ne-um, or by the Cai-a-was, or any other The C. S. to pay Prairie tribe, they will also bring them in, to be restored to liberty. And suitable rewards. the Confederate States agree that if any prisoners are so brought in and restored, suitable rewards shall be given the band that brings them in, for doing so. But this article creates no obligation to deliver up Mexicans who may be prisoners.

Comanches held ARTICLE XIV. The Confederate States also agree, that if there be as prisoners to be any person or persons held as prisoners in Texas or any other of the Con- delivered up and federate States, or in the Cherokee, Mus-ko-ki, Seminole, Choctaw or restored to their Chickasaw Nation who are of the Ne-um or Comanches, that all such bands. persons shall be set free and delivered up and restored to their band without charge or expense to the Ne-um.

The C. S. ask ARTICLE XV. The Confederate States ask nothing of the bands of nothing of the Co- the Ne-um, except that they will settle upon their reserves, become manches except industrious, prepare to support themselves, and live in peace and quiet- that they will set- ness; and in order to encourage and assist them in their endeavors to tle upon the r re- become able to support themselves, the Confederate States agree to fur- serves, live peace- nish them rations of provisions in the same manner as they are now ably, &c., and agree to furnish doing for the Wichitas and other tribes and bands settled upon reserves, them with rations, to include also sugar and coffee, salt, soap and vinegar, for such time as stocks, agricultu- may be necessary to enable them to feed themselves. They agree to ral implements, furnish each of the said bands of the Ne-um with twenty cows and calves &c. for every fifty persons contained in the same, and one bull for every forty cows and calves; and also other stock at the discretion of the superin- tendent when they desire to have the same; all of which animals shall be distributed by the agent to such persons and families as shall, in his judg- ment, be most likely to take care of them. And they also agree to furnish for the use of the said bands of the Ne-um, such number of draught oxen, wagons, carts, ploughs, shovels, hoes, pick-axes, spades, scythes, rakes, axes and seeds as may be necessary to enable them to farm successfully. They also agree to furnish the said bands of the Ne-um, annually, with such quantities as the agent shall estimate for, and the superintendent require, of all such articles as are mentioned and contained in schedule here- unto annexed, marked A, to be issued and delivered to them by the agent.

ARTICLE XVI. The Confederate States will maintain one agency for the Agency for the tribes and bands now settled upon the reserves in the said leased country, tribes and bands. and for the said four bands and all the other bands of the Ne-um that may settle therein; which agency shall be kept either at the present agency house or some other convenient location, at which the agent shall con- tinually reside; and they do promise the said four bands and all the other bands of the Ne-um that may settle in reserves, that they sh ll n ver be abandoned by the agent, and that he shall not be often nor for any long time away from his agency.

ARTICLE XVII. The Confederate States will employ and pay one inter- *Interpreter; blacksmith, striker and wagon maker.* preter for all the bands of the Ne-um settled upon the reserves; and an additional blacksmith, another striker, and another wagon-maker, shall be employed for the bands of the Neum alone, when the said four bands of the Neum shall have come in and settle upon reserves. The interpreter, blacksmith, striker and wagon-maker shall reside with some one of the bands. The Confederate States will also furnish, from time to time, *Tools and supplies of iron, steel and wood.* such tools and such supplies of iron, steel and wood as may be needed for the work of the said bands; and will also furnish them with medicines *Medicines and medical services.* and medical advice, at the agency, where a physician shall be employed to reside, for their benefit exclusively. And they will also employ, for five years and as much longer as the President shall please, a farmer for each *Farmer for each reserve.* reserve, to instruct them in cultivating the soil, so that they may soon be able to feed themselves; and will erect such a number of horse-mills, to *Grist mills.* grind their corn, as the superintendent shall consider to be necessary, in order to accommodate all.

ARTICLE XVIII. The Confederate States also agree to erect such build- *Erection of buildings.* ings for the mills, and the blacksmith shops, and houses for the farmers, interpreters and physicians as have been erected among the other Indian tribes, and also to assist the said Indians in building houses for themselves, and in digging wells for water, and opening their lands.

ARTICLE XIX. The said four bands agree to remain upon their reserves, *Bands agree to remain upon their reserves.* when they shall have settled thereon, and not, at any time, to leave them in order to make crops elsewhere. And, if they should leave them, the Confederate States shall not be bound any longer to feed them or make them presents, or give them any assistance.

ARTICLE XX. The Confederate States also agree to furnish each warrior *Rifle and ammunition to be furnished each warrior.* of the said four bands, who has not a gun, with a flint-lock rifle and ammunition, which he agrees never to sell or give away, and the Confederate States will punish any trader or other white man who may purchase one from them.

ARTICLE XXI. The Confederate States will invite all the other bands *Promises made by the C. S. to the Comanches, should they settle within the leased country and atone for crimes committed.* of the Ne-um or Comanches to abandon their wandering life and settle within the leased country aforesaid; and do promise them, in that case, the same protection and care as is hereby promised to the tribes and bands now residing therein; and that there shall be allotted to them reserves of good land, of sufficient extent, to be held and owned by them forever; and that all the other promises made by these articles, shall be considered as made to them also, as well as to the tribes and bands now residing on reserves; and that the same presents shall be made to them, and assistance given them in all respects; and the same things, in all respects, are also hereby offered the Cai-a-was and agreed to be given them, if they will settle in said country, atone for the murders and robberies they have lately committed, and show a resolution to lead an honest life; to which end the Confederate States send the Cai-a-was, with this talk, the wampum of peace and the bullet of war, for them to take their choice, now and for all time to come.

ARTICLE XXII. The Confederate States hereby guarantee to the mem- *Indemnity for horses or other property killed or stolen. Proviso.* bers of the aforesaid four bands full indemnity for any horses or any other property that may be killed or stolen from them by any citizen of the Confederate States or by any other Indians: *Provided*, That the property, if stolen, cannot be recovered and restored, and that sufficient proof is produced, to satisfy the agent that it was killed or stolen within the limits of the Confederate States.

Payment to be. **ARTICLE XXIII.** The Seminoles having asked the Confederate States to made to the Seminoles for horses pay them for certain horses stolen from them by some of the Ne-um, two stolen, according years ago, and which the United States were bound to pay for if they to the annexed could not be recovered, the Confederate States have accordingly agreed to schedule. do so, at the time of making the treaty lately with the Seminoles; and they do hereby agree, in order that the Neum may not hereafter be troubled about the horses so taken, to pay for them the sums, and to the persons, mentioned in the schedule thereof hereunto annexed; but as the Seminoles allege that one or more of their horses is now here. in the possession of some of the No-co-ni, Ta-ne-i-weh, Ya-pa-rih-ca or Co-cho-tih-ca band of Ne-um, it is agreed that, if it be so, such horse or horses shall be given up, and the person in possession shall be compensated for the loss of the same. To this end, the Chiefs will let the Seminoles see all their horses; and, after this time, it is distinctly understood that no one can get any right to property by stealing it, and that no compensation will ever again be made to any one who has given up stolen property. And the Confederate States do hereby agree with the several persons from whom horses were stolen, and the heirs of such of them as are deceased, and whose names are found in the said schedule B, hereunto annexed, that they will pay, immediately upon the ratification of this treaty, through the agent for the Seminoles, the amount of loss sustained by each respectively, according to the said schedule, except for such horses as may be returned as above provided for and noted as returned on the said schedule.

Settlement of **ARTICLE XXIV.** If any difficulty should hereafter arise between any of difficulties between the said four bands or any of their members, or between any of them and the bands on account of injuries any of the other tribes or bands settled on reserves, in consequence of to persons or prop- the killing of any one, of the stealing or killing of horses, cattle or other erty. stock, or of injury in any other way to person or property, the same shall be submitted to the agent of the Confederate States, who shall settle and decide the same equitably and justly, to which settlement all parties agree to submit, and such atonement and satisfaction shall be made as he shall direct.

No private re- **ARTICLE XXV.** In order that the friendship which now exists between venge or retalia- the said several tribes and bands of Indians, now or hereafter settled in tion to be taken for injuries. the said leased country, and the Choctaws and Chickasaws and the people of the Confederate States, may not be interrupted by the conduct of individuals, it is hereby agreed, that if any white man or any Choctaw or Chickasaw injures an Indian of any one of said tribes and bands, or if any one them injuries a white man or a Choctaw or Chickasaw, no private revenge or retaliation shall take place, nor shall the Choctaws or Chicka-saws try the person who does the wrong, and punish, him in their courts, Offenders to be but he shall be tried and punished by the Confederate States; and the life tried and punished by the C. S. of every person belonging to said tribes and bands shall be of the same Punishment for value as the life of a white man; and any Indian or white man who kills killing without one of them without cause, shall be hung by the neck until he is dead. cause. **ARTICLE XXVI.** In case either of the bands of the Ne-um, with whom Peace and friendship between this convention is made, should not consent to come in and settle, and the C. S. and such should prefer to continue to live as they have heretofore, then there shall of the bands as still be peace and friendship between them and the people of the Confede-continue to live as they have hereto- rate States, and the Cherokees, Mus-ko-kis, Seminoles, Choctaws and fore. Chickasaws, and all the tribes and bands settled upon reserves in the country aforesaid; and all of the same shall travel, without injury or molestation, through the hunting grounds of the Ne-um, and shall be treated with kindness and friendship.

Texan troops to **ARTICLE XXVII.** It is further hereby agreed by the Confederate States, be withdrawn. that all the Texan troops now within the limits of said leased country shall be withdrawn across Red river, and that no Texan troops shall hereafter be stationed in forts or garrisons in the said country, or be sent into the same, except in the service of the Confederate States and when on the war-path against the Cai-a-was or other hostile Indians.

ARTICLE XXVIII. It is further agreed by the chiefs and head men of the bands of the Ne-um who have signed this convention, that upon their return to their bands they will take this talk and the wampum of peace from the Confederate States and from the Mus-ko-kis, Seminoles, Choctaws and Chickasaws, to the bands of the Ne-um, and tell them what they have seen and heard, and persuade them also, if they can, to come in and settle upon reserves in the leased country, and at any rate to make peace by the time when the leaves fall before the next snows. *Other bands of Indians to be persuaded to come in and settle upon reserves and to make peace.*

ARTICLE XXIX. It is agreed by the parties, that the making of this Convention shall in no wise interrupt the friendly relations between the Ne-um and the people of Mexico; and that the Confederate States desire that perfect peace should exist between the Ne-um and all the Mexicans. *Friendly relations between the Ne-um and the people of Mexico not interrupted by this treaty.*

ARTICLE XXX. This convention shall be obligatory on the bands whose chiefs and head men sign the same from the day of its date, and on the Confederate States from and after its ratification by the proper authority. *When this Convention to be obligatory.*

In perpetual testimony whereof, the said Albert Pike, as Commissioner, with plenary powers, of the Confederate States of America to the Indian nations and tribes west of Arkansas, for and on behalf of the said Confederate States, doth now hereunto set his hand and affix the seal of his arms; and Wi-na-hi-hi or the Drinking Eagle, Chief of the No-co-ni band of the Ne-um, and the undersigned head men of the same, for and in behalf of that band; and the same Wi-na-hi wa, Chief of the No-co-nis, by special authorization and direction of Po-ho-wi-ti-quas-so, or Iron Shirt, the Chief of the Ta-ne-i-weh band of the Ne-um, who has been present but is now absent mourning for a relative deceased, with Ke-e-na-toh-pa a head man of the Ta-ne-i-weh band, for and on behalf of the same; and Te-hi-a-quah, Chief of the Ya-pa-rih-ca band of the Ne-um, with the undersigned head men of the same, for and on behalf of the Ya-rih-ca band; and Ma-a-we, Chief of the Co-cho-tih-ca band of the Ne-um, with the undersigned head men of the same, for and on behalf of the Co-cho-tih-ca band, do now hereunto respectively set their hands and affix their seals.

{ SEAL. }

Done at the Witchita Agency aforesaid, on the twelfth day of August, in the year of our Lord, one thousand eight hundred and sixty-one.

ALBERT PIKE,
Commissioner of the Confederate States to the Indian Nations and tribes west of Arkansas.

QUI-NA-HI-WI,
Principal Chief of the Noconi Band.
O-TE,
Sub-Chief of the Noconis.
KE-PA-HE-WA,
Sub-Chief of the Noconis.
CHO-O-SHI,
Retired Chief of the Noconis.
PO-HO-WI-TI-QUAS-SO,
Principal Chief of Ta-ne-i-weh Band, by
QUI-NA-HI-WI,
Principal Chief of the Noconi Band.
KE-E-NA-TOH-PA,
Sub-Chief of the Te-ne-wi Band.

TE-HI-A-QUAH,
Chief of the Ya-pa-rih-ca Band.
BIS-TE-VA-NA,
Principal Chief of the Ya-pa-rih-ca Band.
PE-HAI-E-CHI,
Chief of the Ya-pa-rih-ca Band.
MA-A-WE,
Principal Chief of the Co-cho-tih-ca Band.
CHO-CO-RA,
Chief of the Co-cho-tih-ca Band.
TE-CO-WE-WIH-PA,
Chief of the Co-cho-tih-ca Band.

Signed, sealed and copies exchanged in presence of us.

WM. QUESENBURY,
Secretary to the Commission.
E. RECTOR,
Superintendent of Indian Affairs for the Confederate States.
M. LUPER,
Agent of the Wichita and affiliated bands of the Confederate States.
MOTY KINNAIRD,
Principal Chief of the Mus-ko-kis.
JOHN JUMPER,
Principal Chief of the Seminoles.

CHILLY McINTOSH,
ISRAEL G. VORE,
W. WARREN JOHNSON.
W. L. PIKE,
JESSE CHISHOLM,
H. P. JONES,
CHARLES B. JOHNSON,
J. J. STURM,
WM. SHIRLEY,
WM. H. FAULKNER.

To the Indian names are subjoined marks.

SCHEDULE A.

Of articles of merchandise, &c., agreed to be furnished annually, under the foregoing Convention, to the Comanches, Wichita, Huecos, Cado, Hadachos, Anadaghcos, Tahuacaros, Kichais, Aionais, Shawnees and Delawares living in reserves in the country leased from the Choctaws and Chickasaws.

Blue drilling, warm coats, calico, plaid check, regatta cotton shirts, woolen shirts, beads, camp kettles, knives and forks, nails, augers, chopping axes, locks, hats, white drilling, brown domestic, thread, yarn and twine, ribbons, assorted colors, combs, butcher knives, large iron-spoons, hatchets and hammers, gimlets, fish-hooks, red, white and blue blankets, red and blue list cloth, shawls and handkerchiefs, shoes for men and women, tin-cups and buckets, coffee-pots and dippers, needles, scissors and shears, ammunition, including powder, lead, flints and percussion caps, tobacco.

This is schedule A, of the treaty with the four bands of the Ne-um, to which it is annexed as part thereof.

ALBERT PIKE, *Commissioner.*

SCHEDULE B.

Of the citizens of the Seminole Nation who are to be paid under the 23d article of the foregoing treaty for the horses stolen from them by the Comanches and other tribes of Indians; and of the amounts to be paid for horses stolen by marauding bands of the Prairie Indians, in November, 1859, and November, 1860.

Names of claimants.	Number of horses stolen.	Value of horses stolen.	Amounts to be paid.
Pas-co-fa............................	6	2 at $75 each,	$150
		3 " 50 "	150
		1 " 70 "	70, $370
Jenny..............................	4	1 " 60 "	60
		1 " 50 "	50
		1 " 40 "	40
		1 " "	80, 230
Amount carried forward,....			$600

SCHEDULE B.—Continued.

Names of claimants.	Number of horses stolen.	Value of horses stolen.	Amounts to be paid.
Amount brought forward,...			$600
O-i-ous Hacho........	2	1 at $65	
		1 " 50,	115
Cho la Fic si-co..............	1	50,	50
Fos Hut-chi................	6	1 75	
		1 35	
		2 " 40 each. 80	
		2 " -50 " 100,	290
Api-i-ca...............	2	1 50	
		1 35,	85
Ki-tis-ti a-ni............	3	2 " 50 each. 100	
	1	20 20,	120
I-o-fa-la Fic-si-co.........	1	1	75
Ka-pit-cha Tust-i-nuc-ochi..	2	1 " 60 60	
		1 " 40 40,	100
A-i-ma-mi.............	3	1 " 30 30	
		2 " 16 each. 32,	62
Fic-lum-mi...............	2	2 " 60 "	120
Hal-pa-ta Fic-si-co.........	1		75
Toh-kul-ka......	2	2 at 50 each.	100
Pa-ho-si................	2	1 " 60	
		1 " 40	100
Mary...............	2	Mare and colt.	50
Kat-cha Ha-cho-chi........	2	1 at 50	
		1 " 40	90
Fos Hut-chi Hacho.........		1 " 40	40
Ni-ha Fic-si-co............	2	2 " 40	80
Ta-co-sa Hacho............	1	1 " 50	50
Kat-cho-chi............	2	1 " 40 40	
		1 " 20 20	60
Nalth-ka-put Tus ti-nuk-ki..	6	1 " 30	
		1 " 35	
		1 " 40	
		1 " 25	
		2 " 20 each. 40,	170
Sa-ho-tah-ki.............	8	3 " 30 " 90	
		3 " 25 " 75	
		1 " 20 " 20	
		1 " 10 " 10,	195
George Cloud.........	1		45
Fos-hut-chi Co-cho-ni........	5	1 " 50	
		1 " 60	
		1 " 35	
		1 " 25	
		1 " 20	190
Sup-pa-ho-ho-yi.........	3	1 " 50	
		1 " 45	
		1 " 35	130
Kat-cha Fic-si-co.........	2	1 " 60	
		1 " 50	110
Oc-tai-ah-chi.........	2	1 " 50	
		1 " 30	80
Sen-wi-i-ca........	4	2 " 40 ea. 80	
		1 " 35 35	
		1 " 20 20,	135
Pa-hos Hacho...........	1		45
Pa-lut-ho-ho-eyi.........	1		50
Tus-ti-nuk Chap-co.........	2	1 " 45 45	
		1 " 30 30,	75
			$3,487

Received of **Albert Pike**, Commissioner of the Confederate States to the Indian Nations west of Arkansas, the sum of forty dollars in full payment of the within mentioned amount of forty dollars agreed to be paid to me.

Witness:

W. WARREN JOHNSON.

FOS-HUT-CHI HACHO,

This and the two preceding folios are Schedule B, of the treaty with the four bands of the Ne-um, to which they are annexed as a part thereof.

ALBERT PIKE, *Commissioner.*

RATIFICATION.

Dec. 21, 1861.

Ratification by Congress of the foregoing treaty.   *Resolved,* (two thirds of the Congress concurring,) That the Congress of the Confederate States of America do advise and consent to the ratification of the articles of a Convention made by Albert Pike, Commissioner of the Confederate States to the Indian Nations west of Arkansas, in behalf of the Confederate States, of the one part, and the No-co-ni, Ta-nie-we, Co-cho-tih-ca and Ya-pa-rich-ca ' Bands of the Ne-um or Camanches of the Prairies and Staked Plain, by their Chiefs and head men, who signed the same articles, of the other part, concluded at the Wichita Agency, near the False Washita river, in the country leased from the Choctaws and Chickasaws, on the twelfth day of August, in the year of our Lord, one thousand eight hundred and sixty-one, with the following amendments, to-wit:

Amendments.   1st. In the last paragraph of article thirteen where occur the words, "but this article creates no obligation to deliver up Mexicans who may be prisoners." Strike out all after the words "up" and insert in lieu thereof the following words: other prisoners than inhabitants of the Confederate States or Territories thereof.

2d. Strike out all of article twenty.

3d. Strike out all of article twenty-seven.

TREATY WITH THE OSAGES,

OCTOBER 2, 1861.

ARTICLES OF A CONVENTION

October 2, 1861.

Entered into and concluded at Park Hill, in the Cherokee Nation, on the second day of October, in the year of our Lord, one thousand eight hundred and sixty-one, between the Confederate States of America, by Albert Pike, their Commissioner, with full powers, appointed by the President, by virtue of an Act of the Congress in that behalf, of the one part, and the Great Osage Tribe of Indians, by its Chiefs and Headmen, who have signed these articles, of the other part.

ARTICLE I. The Great Osage Tribe of Indians and all the persons thereof, do hereby place themselves under the laws and protection of the Confederate States of America, in peace and war, forever, and agree to be true and loyal to them under all circumstances. *The Osage under the protection of the C. S.*

ARTICLE II. The Confederate States of America do hereby promise and firmly engage themselves to be, during all time, the friends and protectors of the Great Osage Tribe of Indians, and to defend and secure them in the enjoyment of all their rights; and that they will not allow them henceforward to be in any wise troubled or molested by any power or people, State or person whatever. *The C. S. assume the protectorate.*

ARTICLE III. The Confederate States of America do hereby assure and guarantee to the Great and Little Osage Tribes of Indians the exclusive and undisturbed possession, use and occupancy, during all time, as long as grass shall grow and water run, of the country heretofore secured to them by treaty with the United States of America, and which is described in the treaty of the second day of June, in the year of our Lord, one thousand eight hundred and twenty-five, as being thus bounded, that is to say: Beginning at a point due east of White Hair's Village, and twenty-five miles west of the western boundary line of the State of Missouri, fronting on a north and south line, so as to leave ten miles north and forty miles south of the point of said beginning, and extending west, with the width of fifty miles, to the western boundary of the lands ceded and relinquished by said nations by that treaty, which lands shall not be sold or ceded by the said tribes, nor shall any part thereof, to any nation or people, except to the Confederate States, or to any individuals whatever; and the same shall vest in the Confederate States, in case the said tribes become extinct or abandon the same. *The Osages to have the possession and use of the country secured to them by the treaty with the U. S.* *Boundaries.*

Reservation of lands for Indian agency. **ARTICLE IV.** The right is hereby reserved to the Confederate States to select, in any unoccupied part of said country, a tract of two sections of land, as a reserve and site for an agency for the said tribes, which shall revert to the said tribes whenever it shall cease to be occupied for an agency.

Establishment of forts and military posts. **ARTICLE V.** The Confederate States shall have the right to establish in the said country such forts and military posts as they may deem necessary, and shall have the right to select for each such fort or post a tract of land Proviso. one mile square, on which such fort or post shall be established: *Provided,* That if any person or persons have any improvements on any tract so selected, the value of such improvements shall be paid by the Government to the owner thereof.

Persons not to settle upon the agency reserve, nor upon any reserve for forts, &c. **ARTICLE VI.** No person whatever, shall be permitted to settle or reside upon the agency reserve, when it shall have been selected, except by the permission of the agent; nor upon any reserve for a fort or military post, except by the permission of the commanding officer; and every such reserve, for the agency or the forts or military posts, shall be within the sole and exclusive jurisdiction of the Confederate States.

Free navigation of water courses. **ARTICLE VII.** The Confederate States shall forever have the right of free navigation of all navigable streams and water courses, within or running through the country hereby assured and guaranteed to said tribes.

The Osage country not to be included within the bounds of any State or Territory, or to be under the laws thereof. **ARTICLE VIII.** The Confederate States hereby guarantee that the country hereby secured to said Great and Little Osage Tribes shall never be included within the bounds of any State or Territory, nor shall any of the laws of any State or Territory ever be extended over, or put in force within, any part of the said country; and the President of the Confede-Protection against other or rate States will cause the said tribes to be protected against all molestation tribes or persons. or disturbance at the hands of any other tribe or nation of Indians, or of any other person whatever; and he shall have the same care and superintendence over them as was heretofore had by the President of the United States.

Hunting and killing of game. **ARTICLE IX.** The members of the said Great and Little Osage Tribes of Indians shall have the right, henceforward, of hunting and killing game, in all the unoccupied country west of the possessions of the Cherokees, Seminoles, Choctaws and Chickasaws, without molestation from any quarter, being, while so engaged therein, under the protection of the Confederate States.

Perpetual peace and brotherhood between the Osages and other tribes. **ARTICLE X.** There shall be perpetual peace and brotherhood between the Great and Little Osage Tribes of Indians, and the Cherokees, Musko-kies, Seminoles, Choctaws and Chickasaws, and the bands of Wichitas, Cado Hadachos, Huecos, Tawacaros, Anadaghcos, Toncawes, Kichais, Aionais, Shawnees and Delawares, living in the country leased from the Choctaws and Chickasaws, and the Peneteghca, Noconi, Taneiwe, Yapa-Injuries, &c , to be forgiven and forgotten. rilica and Cochotihca bands of the Neum or Comanches; and every injury or act of hostility which either has heretofore sustained or met with at the hands of the other, shall be forgiven and forgotten.

The Osages and other nations to be good neighbors to each other. **ARTICLE XI.** The Great and Little Osage Tribes of Indians, and the said several other nations, tribes and bands shall henceforth be good neighbors to each other, and there shall be a free and friendly intercourse among them. And it is hereby agreed by the said Great Osage Tribe, as has already been agreed by all the others except the Little Osage Tribe, that Right of property in horses, cattle and stock. the horses, cattle and other stock and property of each nation, tribe or band, and of every person of each, is his or its own; and that no person belonging to the Great Osage Tribe shall, or will hereafter, kill, take away or injure any such property of another tribe or band, or of any member of any other tribe or band, or in any other way do them any harm.

Perpetual peace **ARTICLE XII.** Especially there shall be perpetual peace and friendship between said Great Osage Tribe and the Cherokees, Mus-ko-kies, Seminoles, Choctaws and Chickasaws, and the Chiefs and headmen of the said Great Osage Tribe shall do all in their power to take and restore any negroes, horses or other property stolen from white men, or from persons belonging to either of said five nations, and to catch and give up any person among them, who may kill or steal, or do any other evil act.

and friendship with the Cherokees and other Indian nations.

Return of stolen property.

ARTICLE XIII. In order that the friendship now established between the said Great Osage Tribe of Indians and the Confederate States and the other Indian nations, tribes and bands aforesaid, may not be interrupted by the misconduct of individuals, or bands of individuals, it is hereby agreed that for injuries done by individuals, no private revenge or retaliation shall take place, but instead thereof, complaint shall be made by the said Great Osage Tribe of Indians, when any individual thereof is injured, to the agent of the Confederate States for the Osages and other tribes, who shall investigate the complaint, and, if he finds it well-founded, shall report the same to the Superintendent, who will cause the wrong to be redressed, and the person or persons doing the wrong to be arrested, whether he be a white man or an Indian: and he or they shall be tried for the same agreeably to the laws of the Confederate States or of the State or Territory against which he may have offended, and be punished in the same manner and with the same severity as if the injury had been done to a white man. And it is also agreed, that if any member of the Great Osage tribe shall do any injury to the person or property of any white man or of a member of any other Indian nation or tribe under the protection of the Confederate States, the offender shall be given up to the agent, upon complaint made to him and on his demand, the wrong shall be redressed by him, and the offender be tried for the offence agreeably to the laws of the Confederate States, or of the State, Territory or nation against which he may have offended: *Provided*, That he shall be punished in no other manner nor with any greater severity than a citizen of the Confederate States, or of such State, Territory or nation would be, if he had committed the same offence.

No private revenge or retaliation to be taken for injuries done to the Osages.

Mode of redress.

Trial and punishment of wrong doer.

Redress for injuries done by the Osages.

Proviso.

ARTICLE XIV. It is hereby further agreed that the Chiefs of the Great Osage tribe shall use every exertion in their power to recover any horses or other property that may be stolen from any citizen of the Confederate States or from any member of any other Indian tribe under the protection of the Confederate States by any person or persons whatever, and found within the limits of their country; and the property so recovered shall be forthwith delivered to the owner or to the agent to be restored to him. If in any case the right to the property claimed is contested by the person in possession, the agent shall summarily investigate the case, and upon hearing the testimony of witnesses, shall decide the right to the property, and order it to be retained or delivered up accordingly. Either party may appeal from his decision to the superintendent, whose decision shall be final in all cases, the property, in the meantime, remaining in the custody of the agent. If in any case the exertions of the Chiefs to cause the restoration of stolen property prove ineffectual, and the agent is satisfied from the testimony that it was actually stolen, or received with knowledge of its being stolen, by any person belonging to the Great Osage tribe, he shall so report to the superintendent, with a copy of the testimony; which shall for that purpose be always reduced to writing; and the superintendent shall, if satisfied from the testimony, deduct from the annuity of the tribe a sum equal to the value of the property stolen.

Horses or other property stolen to be returned to owner.

Proceeding where right to property is contested.

Appeal.

When restitution cannot be made the value of the property stolen to be deducted from the annuity of the tribe.

ARTICLE XV. The Confederate States hereby guarantee full and fair payment to the owner, of the actual and full value of all horses and other property stolen from any person or persons belonging to the Great Osage tribe, by any citizen of the Confederate States, or by any Indian of any

When the value of the property stolen will be paid by the C. S. to the owner.

other nation or tribe under their protection, in case the same cannot be recovered and restored, and upon sufficient proof being made before the superintendent or any agent of the Confederate States for any of such nations or tribes, that such property was actually stolen by a citizen, or citizens of the Confederate States, or by an Indian or Indians of any nation or tribe under their protection.

Agent and inter- ARTICLE XVI. An agent for the Great and Little Osage tribes, the
preter. Quapaws, Senecas and Senecas and Shawnees shall be appointed by the President, and an interpreter for the Great and Little tribes of Osages, for their protection and that their complaints may be heard by, and their
Where to reside. wants made known to the President. The agent shall reside continually in the country of one or the other of said tribes or bands, and the inter-
Not to be absent preter shall reside among either the Great or Little Osages; and neither
without leave. of them shall ever be absent from their posts, except by the permission of the superintendent.

No war to be ARTICLE XVII. None of the braves of the Great Osage tribe shall go
waged or councils upon the war-path, against any enemy whatever, except with the consent
held, except with
the consent of the of the agent, or unless it be to pursue hostile bands of white men or
agent. Indians entering their country and committing murder, robbery, or other outrage when immediate pursuit is necessary; nor shall hold any talks or councils with any white men or Indians without his knowledge and consent. And they especially agree to attend no councils or talks in the country of any people, or with the officers or agents of any people, with whom the Confederate States are at war; and in case they do so, all the benefits secured to them by this treaty shall immediately and forever cease.

Who may live ARTICLE XVIII. The Confederate States will not permit any improper
in the Osage persons to reside or be in the Great or Little Osage country, but only such
country. persons as are employed by them, their officers or agents, and traders licensed by them, who shall sell to the Osages and buy from them, at fair prices, under such regulations as the President shall make from time to time.

The stealing of ARTICLE XIX. To steal a horse or any other article of property from a
property regarded
as disgraceful. white man or an Indian not at war with the Confederate States, shall always be regarded as disgraceful, and the Chiefs of the Osages will discountenance and prevent it by every means in their power. For if they should not there never could be any permanent peace.

The C. S. wish ARTICLE XX. The Confederate States wish the Osages to settle upon
the Osages to set-
tle upon their and cultivate their land, build houses and dig wells, and by industry
lands, build become enabled to support themselves; and in order to encourage and
houses, &c., and assist them and because of the chattels and articles promised to the Great
agree to furnish
them with stock, Osages and and Little Osages by the treaty of the eleventh day of Jan-
farming imple- uary, A. D., one thousand eight hundred and thirty-nine, a considerable
ments, &c. portion never was furnished them, to-wit: twelve hundred hogs, seven hundred ploughs, seven hundred sets of horse-gear, eight hundred axes, and eight hundred hoes, the Confederate States agree to give them twelve hundred breeding hogs, fifty yoke of oxen with ox-wagons, horse-gear, ploughs, yokes, axes, spades and hoes, and other useful implements, to the value of fifteen thousand dollars, at the first cost in the place in the Confederate States where the same shall be purchased; of which stock, nine hundred hogs, forty yoke of oxen, and such implements as aforesaid to the value of eleven thousand dollars shall be given to the Great Osages, and the residue to the Little Osages if they unite in this treaty. But such stock and implements shall only be issued from time to time, and to such persons as shall be reported by the agent to the superintendent to be engaged or ready to engage in farming, and who will take care of and profitably use the same, and be benefitted by them, and not sell, waste or destroy the same; upon which reports, and so only, the superinten

dent shall cause the issue to such persons only, of so much of said stock, and so many of said implements as he would be entitled to upon a distribution of all *per capita;* and it shall be the duty of the Chiefs and of the agent to see that what is so issued is not destroyed or wasted; and if waste or destruction can in no otherwise be prevented, to reclaim the same and issue them elsewhere.

ARTICLE XXI. The Confederate States also agree to build and put in running order a grist and saw mill, at some suitable point in the Osage country, and to employ a miller for each mill for the term of nine years from the date of this treaty, and an assistant to each for the same time; the latter to be selected from the Osage Nation, and each of them to receive two hundred and twenty-five dollars per annum as his compensation; and each miller shall be furnished with a dwelling house; this article being agreed to by the Confederate States because the mill erected by the United States, under the treaty of the year one thousand eight hundred and thirty-nine, was burned down after being in operation only six years. Building of grist and saw mills and the employment of millers and assistants.
Compensation of millers and assistants.

ARTICLE XXII. The Confederate States also agree, that the agent for the Osages shall be authorized to employ, for and during the term of ten years from the day of the signing of this treaty, ten agricultural and other laborers, to assist the Great and Little Osages in opening and preparing for cultivation their fields, and building their houses, who shall be, at all times, under the control and direction of the agent. Agent to employ agricultural and other laborers.

ARTICLE XXIII. For the same purpose, the Confederate States will also provide, furnish and support for and during the term of twenty years from the date of this treaty, for the Great Osages upon and after the ratification of this treaty, and for the Little Osages when they shall become parties to this treaty, to each a blacksmith and an assistant who shall be one of their own people, and for each, annually, a sufficient supply of coal, with five hundred pounds of iron and sixty pounds of steel to the blacksmsth for the Great Osages, and two hundred and fifty pounds of iron and twenty-five pounds of steel to the blacksmith for the Little Osages, that their farming utensils, tools and arms may be seasonably repaired; and also one wagon-maker for each; and will furnish each smith and wagon-maker with the necessary tools and with a shop, and the wagon-maker with the necessary wood and other materials from time to time. Blacksmith and assistant.
Coal, iron and steel.
Wagon-maker.
Tools and shop to smith and wagon-maker, and wood, &c., for the latter.

ARTICLE XXIV. The Confederate States will also furnish, at proper places, the Great and Little Osages with such medicines as may be necessary, and will employ a physician for each, who shall reside among them, during the pleasure of the President. Medicines and medical service.

ARTICLE XXV. The Confederate States also agree to furnish each warrior of said Great Osage tribe, who has not a gun, with a good rifle and a supply of powder and lead and percussion caps or flints, as soon as it may be found practicable. The arms and ammunition are never to be given away, sold or exchanged, and the Chiefs will punish any one who so disposes of either; and the Confederate States will severely punish any trader or other white man who may purchase either from them. Rifle, ammunition, caps, &c., to be furnished each warr.or.

ARTICLE XXVI. No State or Territory shall ever pass laws for the government of the Osage people; and except so far as the laws of the Confederate States are in force in their country, they shall be left free to govern themselves, and to punish offences committed by one of themselves against the person or property of another: *Provided,* That if one of them kills another, without good cause or justification, he shall suffer death, but only by the sentence of the Chiefs, and after a fair trial, all private revenge being strictly forbidden. The Osages left free to govern themselves.
Proviso.

ARTICLE XXVII. Every white man who marries a woman of the

White man who Osages, and resides in the Osage country, shall be deemed and taken, marries a woman even after the death of his wife, to be an Osage and a member of the of the Osages tribe in which he resides, so far as to be subject to the laws of the tribe deemed to be an Osage, so far as to in respect to all offences committed in its country against the person or be subject to the property of another member of the tribe, and as not to be considered a white laws of the tribe. man committing such offences against the person or property of an Indian, within the meaning of the acts of the Congress of the Confederate Negroes and mu- States. And all negroes and mulattoes, bond or free, committing any lattoes in like man- such offence in said country shall, in like manner, be subject to the laws ner subject to the laws of the tribe. of the tribe.

Military and ARTICLE XXVII. The Confederate States shall have the right to other roads. establish, open and maintain such military and other roads through any part of the Osage-country, as the President may deem necessary, without making any compensation for the right of way, or for the land, timber . Compensation or stone used in constructing the same ; but if any other property of the for property used tribe, or any other property or the improvements of an individual be or injured. used or injured therein, just and adequate compensation shall be made.

Granting of right ARTICLE XXIX. The Confederate States may grant the right of way of way for rail- for any railroad through any part of the said country; but the company roads. to which any such right may be granted shall pay the tribe therefor such sum as shall, in the opinion of the President, be its fair value; and shall also pay to individuals all damages done by the building of said road to their improvements or other property to such amount in each case as commissioners appointed by the President shall determine.

Intrusions and ARTICLE XXX. The agent of the Confederate States for the Osages settlement upon and other bands shall prevent all intrusions by hunters and others, upon the lands of the the lands of the Osages, and permit no white men or other Indians to Osages to be pre-settle thereon, and shall remove all such persons, calling, if necessary, vented. upon the military power for aid ; and the commanders of military posts in that country shall be required to afford him such aid upon his requisition.

Purchasers from ARTICLE XXXI. If any trader or other person should purchase from the Osages of arti- any Osage any of the cattle or other chattels or articles given him by cles given them by the Confederate States, he shall be severely punished. the C. S., to be punished.

The Osages may ARTICLE XXXII. The Great and Little Osages may allow persons of allow other In- any other tribe of Indians to settle among them, and may receive from dians to settle them for their own benefit compensation for such lands as they may sell among them. or assign to such persons.

Who not to pas- ARTICLE XXXIII. No citizen or inhabitant of the Confederate States ture stock on their or member of any friendly nation or tribe of Indians shall pasture stock lands. on the lands of the Osages ; but all such persons shall have full liberty, Liberty given to at all times, and whether for business or pleasure, peaceably to travel in travel in their their country, on the roads or elsewhere, to drive their stock through country, and drive the same and to halt such reasonable time on the way as may be neces-stock through the same. sary to recruit their stock, such delay being in good faith for that purpose and for no other.

Fugitives from ARTICLE XXXIV. Any person duly charged with a criminal offence justice to be sur- against the laws of the Confederate States, or of any State, or Territory, rendered. or of any Indian nation or tribe under the protection of the Confederate States, escaping into the Osage country, shall be promptly taken and delivered up by the Chiefs of the Osages, on the demand of the proper authority of the Confederate States, or of the State, Territory, nation or tribe within whose jurisdiction the offence shall be alleged to have been committed.

Laws declared ARTICLE XXXV. In addition to the laws of the Confederate States to be in force in expressly applying to the Indian country, so much of their laws as pro-the Osage country. vides for the punishment of crimes amounting to felony at common law or by statute against their laws, authority or treaties, and over which the courts of the Confederate States have jurisdiction, including the counterfeiting the coin of the United States or of the Confederate States, or any other current coin, or the securities of the Confederate States, or the uttering of such counterfeit coin or securities; and so much of said laws as provides for punishing violations of the neutrality laws, and resistance to the process of the Confederate States; and all the acts of the provisional Congress providing for the common defence and welfare; so far as the same are not locally inapplicable; and the laws providing *Jurisdiction of* for the capture and delivery of fugitive slaves shall be in force in the *district court of the* Osage country; and the district court for the Chalahki district, when *Chalahki district.* established, shall have exclusive jurisdiction to try, condemn and punish offenders against those laws, to adjudge and pronounce sentence, and cause execution thereof to be done.

ARTICLE XXXVI. Whenever any person who is a member of the *Any member of* Great or Little Osage tribe shall be indicted for any offence in any court *the Osage tribe in-* of the Confederate States, or in a State court, he shall be entitled as of *of the C. S. or* common right to subpœna, and if necessary to compulsory process for *State court enti-* all such witnesses in his behalf as his counsel may think material for *tied to process for* his defence; and the costs of process for such witnesses, and of the ser- *Costs of process* vice thereof, and fees and mileage of such witnesses shall be paid by the *and fees and mile-* Confederate States; and whenever the accused is not able to employ *age of witnesses.* counsel, the court shall assign him one experienced counsel for his *When accused* defence, who shall be paid by the Confederate States a reasonable com- *counsel.* pensation for his services, to be fixed by the court and paid upon the certificate of the judge.

ARTICLE XXXVII. It is hereby declared and agreed that the insti- *Existing laws,* tution of slavery in the said Great and Little Osage tribes is legal, and *usages and cus-* has existed from time immemorial; that slaves are personal property; *slavery, declared* that the title to slaves and other property having its origin in the said *binding.* tribes is to be determined by the laws and customs thereof; and that the slaves and personal property of every person domiciled in the country of the said tribes, shall pass and be distributed at his or her death, in accordance with the laws, usages and customs of the said tribes, which may be proved by oral evidence, and shall everywhere be held valid and binding within the scope of their operations. And if any slaves escape *Laws of the C.* from any of said tribes, the laws of the Confederate States for the *S. for the capture* capture and delivery of fugitive slaves shall apply to such cases, whether *and delivery of fa-* they escape into a State or Territory or into any Indian nation or *ply.* tribe under the protection of the Confederate States; the obligation upon each such State, Territory, nation or tribe to deliver up the same, being in every case as complete as if they had escaped from a State, and the mode of procedure the same.

ARTICLE XXXVIII. The Great Osage Tribe of Indians hereby makes *The Great Osage* itself a party to the existing war between the Confederate States and the *Tribe makes itself* United States of America, as the ally and ward of the former; and, in *a party to the ex-* consideration of the protection guaranteed by this treaty, and of their *agrees to furnish* common interests hereby agrees to raise and furnish, whenever they *men for the service.* shall be called on, a force of five hundred men for the service of the Confederate States, or any less number, who shall receive the same pay *Pay and allow-* and allowances as other troops of the same class in that service, and *ances of the men.* remain in the service as long as the President shall require; and, also, *How long to* to furnish any number of young men for scouts and runners, required by *serve.* any general or other commanding officer of the Confederate States in *ners.* the Indian country, who shall receive such compensation as such officer *Compensation.* shall fix.

ARTICLE XXXIX. In consideration of the loyalty of the Great

Osage Tribe, and of their readiness to place themselves under the protection of the Confederate States, and of their poverty, and of the great losses in horses and other property, sustained by them at the hands of lawless persons for many years, the Confederate States do hereby agree to expend for the benefit of the Great and Little Osage Tribes, for the full term of twenty years from the date of this treaty, the sum of fifteen thousand dollars annually, of which sum five thousand dollars per annum shall be added to the interest on the school fund of the nation, hereinafter provided for, and ten thousand dollars shall be divided fairly in each year, after the Little Osage Tribe shall have united in this convention, between the two tribes in proportion to the number of souls in each ; and the said sum of ten thousand dollas shall, in each year, be applied by the Superintendent to the purchase of such articles of clothing household utensils, blankets and other articles, as shall tend to the comfort of the Osages, and encourage them in their endeavors to improve, and which articles the agent shall distribute among them, in the same manner, and nearly as possible, as moneys would be distributed *per* *capita: Provided,* That in the distribution any person may be excluded by him, if reported by the chiefs to be worthless, idle or dissolute, or a bad and mischievous person ; and that he may do the same upon his own knowledge, taking care, as far as may be, that only the good and worthy shall be the recipients of the bounty of the Government of the Confederate States.

ARTICLE XL. It is hereby agreed and ascertained, that by the sixth article of the treaty with the Great and Little Osages, of the second day of June, A. D., one thousand eight hundred twenty-five, it was agreed that from the lands ceded and relinquished by the Osages by that treaty, a reservation should be made of fifty-four tracts of land, of a mile square each, to be laid off under the direction of the President of the United States, and sold for the purpose of raising a fund to be applied to the support of schools, for the education of the Osage children, in such manner as the President might deem advisable for the attainment of that end ; that fifty-four sections of land were accordingly selected, and afterwards sold, and the proceeds of the same amounted to thirty-one thousand seven hundred and twenty-four dollars and two cents, which sum remains invested as follows, that is to say :

In six per cent. stock of the State of Missouri, seven thousand dollars ;

In United States six per cent. loan of one thousand eight hundred and forty-two, twenty-four thousand six hundred and seventy-nine dollars and fifty-six cents;

And in United States six per cent. loan, of one thousand eight hundred and forty-seven, forty-four dollars and forty-six cents ;

And as it will be useless for the Osages hereafter to expect anything from the justice of the United States, and the Confederate States do not desire that they should hereafter look to that quarter for any moneys; it is, therefore, further hereby agreed, that the Confederate States will hereafter pay, annually, on the first day of January in each year, perpetually, commencing with the year one thousand eight hundred and sixty-two, for the benefit of the Great and Little Osage Tribes, the sum of one thousand nine hundred and three dollars and forty-four cents, being the annual interest on said sums of money so as aforesaid in United States stocks and stocks of the State of Missouri, at the rate of six per cent. per annum, and will look to the State of Missouri for the payment of the principal and interest of said sum of seven thousand dollars, as invested in stocks of that State. To which sum shall be annually added, on the same day, commencing with the same year, the sum of five thousand dollars, part of the annuity provided for in the xxxix. article of this treaty, and the whole shall be applied by the agent to the support and maintainance of the Osage manual labor school, now in operation at the mission on the Neosho river, as the said interest has heretofore been applied. *Additional payment under article xxxix. of this treaty. Whole to be applied to support of Osage manual labor school.*

ARTICLE XLI. A tract of land of the quantity of two sections, or two tracts of one section each, to be selected by the agent of the Confederate States for the Osages and other tribes, and in which or one of which, the present site of the mission and its buildings is to be included, is hereby forever dedicated to the use of the Osage manual labor school, to be under the exclusive control of those who have charge of that institution, and for its exclusive use; and not to be sold or disposed of, or applied to any other use or purpose whatsoever. *Dedication of land to the school.*

ARTICLE XLII. All just claims and demands against the United States, of the Great Osage Tribe, or of any individual or individuals thereof, not herein specified, arising or due under former treaties with the United States, are hereby assumed, and shall, after the restoration of peace, be investigated by the President, and so far as they are found to be just, shall be paid in full by the Confederate States; and all provisions of the several treaties with the United States, made by the Osages, under which any rights or privileges were secured or guaranteed to the Great Osage Tribe, or to any individual or individuals of the same, and the place whereof is not supplied by any provision of this treaty, and the same not being obsolete or no longer necessary, and so far as they are not annulled, repealed, changed or modified by subsequent treaties or statutes, or are not so by this treaty, are hereby continued in force, as if the same had been made with the Confederate States. *Claims of the Great Osage Tribe against the C. S., under former treaties continued in force as if the treaties were made with the C. S.*

ARTICLE XLIII. A general amnesty of all past offences against the laws of the United States or of the Confederate States, committed before the signing of this treaty, by any member of the Great Osage Tribe, as such membership is defined by this treaty, is hereby declared; and all such persons, if any, charged with any such offence, shall receive from the President full and free pardon, and if imprisoned, or held to bail, before or after conviction, shall be discharged. *General amnesty declared.*

ARTICLE XLIV. The Confederate States of America hereby tender to the Little Osage Tribe the same protection and guarantees as are hereby extended and given to the Great Osage Tribe, and the other benefits offered them specifically by this treaty; and if the said Little Osage Tribe shall give no aid to the enemies of the Confederate States, and shall, within one year from the day of the signing of this treaty, enter into a convention whereby they shall unite in this treaty, and accept and agree to all the terms and conditions of the same, then it shall, to all intents and purposes, be regarded as having been made with them originally, and they be deemed and taken to be parties thereto, as if they were now to sign the same. *The C. S. tender to the Little Osage Tribe the same protection and guarantees as are extended and given to the Great Osage Tribe. How the Little Osage Tribe may become a party to this treaty.*

ARTICLE XLV. This convention shall be obligatory on the Great Osage Tribe of Indians from the day of its date, and on the Confederate States from and after its ratification by the Senate or provisional Congress. *When this treaty to take effect.*

In perpetual testimony whereof, the said Albert Pike, as Commissioner, with plenary powers, on the part of the Confederate States, doth now hereunto set his hand and affix the seal

{ SEAL. } of his arms; and, the undersigned, Chiefs and headmen of the Great Osage Tribe of Indians, do hereunto set their hands and affix their seals.

Thus done in duplicate, at the place and upon the day, in the month and year first aforesaid.

ALBERT PIKE,

Commissioner of the Confederate States to the Indian Nations west of Arkansas.

KA-HI-KE-TUNG-KA,
Chief of Clermont Band Great Osages.
PA-HIU-SKA,
Chief of White Hairs Band.
CHI-SHU-HUNG-KA.
Chief of Big Hill Band.
SHON-TAS-SAP-PE or BLACK DOG.
Chief of Black Dog's Band.
SHA-PE-SHING-KA or BEAVER,
Second Chief of White Hair's Band.
WASH-KA-CHE,
Second Chief of Clermont's Band.
TA-WAN-CHE-HE, or TALL CHIEF,
Second Chief of Big Hill Band.
WA-HO PEK-EH,
Second Chief of Black Dog's Band.
WA-TA-EN-KA, or DRY FEATHER,
Councillor of Clermont's Band.
KAN-SE-KA-HRI,
Councillor of Big Hill Band.
KA-HI-KE WA-TA-EN-KA,
KA-HI-KE SHING-KA,
CHI-SHO-WATA-ENG-KA,
E-E SHI KA-HRI,
SHO-MEH-KAS-SI,
NI-IH-KA KI-PA-NA,
SA-PEH-KU-YEH,
WA-A-HAN-HA,
HA-KA-SHE,
WA-NO-PAH-SHE,
SHING-KAKA-HU-KE,
WA-CHE-WA-HE,

NA-HIN-TA-PI,
AH-KIH-TA-TUNG-KA,
WAH-KAN-TA-CHI-LEH-
NI-KA-KA-HRI,
SHA-A KE-TO-PA,
TO-TI-NA-HE,
O-LO-ING KA-SHI,
KA-WA-SI,
WA-SHA-SHI WA-SHA-ON-CHI,
WA-HU-NOMP-I,
WA-AK-AN-CHI-LE,
O-KI-PA-HRA,
TRE-NOM-PA-SHI,
A-KI-KO-SHA,
WA-TO-KI-KA,
O-SHANG-KE-TUNG-KA,
CHE-E-SE-TUNG-KA,
WA-TA-SHO-WE,
I-KA-SHA-PE,
A-NO-HRA-PI,
MIN-CHE-EH-NA,
WA-CHE-NA-SHI,
MA-HING-KA-HE,
TAN-WA-SHING-KA,
MIINK-SHES-KA,
TO-TA-NA-SHE,
KA-WA-KA-HII-KI,
MU-KA-KE-SHING KA,
GESSO CHOUTAU,
AUGUSTUS C-PTAIN,
LOUIS J. CHOUTEAU.

Signed, sealed and delivered in presence of us.

WM. QUESENBURY,
Secretary to the Commissioner.
E. RECTOR,
Superintendent of Indian Affairs.
Cofederate States.
ANDREW J. DORN,
Agent for Osages and other tribes,
Confederate States.
LOUIS P. CHOUTEAU,
Confederate States Interpreter for
Osages.
JOHN DREW,
GEORGE M. MURRELL,
J. W. WASHBOURNE,
W. WARREN JOHNSON,

To the Indian names are subjoined marks.

Dec. 20, 1861.

RATIFICATION.

Ratification by
Congress of the
foregoing treaty
with the Great
Osage Tribe. *Resolved,* (two-thirds of the Congress concurring,) That the Congress of the Confederate States of America do advise and consent to the ratification of the articles of a convention made by Albert Pike, Commissioner of the Confederate States to the Indian nations west of Arkansas, in behalf of the Confederate States, of the one part, and the Great

Osage Tribe of Indians, by its Chiefs and headmen, who signed the
same articles, of the other part, concluded at Park Hill, in the Cherokee
Nation, on the second day of October, in the year of our Lord, one
thousand eight hundred and sixty-one, with the following amendment :

AMENDMENT.

In article thirty-six, at the end of the words "or in a State Court," insert the following words : "Subject to the laws of the State." **Amendment.**

TREATY WITH THE SENECAS AND SENECAS

AND SHAWNEES.

OCTOBER 4TH, 1861.

ARTICLES OF A CONVENTION

Oct. 4, 1861.

Entered into and concluded at Park Hill, in the Cherokee Nation, on the fourth day of October, in the year of our Lord, one thousand eight hundred and sixty-one, between the Confederate States of America, by Albert Pike, their Commissioner, with full powers, appointed by the President, by virtue of an act of Congress in that behalf, and the Seneca tribe of Indians, formerly known as the Senecas of Sandusky, and the Shawnees of the tribe or confederacy of Senecas and Shawnees, formerly known as the Senecas and Shawnees of Lewistown, or the mixed bands of Senecas and Shawnees, each tribe for itself, by its Chiefs and warriors, who have signed these articles, of the other part.

The Senecas and Shawnees under the protection of the C. S.

ARTICLE I. The Seneca tribe of Indians, formerly known as the Senecas of Sandusky, and the Shawnees of the tribe or confederacy of Senecas and Shawnees, formerly known as the Senecas and Shawnees of Lewistown, or the mixed bands of Senecas and Shawnees and all the persons of each, do hereby place themselves under the laws and protection of the Confederate States of America, in peace and war forever, and agree to be true and loyal to them under all circumstances.

The C. S. assume the protectorate.

ARTICLE II. The Confederate States of America do hereby promise and firmly engage themselves to be, during all time, the friends and protectors of the Seneca tribe of Indians, formerly known as the Senecas of Sandusky, and the Shawnees of the tribe or confederacy of Senecas and Shawnees, formerly known as the Senecas and Shawnees of Lewistown or the mixed bands of Senecas and Shawnees, and to secure and defend them in the enjoyment of all their rights, possessions and property; and that they will not allow them henceforward to be in any wise troubled or molested by any power or people, State or person whatever.

Guarantee to the tribes of the country secured to them by treaties with and patents from the U. S.

ARTICLE III. The Confederate States of America do hereby assure and guarantee to the Seneca tribe aforesaid, and to the Senecas and Shawnees, formerly known as the Senecas and Shawnees of Lewistown or the mixed bands of Senecas and Shawnees, in case the Senecas thereof should hereafter unite in this treaty, by a convention for that purpose made and concluded, or to the Shawnees thereof aforesaid alone, in case the said Senecas thereof should refuse so to unite herein, to each tribe or band respectively, the title in fee simple, as long as each, respectively, shall exist as a nation and remain thereon, and the exclusive possession and undisturbed use, occupancy and enjoyment, as long as grass shall grow and water run, of the country heretofore secured to each respectively, by treaties with, and patents from, the United States of America; and which countries are thus described and ascertained, that is to say:

By the treaty with the Senecas of Sandusky made and concluded on the twenty-eighth day of February, A. D., one thousand eight hundred and thirty-one, a country was ceded and granted to that tribe, therein described as "a tract of land situate on and adjacent to the northern boundary of the lands heretofore granted to the Cherokee Nation of Indians, and adjoining the boundary of the State of Missouri, which tract shall extend fifteen miles from east to west, and seven miles from north to south, containing about sixty-seven thousand acres. be the same more or less."

By the treaty made and concluded with the mixed bands of Seneca and Shawnee Indians residing at and around Lewistown, on the twentieth day of July, in the same year, a country was ceded and granted to these bands therein described as "a tract of land to contain sixty thousand acres, to be located under the direction of the President of the United States, contiguous to the lands granted to the Senecas of Sandusky by the treaty made with them at the city of Washington, on the twenty-eighth of February, eighteen hundred and thirty-one,' and the Cherokee settlements; the east line of said tract shall be within two miles of the west lines of the lands granted to the Senecas of Sandusky, and the south line shall be within two miles of the north line of the lands held by the Cherokees;" and by the treaty made and concluded on the twenty-ninth day of December, A. D., one thousand eight hundred and thirty-two, with the united nation or tribe of Senecas and Shawnees, by which that united tribe ceded, relinquished and quit—claimed to the United States all their lands west of the Neosho or Grand river, the United States agreed to grant by patent, in the manner thereinafter mentioned, the country therein described as follows, that is to say: "The following tract of land lying on the east side of Neosho or Grand river, viz: Bounded on the east by the west line of the State of Missouri; south by the present established line of the Cherokee Indians; west by Neosho or Grand river; and north by a line running parallel with said south line, and extending so far from the present north line of the Seneca Indians from Sandusky, as to contain sixty thousand acres, exclusive of the land now owned by said Seneca Indians, (which said boundaries include, however, all the land heretofore granted· said Senecas of Sandusky, on the east side of Grand river;" and which country included within said boundaries, the United States thereby agreed to grant, by two letters patent; the north half, in quantity, to the mixed bands of the Senecas and Shawnees of Ohio, or of Lewistown, and the south half to the Senecas from Sandusky; the whole to be occupied, in common, so long as the said tribes or bands should desire the same, and the grant to be in fee simple, but the lands not to be sold or ceded without the consent of the United States; which lands shall not be sold or ceded by the said tribes or bands, nor shall any part thereof to any nation or people, except to the Confederate States, or to any individuals whatever, except as hereinafter provided; and the same shall vest in the Confederate States, in case the said tribes or bands, respectively, become extinct or abandon the same.

Lands not to be sold or ceded except to the C. S.

ARTICLE IV. The Seneca tribe of Indians aforesaid, and the Senecas and Shawnees alone, aforesaid, as the case may be, may respectively, by a majority vote of the whole people of each, respectively, receive and

May receive as members of the tribe or permit to settle upon their

lands, the Indians incorporate, each in itself, as members of the tribe, or permit to settle of certain other and reside upon the lands of the tribe, such Shawnees of Kansas, or Indians. dians of any other tribe, in amity with the Confederate States, as to it May sell or lease may seem good; and may sell such Indians portions of land, in fee or by land to such In- less estate, or lease them portions thereof for years or otherwise, and dians. Who entitled to receive to its own use the price and consideration of such sales or leases; and vote, hold office, it alone shall determine who are citizens of the tribe entitled to vote at share in annuities elections, hold office or share the annuities or other moneys of the tribe or the common or in the common lands: *Provided*, That when persons of another tribe lands. Proviso. shall once have been received as members of either of said tribes, they shall not be disfranchised or subjected to any other restrictions upon the right of voting, than such as shall apply to the Senecas or Senecas and Shawnees respectively, themselves. But no Indians of any other tribe or band than these shall be permitted to come within their country to reside without the consent and license of the people of each tribe respectively.

Reservation of ARTICLE V. The right is hereby reserved to the Confederate States to land for Indian select in any unoccupied part of the country of either of said tribes or agency. bands, if they should desire to do so, a tract of land one mile square as a reserve and site for an agency, for the said tribes and for the Quapaws and Osages, which shall revert to the tribe in whose country it is selected with the buildings thereon, whenever it shall cease to be occupied as an agency.

Forts and mili- ARTICLE VI. The Confederate States shall have the right to establish tary posts. in the said country such forts and military posts as they may deem necessary, and shall have the right to select for each such fort or post a Proviso. tract of land one mile square, on which such fort or post shall be established: *Provided*, That if any person have any improvements on any tract so selected, the value of such improvements shall be paid by the Government to the owner thereof.

No settlement ARTICLE VII. No person whatever shall be permitted to settle or permitted upon the reside upon the agency reserve, when it shall have been selected, except agency reserve or the reserve for by the permission of the agent, nor upon any reserve for a fort or military forts, &c. post, except by the permission of the commanding officer; and every such reserve, for the agency, or for forts or military posts, shall be within the sole and exclusive jurisdiction of the Confederate States.

The country of ARTICLE VIII. The Confederate States hereby guarantee that the the tribes not to be country hereby secured to the said Senecas and Senecas and Shawnees included within the bounds of any shall never be included within the bounds of any State or Territory, nor State or Territory shall any of the laws of any State or Territory ever be extended over, or or to be under the put in force within any part of the said country; and the President of the laws thereof. Confederate States will cause the said tribes to be protected against all Protection molestation or disturbance at the hands of any other tribe or nation of against other tribes or persons. Indians, or of any other person or persons whatever; and he shall have the same care and superintendence over them as was heretofore had by the President of the United States.

Hunting and ARTICLE IX. The members of the said Seneca tribe and the said Seneca killing of game. and Shawnee mixed bands shall have the right, henceforward, of hunting and killing game, in all the unoccupied country west of the possessions of the Cherokees, Seminoles, Choctaws and Chickasaws, without molestation from any quarter, being while so engaged therein under the protection of the Confederate States.

Perpetual peace ARTICLE X. There shall be perpetual peace and brotherhood between and brotherhood the Seneca tribe and the Shawnees aforesaid, and the Osages, Cherokees, between the Sene- cas and Shawnees Muskokis, Seminoles, Choctaws and Chickasaws and the bands of the and other tribes. Wichitas, Cado Hadachos, Huecos, Ta-na-ca-ros, Ana-dagh-cos, Ton-ca-wes, Ki-chais, Ai-nais, Shawnees and Delawares living in the country leased from the Choctaws and Chickasaws, and the Pen-e-tegh-ca, No-co-ni, Fanei-we, Ya-pa-rih-ca and Co-cho-tih-ca bands of the Ne-um or Comanches; and every injury or act of hostility which either has heretofore sustained or met with at the hands of the other, shall be forgiven and forgotten.

Injuries, &c., to be forgiven and forgotten.

ARTICLE XI. The Seneca tribe and the Shawnees aforesaid, and the said several other nations, tribes and bands shall henceforth be good neighbors to each other, and there shall be a free and friendly intercourse among them. And it is hereby agreed by the said Seneca tribe and the said Shawnees, as has already been agreed by all the others, that the horses, cattle and other stock and property of each nation, tribe or band, and every person of each, is his or its own; and that no person belonging to the Senecas or Shawnees aforesaid, shall or will hereafter kill, take away or injure any such property of another tribe or band or of any member of any other tribe or band, or in any other way do them any harm.

The Senecas and Shawnees and other tribes to be good neighbors to each other.

Right of property in horses, cattle, &c.

ARTICLE XII. Especially there shall be perpetual peace and friendship between said Senecas and Shawnees aforesaid, and the Osages, Quapaws, Cherokees, Muskokis, Seminoles, Choctaws and Chickasaws; and the Chiefs and headmen of the said Seneca tribe and Shawnees shall do all in their power to take and restore any negroes, horses or other property stolen from white men or from persons belonging to either of said five nations; and to catch and give up any person among them who may kill or steal or do any other evil act.

Perpetual peace and friendship with the Osages and other Indian nations.

Return of stolen property.

ARTICLE XIII. In order that the friendship now established between the Seneca tribe and Shawnees, the Confederate States and the other Indian nations, tribes and bands aforesaid, may not be interrupted by the misconduct of individuals, or bands of individuals, it is hereby agreed that for injuries done by individuals no private revenge or retaliation shall take place, but instead thereof complaint shall be made by the said Seneca tribe and Shawnees when any individual thereof is injured, to the agent of the Confederate States for the Osages and other tribes, who shall investigate the complaint, and if he finds it well founded shall report the same to the superintendent, who will cause the wrong to be redressed, and the person doing the wrong to be arrested, whether he be a white man or an Indian; and he or they shall be tried for the same agreeably to the laws of the Confederate States or of the State or Territory against which he may have offended, and be punished in the same manner and with the same severity, as if the injury had been done to a white man. And it is also agreed that if any member of the Seneca tribe or any one of the Shawnees shall do any injury to the person or property of any white man or of a member of any other Indian nation or tribe under the protection of the Confederate States, the offender shall be given up to the agent upon complaint made to him, and on his demand, the wrong shall be redressed by him, and the offender be tried for the offence, agreeably to the laws of the Confederate States or of the State, Territory or nation against which he may have offended : *Provided*, That he shall be punished in no other manner nor with any greater severity than a citizen of the Confederate States or of such State, Territory or nation would be, if he had committed the same offence.

No private revenge or retaliation to be taken for injuries.

Mode of redress.

Trial and punishment of wrong doer.

Redress for injuries done by the Senecas and Shawnees

Proviso.

ARTICLE XIV. It is hereby further agreed that the Chiefs of the Senecas and of the Shawnees shall use every exertion in their power to recover any horses or other property that may be stolen from any citizen of the Confederate States or from any member of any other Indian nation or tribe under the protection of the Confederate States, by any person or persons whatever, and found within the limits of their country; and the property so recovered shall be forthwith delivered to the owner or to the agent to be restored to him. If in any case the right to the property claimed is contested by the person in possession, the agent shall summarily investigate the case, and upon hearing the testimony of witnesses, shall decide the right to the property, and order it to be retained or delivered up

Horses or other property stolen to be returned to owner.

Proceeding where right to property is contested.

Appeal.
accordingly. Either party may appeal from his decision to the superintendent, whose decision shall be final in all cases, the property, in the mean-

Where restitution cannot be made the value of the property stolen to be deducted from the annuity of the tribe.
time, remaining in the custody of the agent. If, in any case, the exertions of the Chiefs to cause the restoration of stolen property prove ineffectual, and the agent is satisfied from the testimony that it was actually stolen, or received with knowledge of its being stolen, by any person belonging to the Seneca tribe or by any one of the Shawnees, he shall so report to the superintendent, with a copy of the testimony, which shall for that purpose be always reduced to writing; and the superintendent shall, if satisfied from the testimony, deduct from the annuity of the tribe a sum equal to the value of the property stolen.

When the value of the property stolen will be paid by the C. S. to the owner.
Article XV. The Confederate States hereby guarantee full and fair payment to the owner of the actual and full value of all horses and other property stolen from any person or persons belonging to the Seneca tribe, or being of the Shawnees aforesaid, by any citizen of the Confederate States or by any Indian of any other nation or tribe under the[ir] protection, in case the same cannot be recovered and restored, and upon sufficient proof being made before the superintendent or any agent of the Confederate States for any such nations or tribes, that such property was actually stolen by a citizen or citizens of the Confederate States or by an Indian or Indians of any nation or tribe under their protection.

Agent and interpreter.
Article XVI. An agent for the Great and Little Osage tribes, the Quapaws, Senecas and Senecas and Shawnees shall be appointed by the President, and an interpreter for the Seneca tribe and one for the Shawnees for their protection, and that their complaints may be heard by, and their

Where to reside.
wants made known to the President. The agent shall reside continually in the country of one or the other of said tribes or bands, and the inter-

Not to be absent without leave.
preter shall reside continually among the people for whom he is employed, and neither of them shall ever be absent from their posts, except by the permission of the superintendent.

No councils to be held except with the consent of the C. S.
Article XVII. The Senecas and the Senecas and Shawnees shall hold no talks or councils with any white men or Indians without the knowledge and consent of the agent of the Confederate States. And they especially agree to attend no councils or talks in the country of any people or with the officers or agents of any people with whom the Confederate States are at war; and in case they do so, all the benefits secured to them by this treaty shall immediately and forever cease.

Who may live in the country of the tribes.
Article XVIII. The Confederate States will not permit any improper persons to reside or be in the country of the Senecas, or in that of the Senecas and Shawnees, but only such persons as are employed by them, their officers or agents, and traders licensed by them, who shall sell to the said Indians and buy from [them] at fair prices, under such regulations as the President shall make from time to time.

Tribes left free to govern themselves.
Article XIX. No State or Territory shall ever pass laws for the government of the Seneca tribe or of the Seneca and Shawnee people; and except so far as the laws of the Confederate States are in force in their country, they shall be left free to govern themselves, and to punish offences committed by one of themselves against the person or property of another:

Proviso.
Provided, That if one of them kills another, without good cause or justification, he shall suffer death, but only by the sentence of the Chiefs, and after a fair trial, all private revenge being strictly forbidden.

White man who marries a woman of the Senecas or the Shawnees deemed to be a member of such tribe, so far as to
Article XX. Every white man who marries or has married a woman of the Senecas or of the Shawnees and resides in the Seneca or Seneca and Shawnee country, respectively, shall be deemed and taken even after the death of his wife, to be a member of the tribe in which he marries or has married, so far as to be subject to its laws in respect to all offences committed in its country against the person or property of another member of

the tribe and as not to be considered a white man committing such offence be subject to its against the person or property of an Indian, within the meaning of the laws. act of Congress of the Confederate States. And all negroes and mulat- Negroes and mu- toes, bond or free, committing any such offence in said country shall, in lattoes in like man- like manner, be subject to the laws of the tribe. laws.

ARTICLE XXI. The Confederate States shall have the right to establish, Military and open and maintain such military and other roads through any part of the other roads. Seneca or Seneca and Shawnee country as the President may deem neces- sary, without making any compensation for the right of way, or for the land, timber or stone used in constructing the same; but if any other property of the tribe, or any other property or the improvements of an indi- vidual be used or injured therein, just and adequate compensation shall be made.

ARTICLE XXII. The Confederate States may grant the right of way for Right of way for any railroad through any part of the Seneca or Seneca and Shawnee railroads. country; but the company to which any such right of way may be granted shall pay the tribe therefor through whose country any part of the road runs such sums as in the opinion of the President be its fair value; and Payment of shall also pay to individuals all damages done by the building of said damages to indi- road to their improvements or other property to such amount in each case viduals. as commissioners appointed by the President shall determine.

ARTICLE XXIII. The agent of the Confederate States for the Osages Intrusions and and other tribes shall prevent all intrusions by hunters and others upon the settlement upon lands of the Senecas and of the Senecas and Shawnees, and permit no Senecas and Shaw- white men or other Indians to settle thereon, and shall remove all such nees to be pre- persons, calling, if necessary, upon the military power for aid; and the vented. commanders of military posts in that or the adjoining country shall be required to afford him such aid upon his requisition.

ARTICLE XXIV. No citizen or inhabitant of the Confederate States Who not to pas- or member of any friendly nation or tribe of Indians shall pasture stock ture stock on their on the lands of the Senecas or Senecas and Shawnees, but all such lands. persons shall have full liberty, at all times, and whether for business or travel in their pleasure, peaceably to travel in their country, on the roads or elsewhere, country, and drive to drive their stock through the same and to halt such reasonable time stock through the on the way as may be necessary to recruit their stock, such delay being same. in good faith for that purpose and for no other.

ARTICLE XXV. Any person duly charged with a criminal offence Surrender of against the laws of the Confederate States, or of any State or Territory, fugitives from jus- or of any Indian nation or tribe, under the protection of the Confederate tice. States, escaping into the Seneca or Seneca and Shawnee country, shall be promptly taken and delivered up by the Chiefs of the Senecas or Senecas and Shawnees, on the demand of the proper authority of the Confederate States, or of the State, Territory, nation or tribe within whose jurisdiction the offence shall be alleged to have been committed.

ARTICLE XXVI. In addition to the laws of the Confederate States, Laws declared expressly applying to the Indian country, so much of their laws as to be in force. provides for the punishment of crimes amounting to felony at common law, or by statute against their laws, authority or treaties, and over which the courts of the Confederate States have jurisdiction, including the counterfeiting the coin of the United States or of the Confederate States, or any other current coin, or the securities of the Confederate States, or the uttering of such counterfeit coin or securities; and so much of said laws as provides for punishing violations of the neutrality law, and resistance to the process of the Confederate States; and all the acts of the provisional Congress providing for the common defence and welfare, so far as the same are not locally inapplicable; and the laws providing for the capture and delivery of fugitive slaves, shall be in

Jurisdiction of district court for the Chalahki district.

force in the Seneca and the Seneca and Shawnee country; and the district court for the Chalahki District, when established, shall have exclusive jurisdiction to try, condemn and punish offenders against those laws, to adjudge and pronounce sentence, and cause execution thereof to be done.

Any Seneca or Shawnee indicted in any court of the C. S. entitled to process for witnesses. Costs of process and fees and mileage of witnesses. When accused may be assigned counsel.

ARTICLE XXVII. Whenever any person, who is a member of the Seneca or Seneca and Shawnee tribe, shall be indicted for any offence in any court of the Confederate States, or in a State court, he shall be entitled, as of common right, to subpœna, and, if necessary, to compulsory process for all such witnesses in his behalf as his counsel may think material for his defence; and the costs of process for such witnesses and of the service thereof, and fees and mileage of such witnesses shall be paid by the Confederate States; and whenever the accused is not able to employ counsel, the court shall assign him one experienced counsel for his defence, who shall be paid, by the Confederate States, a reasonable compensation for his services, to be fixed by the court and paid upon the certificate of the judge.

Existing laws, usages and customs in regard to slavery declared binding.

ARTICLE XXVIII. It is hereby declared and agreed that the institution of slavery in the said Seneca and Seneca and Shawnee Tribes is legal, and has existed from time immemorial; that slaves are personal property; that the title to slave and other property having its origin in either of the said tribes is to be determined by the laws and customs thereof; and that the slaves and personal property of every person domiciled in the country of either of the said tribes shall pass and be distributed at his or her death, in accordance with the laws, usages and customs of the said tribes, which may be proved by oral evidence, and shall everywhere be held valid and binding within the scope of their operations. And if any slaves escape from either of the said tribes, the laws of the Confederate States for the capture and delivery of fugitive slaves shall apply to such cases, whether they escape into a State or Territory, or into any Indian nation or tribe under the protection of the Confederate States; the obligation upon each such State, Territory, nation or tribe to deliver up the same being, in every case, as complete as if they had escaped from a State, and the mode of procedure the same.

The tribes made a party to the existing war, and agree to furnish aid.

ARTICLE XXIX. The Seneca Tribe and the Shawnees of the Seneca and Shawnee Tribe, hereby make themselves parties to the existing war between the Confederate States and the United States of America, as the allies and wards of the former; and, in consideration of the protection guaranteed by this treaty, and of their common interests, hereby agree to aid in defending their country against any invasion thereof by the common enemy; and it is agreed that all warriors furnished by them for the service of the Confederate States, and which shall be mustered into that service, shall receive the same pay and allowances as other troops of the same class therein, and remain in the service as long as the President shall require.

Pay of the warriors.

How long to serve.

Debts due by the U. S. to the Seneca tribe.

ARTICLE XXX. It is further agreed and ascertained, by and between the Confederate States and the said Seneca Tribe of Indians, formerly known as the Senecas of Sandusky, that the United States of America were, while the several States of the Confederacy were members of the same, and still remain indebted to the said Seneca Tribe, and had and still have in their hands money's in trust for the said tribes, as follows, that is to say:

By the fourth article of the treaty made with the Wyandot, Seneca and other tribes of Indians, on the twenty-ninth day of September, A. D., one thousand eight hundred and seventeen, the United States agreed and bound themselves to pay annually, forever, to the Seneca tribe, the sum of five hundred dollars, in specie, at Lower Sandusky;

By the fourth article of the treaty made the seventeenth day of September, A. D., one thousand eight hundred and eighteen, with the Wyandot, Seneca, Shawnee and Ottawa tribes of Indians, the United States agreed and bound themselves to pay, to the Senecas of Sandusky, an additional annuity of five hundred dollars forever ;

By the eighth article of the treaty with the Seneca Tribe of Sandusky, made on the twenty-eighth day of February, A. D., one thousand eight hundred and thirty-one, the United States agreed to sell the land thereby ceded to them by the said tribe, by that treaty; and it was that after certain deductions therefrom to be made, as therein specified, any balance that might remain, of the proceeds of sale of such lands, should constitute a fund for the future exigencies of the tribe, on which the United States would pay to the Chiefs of the tribe, for the use and general benefit of the tribe, annually, five per centum as annuity; which sales being accordingly effected, the fund thus created amounted to five thousand dollars, which was invested by the United States, and yet remains invested, in five per cent. stock of the State of Kentucky, now held by the United States ;

It is further hereby agreed and ascertained, by and between the Confederate States and the Shawnees, of the said Senecas and Shawnees of Lewistown, that the United States of America were, while the several States of the Confederacy were members of the same, and still remain, indebted to the mixed bands of Senecas and Shawnees, and had and still have in their hands moneys in trust for the said tribe, as follows, that is to say : *Debts due by the U. S. to the mixed bands of, Senecas and Shawnees.*

By the fourth article of the treaty, made with the Wyandot, Seneca, Shawnee and Ottawa tribes, on the seventeenth day of September, A. D., one thousand eight hundred and eighteen, the United States agreed and bound themselves to pay, " to the Shawnees and to the Senecas of Lewistown," an additional annuity of one thousand dollars forever;

By the eighth article of the treaty made with the mixed band of Seneca and Shawnee Indians, residing at and around Lewistown in the State of Ohio, on the twentieth day of July, A. D., one thousand eight hundred and thirty-one, the United States agreed to sell the lands ceded to them, by the Senecas and Shawnees, by that treaty; and it was also agreed that, after certain deductions, therein provided for, any balance of the proceeds of such lands that might remain should constitute a fund for the future necessities of the tribes, on which the United States would pay the Chiefs, for the use and general benefit of the said tribes, annually, five per centum, as an annuity, which sales being accordingly effected, the fund thus created amounted to sixteen thousand four hundred and sixty-six dollars and ten cents, which was invested by the United States, and yet remains invested, as follows, that is to say :

Six thousand dollars in five per cent. stock of the State of Kentucky;

Seven thousand dollars in five and a half per cent. stock of the State of Missouri ;

Three thousand dollars in six per cent. stock of the State of Missouri ;

And four hundred and sixty-six dollars and sixty-six cents in the United States six per cent. loan of the year 1847.

Which stocks are held by the United States, and the annual interest thereon amounted to the sum of eight hundred and ninety-two dollars and ninety-six cents.

Therefore, and as the said Senecas and the Shawnees aforesaid are indigent, and have nothing to expect from the justice of the northern States, and will be greatly distressed if the annual payments are not promptly made, and as the Confederate States do not wish them any longer to look

Annual payments agreed to be made by the C. S. to the Senecas and Shawnees. to the northern States or receive any moneys from them, and are willing to make the necessary advances for the States of Missouri and Kentucky; Therefore it is further agreed by the said Confederate States of America, that they will pay annually forever, in each and every year after the day of the signing of this treaty, on the first day of January in each year, commencing with the year one thousand eight hundred and sixty-two, in money;

To the Seneca tribe, formerly known as the Senecas of Sandusky, to the chiefs, for the use and general benefit of the people, one thousand two hundred and fifty dollars;

And to the Shawnees, of the mixed bands of the Senecas and Shawnees, formerly of Lewistown, or to the Senecas and Shawnees together, when the Senecas shall have united in this treaty, but until then, to the Shawnees alone, to the Chiefs, for the use and general benefit of the people, one thousand eight hundred and ninety-two dollars and ninety-six cents.

And it is further agreed by the Confederate States that they will look to the States of Missouri and Kentucky for re-payment of the principal and interest of the said sums so invested in their stocks.

Annuity due by the State of New York to the Cayuga tribe accepted as members of the Seneca tribe. ARTICLE XXXI. Whereas, by the treaty made between the State of New York and the Cayuga tribe of Indians, in the month of June, in the year of our Lord, one thousand eight hundred and fifty, it was agreed that the said State should pay annually thereafter forever, on the first day of June in each year, to that portion of the Cayuga tribe which resided west, the sum of eleven hundred and forty-six dollars, which has been regularly paid until the present year, and the check of the Treasurer of the State of New York on the Commercial Bank of Albany, in that State, for the payment of the year eighteen hundred and sixty-one is in the hands of Andrew J. Dorn, the agent of the Osages and other tribes; and whereas, the Cayugas of the west, to whom the said annuity is payable, reside among and are fully accepted as members of the Seneca tribe aforesaid, with the exception of a few who reside among the Senecas and Shawnees, and the said annuity has, therefore, been in each year, by the consent of all, distributed by the agent among all, the Senecas, formerly known as the Senecas of Sandusky, and such Cayugas as reside among the Senecas and Shawnees, and the Cayugas as are willing it shall forever continue to be distributed; and whereas, by placing themselves under the protection of the Confederate States, the Senecas and Cayugas so entitled to said annuity will forfeit the same, and, in all probability, forever:

The C. S. agree to pay the said annuity. Therefore, it is hereby further agreed by the Confederate States, that they will pay hereafter annually forever, on the first day of January in each year, commencing with the year one thousand eight hundred and sixty-two, to the said Seneca tribe of Indians, including the Cayugas, and to the Cayugas residing among the Senecas and Shawnees jointly, the said sum of eleven hundred and forty-six dollars, in money; and that, if the said check should not be paid, they will also pay the amount thereof, to be in like manner distributed, on the first day of January, *Proviso.* A. D., one thousand eight hundred and sixty-two: *Provided,* That if the State of New York should, at any time hereafter, resume the regular payment of the said annuity, then the Confederate States shall no longer, while it continues to do so, be bound to pay the same.

Annuity to be paid by the C. S. to the Seneca tribe including certain of the Cayugas, Mohawks, Wyandots, and Senecas ARTICLE XXXII. Inasmuch as the Seneca tribe and the Senecas and Shawnees have received among them persons of the Wyandot tribe, to the number of one hundred and thirteen, and have given them land to live on, without charge, and in consideration of the loyalty of the Seneca tribe, including the Cayugas and Mohawks, who are members of the tribe of the

Senecas aforesaid, and of the Wyandots who reside among them, and of of the mixed their great necessities, the Confederate States do hereby further agree that bands. they will expend in each and every year hereafter, for the term of twenty years from the day of the signing of this treaty, commencing with the year one thousand eight hundred and sixty-two, and in the early part of each year, the sum of two thousand four hundred dollars, for the benefit of the Seneca tribe, including the Cayugas and Mohawks, who form part of the tribe of the Shawnees aforesaid, forming part of the mixed bands of Senecas and Shawnees, of the Wyandots residing among each, and of the Senecas of the said mixed bands, if they shall unite in this treaty, but not otherwise, which sum of money shall be annually expended in the pur-   How expended. chase by the superintendent, at first cost at the place of purchase in the Confederate States, of such articles of clothing, blankets, utensils, and other useful articles, as he shall, aided by the report and recommendation of the agent in each year, judge to be most desirable, and as will conduce to the health and comfort of the Indians; and which articles shall be annually   Distribution of distributed by the agent as equally as possible among the persons com-   articles purchased. posing the Seneca tribe as aforesaid, the Shawnees and Wyandots afore- said, and the Senecas of the said mixed bands of Senecas and Shawnees ; in which distribution, however, regard may be had by the agent, by the advice of the Chiefs, to the character and circumstances of the recipients, and the needy who are industrious and worthy be especially provided for, and the idle and disolute not be encouraged.

ARTICLE XXXIII. The Senecas and the Senecas and Shawnees not being   School houses. able to maintain schools among them, and being anxious their children should not grow up in ignorance, the Confederate States hereby agree to build a comfortable school-house in each tribe, and that they will employ, during the term of twenty years, a competent male teacher and a compe-   Teachers; their tent female teacher, pay their salaries and furnish the schools with the   salaries. necessary stationery and such books as are needed for instruction in com-   Stationery and mon schools. The repairs of school-houses shall be made, and fuel fur-   Repairs of school nished, by the Senecas the Senecas and Shawnees and Wyandots them-   houses and fuel. selves ; and the schools shall be open to the children of all alike.

ARTICLE XXXIV. Whenever it shall be desired either by the Sene-   Division of joint cas or the Shawnees of the mixed bands, after the said Senecas shall   annuity between. have united in this treaty, a division of their joint annuity of one thou-   the Senecas and the Shawnees of sand eight hundred and ninety-two dollars and ninety-six cents shall be   the mixed bands. made between them, in the ratio of their numbers, and each band shall thereafter receive to its sole use the share of the said annuity belonging to it, as thus determined, whatever their respective numbers may after- wards be

ARTICLE XXXV. The Confederate States will also furnish the Sene   Medicines ; and cas, formerly of Sandusky, and the Shawnees aforesaid, and the Senecas   medical services. of the mixed bands when they shall have united in this treaty, with such medicines as may be necessary, and will employ a physician for them and for the Quapaws, who shall reside at a convenient place in the country of one or the other tribe, during the pleasure of the President ; and any physician employed shall be discharged by the superintendent and another be employed in his place, in case of incompetency or inat- tention to his duties.

ARTICLE XXXVI. The Confederate States also agree to employ a   Blacksmith and blacksmith for the Senecas, and one for the Senecas and Shawness for,   assistant. and during the term of twenty years from the date of this treaty, and an assistant for each, who shall be one of the Seneca or Shawnee people,   Compensation. and receive a compensation of two hundred and fifty dollars per annum.   Shop and tools, and coal, iron and And they will also furnish each blacksmith a dwelling-house, shop and   steel.

tools, and supply each shop with coal and with six hundred pounds of iron and one hundred pounds of steel annually.

Wagon-maker and wheelwright. ARTICLE XXXVII. The Confederate States will also employ one wagon-maker and wheelwright for the Senecas, and one for the Senecas and Shawnees for, and during the term of, twenty years from the date of **Shop, tools and materials.** this treaty, and furnish each with a dwelling house, shop, tools, and the necessary materials.

Grist and saw mills. ARTICLE XXXVIII. The Confederate States also hereby agree to build and put in running order for the Senecas and the Senecas and Shawnees, at some suitable point in their country, convenient to both, to be selected by the agent, a good grist and saw mill, and to deliver the same, when completed, to the Seneca and Seneca and Shawnee people, whose joint, absolute property it shall at once become. And the Confederate **Millers.** States will also employ, for the term of ten years, an experienced miller for each mill, to be selected, if possible, from among the Senecas or Shawnees, and if such millers can be had at a compensation not exceeding six hundred dollars for each per annum.

Rifle and ammunition for each warrior. ARTICLE XXXIX. The Confederate States hereby agree to furnish each warrior of the Seneca Tribe, and of the Shawnees, aforesaid, and of the Senecas of the mixed bands, aforesaid, when they shall have united in this treaty, who has not a gun, with a good rifle, and also to furnish each warrior of the same, with a sufficient supply of ammunition **Trader to be** during the war.

punished for purchasing articles given by the C. S. ARTICLE XL. If any trader or other person should purchase from the Senecas or Shawnees, aforesaid, any of the articles given them by the **General amnesty declared.** Confederate States, he shall be severely punished.

ARTICLE XLI. A general amnesty of all past offences against the laws of the United States, or of the Confederate States, committed before the signing of this treaty, by any person of the Seneca Tribe, or by any Shawnee of the mixed bands, is hereby declared; and all such persons, if any, charged with any such offence, shall receive from the President full and free pardon, and if imprisoned or held to bail, before or after conviction, shall be discharged.

Protection and guarantees extended to the Senecas of the mixed bands of Senecas and Shawnees. ARTICLE XLII. The Confederate States of America hereby tender to the Senecas, of the mixed bands of Senecas and Shawnees, the same protection and guarantees as are hereby extended and given to the Seneca Tribe, and to the Shawnees aforesaid, and the other benefits offered to the said Senecas specifically by this treaty; and if the said Senecas, of the mixed bands, shall give no aid to the enemies of the **May become parties to this treaty.** Confederate States, and shall, within one year from the day of the signing of this treaty, enter into a convention whereby they shall unite in this treaty, and shall accept and agree to all the terms and conditions of the same, then it shall, to all intents and purposes, be regarded as having been originally made with them also, and they be deemed and taken to be parties hereto as if they were now to sign the same.

When this treaty to take effect. ARTICLE XLIII. This convention shall be obligatory on the Seneca Tribe, and on the Shawnees, aforesaid, of the mixed bands, from the day of its date, and on the Confederate States from and after its ratification by the Senate or provisional Congress.

In testimony whereof, the said Albert Pike, as Commissioner, with plenary powers, on the part of the Confederate States, doth now hereunto set his hand and affix the seal of his arms; and the undersigned, Chiefs and headmen of the Seneca Tribe of Indians, and of the Shawnees of the mixed bands of Senecas and Shawnees, do hereunto set their hands and affix their seals.

{ SEAL. }

Thus done in duplicate, at the place and upon the day, in the month and year first aforesaid.

ALBERT PIKE,
Commissioner of the Confederate States to the Indian Nations west of Arkansas.

LITTLE TOWN SPICER,
Principal Chief of Seneca Tribe.
SMALL CLOUD SPICER,
Second Chief of Seneca Tribe.
MOSES CROW,
Councillor of Seneca Tribe.
JOHN MUSH,
Councillor of Seneca Tribe.
GEORGE SPICER,
Councillor of Seneca Tribe.
JOHN SMITH,
JAMES KING,
ISAAC WARRIOR,
JIM BIG-BONE.
BUCK ARMSTRONG,
JO CROW,

DAVID SMITH,
GEORGE KERON,
C. S. Interpreter for the Seneca Tribe.
[*Warriors of the Seneca Tribe.*]
LEWIS DAVIS,
Principal Chief of the Senecas and Shawnees.
JOSEPH MOHAWK,
Second Chief of the Shawnees.
JOHN TOMAHAWK,
WHITE DEER,
Councillor of the Shawnees.
SILAS DOUGHERTY,
Councillor of the Shawnees.
WILLIAM BARBEE,
C. S. Interpreter for the Shawnees.

Signed, sealed and delivered in presence of us.

WM. QUESENBURY,
Secretary to the Commissioner.
E. RECTOR,
Superintendent of Indian Affairs C. S.
ANDREW J. DORN,
C. S. Agent for Osages, Senecas, etc.
W. WARREN JOHNSON,
LUTHER H. PIKE,
J. W. WASHBOURNE,

To the Indian names are subjoined marks.

RATIFICATION.

Resolved, (two-thirds of Congress concurring,) That the Congress of the Confederate States of America, do advise and consent to the ratification of the articles of a convention, made by Albert Pike, Commissioner of the Confederate States to the Indian nations west of Arkansas, in behalf of the Confederate States, of the one part, and the Seneca Tribe of Indians, formerly known as the Senecas of Sandusky, and the Shawnees of the tribe or confederacy of Senecas and Shawnees, formerly known as the Senecas and Shawnees of Lewistown, or the mixed bands of Senecas and Shawnees, each tribe for itself, by the chiefs and warriors who signed the same articles, of the other part, concluded at Park Hill, in the Cherokee Nation, on the fourth day of October, in the year of our Lord, one thousand eight hundred and sixty-one, withe following amendment:

Dec. 21, 1861.

Ratification by Congress of the treaty with the Senecas and Shawnees.

AMENDMENT.

In article twenty-seven, at the end of the words "or in a State court," add the following words: "subject to the laws of the State."

Amendment.

NOTE.—The amendment was agreed to and ratified by the Senecas and Shawness as a part of the treaty.

25

TREATY WITH THE QUAPAWS.

OCTOBER 4TH, 1861.

ARTICLES OF A CONVENTION

Oct. 4, 1861.   *Entered into and concluded at Park Hill, in the Cherokee Nation, on the fourth day of October, in the year of our Lord, one thousand eight hundred and sixty-one, between the Confederate States of America, by Albert Pike, their Commissioner, with full powers, appointed by the President, by virtue of an Act of the Congress in that behalf, of the one part, and the Quapaw Tribe of Indians, by its Chiefs and warriors, who have signed these articles, of the other part.*

The Quapaws under the protection of the C. S. ARTICLE I. The Quapaw Tribe of Indians, and all the persons thereof, do hereby place themselves under the laws and protection of the Confederate States of America, in peace and in war, forever, and agree to be true and loyal to them under all circumstances.

The C. S. assume the protectorate. ARTICLE II. The Confederate States of America do hereby promise and firmly engage themselves to be, during all time, the friends and protectors of the Quapaw Tribe of Indians, and to defend and secure them in the enjoyment of all their rights; and that they will not allow them henceforward to be in any wise troubled or molested by any power or people, State or person whatever.

Guarantee to the Quapaws of the country secured to them by treaty with the U. S. ARTICLE III. The Confederate States of America do hereby assure and guarantee to the Quapaw Tribe of Indians, the exclusive and undisputed possession, use and occupancy, during all time, as long as grass shall grow and water run, of the country heretofore secured to them by treaty with the United States of America, and which is described in the treaty of the thirteenth day of May, A. D., one thousand eight hundred and thirty-three, as follows, that is to say: "One hundred and fifty sections of land, west of the State of Missouri, and between the lands of the Senecas and Shawnees, not heretofore assigned to any other tribe of Indians;" and as the same was afterwards selected and assigned to said Quapaw Tribe, and is now held and occupied by them; which lands shall not be sold or ceded by said **Lands not to be sold or ceded except to the C. S.** tribe, nor shall any part thereof, to any nation or people, except to the Confederate States, nor to any individuals whatever, except as hereinafter provided, and the same shall vest in the Confederate States, in case the said tribe becomes extinct or abandons the same.

Reservation of land for Indian agency. ARTICLE IV. The right is hereby reserved to the Confederate States to select, in any unoccupied part of said country, if they shall desire to do so, a tract of land, one mile square, as a reserve and site for an agency for the said tribe, which shall revert to the said tribe, with all the buildings thereon, whenever it shall cease to be occupied for an agency.

Forts and military posts. ARTICLE V. The Confederate States shall have the right to establish in the said country such forts and military posts as they may deem necessary, and shall have the right to select for each such fort or post, a tract of land, one mile square, on which such fort or post shall be established:

Provided, That if any person; have any improvements,.on any tract so selected, the value of such improvements shall be paid by the Government .to the owner thereof.

ARTICLE VI. No person whatever shall be permitted to settle or reside upon the agency reserve, when it shall have been selected, except by permission of the agent; nor upon any reserve for a fort or military post, except by the permission of the commanding officer; and every such reserve for forts or military posts, shall be within the sole and exclusive jurisdiction of the Confederate States. *No settlement permitted upon the agency reserve or the reserve for forts, &c.*

ARTICLE VII. The Confederate States hereby agree that the country hereby secured to the said tribe shall never be included within the bounds of any State or Territory, nor shall any of the laws of any State or Territory ever be extended over, or put in force within, any part of the said country; and the President of the Confederate States, will cause the said tribe to be protected against all molestation or disturbance at the hands of any other tribe or nation of Indians, or of any other person or persons whatever; and he shall have the same care and superintendence over them as was heretofore had by the President of the United States. *The country of the Quapaws not to be included within the bounds of any State or Territory or to be under the laws thereof. Protection againstother tribes or persons.*

ARTICLE VIII. The members of the said Quapaw Tribe of Indians shall have the right, henceforward, of hunting and killing game in all the unoccupied country west of the possessions of the Cherokees, Seminoles, Choctaws and Chickasaws, without molestation from any quarter, being, while so engaged therein, under the protection of the Confederate States. *Hunting and killing of game.*

ARTICLE IX. There shall be perpetual peace and brotherhood between the Quapaw Tribe of Indians and the Osages, Senecas, Senecas and Shawnees, Mus-ko-kis, Seminoles, Choctaws and Chickasaws, and the bands of Wichitas, Cado-ha-da-chos, Hue-cos, Ta-wa-caros, An-a-dagh-cos, Ton-ca-wes, Ki-chais, Ai-o-nais, Shawnees and Delawares, living in the country leased from the Choctaws and Chickasaws, and the Pen-e-tegh-ca, No-co-ni, Ta-nei-we, Ya-pa-rih-ca, and Co-cho-tih-ca bands of the Ne-um or Comanches; and every injury or act of hostility which either has heretofore sustained or met with at the hands of the other, shall be forgiven and forgotten. *Perpetual peace and brotherhood between the Quapaws and other tribes. Injuries, &c., to be forgiven and forgotten.*

ARTICE X. The Quapaw Tribe of Indians, and the said several other nations, tribes and bands shall henceforth be good neighbors to each other, and there shall be a free and friendly intercourse among them. And it is hereby agreed by the said Quapaw Tribe, as has already been agreed by all the others that the horses, cattle and other stock and property of each nation, tribe or band, and of every person of each, is his or its own; and that no person belonging to the Quapaw Tribe, shall or will hereafter kill, take away or injure any such property of another tribe or band, or of any member of any other tribe or band, or in any other way do them any harm. *The Quapaws and other tribes to be good neighbors to each other. Right of property in horses, cattle, &c.*

ARTICLE XI. Especially there shall be perpetual peace and friendship between said Quapaw Tribe and the Osages, Senecas, Senecas and Shawnees, Cherokees, Mus-ko-kis, Seminoles, Choctaws and Chickasaws, and the Chiefs and headmen of the said Quapaw Tribe, shall do all in their power to take and restore any negroes, horses or other property stolen from white men or from persons belonging to either of said nations and tribes; and to catch and give up any person among them who may kill or steal or do any other evil act. *Perpetual peace and friendship with the Osages and other Indian nations. Return of stolen property.*

ARTICLE XII. In order that the friendship now established between the said Quapaw Tribe of Indians and the Confederate States and the other Indian nations, tribes and bands aforesaid, may not be interrupted by the misconduct of individuals or bands of individuals, it is hereby agreed that for injuries done by individuals, no private revenge or retaliation shall take place, but instead thereof, complaint shall be made by the said Quapaw Tribe of Indians, when any individual thereof, is *No private revenge or retaliation to be taken for injuries done to the Quapaws. Mode of redress.*

injured, to the agent of the Confederate States for the Osages and other
tribes, who shall investigate the complaint, and if he finds it well-
founded, shall report the same to the Superintendent, who shall cause
the wrong to be redressed, and the person doing to be arrested whether

Trial and pun- he be a white man or an Indian; and he or they shall be tried for the
ishment of wrong same agreeably to the laws of the Confederate States, or of the State or
doer. Territory against which he may have offended, and be punished in the
same manner and with the same severity, as if the injury had been

Redress for in- done to a white man. And it is also agreed that if any member of the
juries done by the Quapaw Tribe shall do any injury to the person or property of any white
Quapaws. man or of a member of any other nation or tribe, under the protection
of the Confederate States, the offender shall be given up to the agent,
upon complaint made to him, and on his demand, the wrong shall be
redressed by him, and the offender be tried for the offence, agreeably to
the laws of the Confederate States, or of the State, Territory or nation

Proviso. against which he may offended: *Provided*, That he shall be punished
in no other manner, nor with any greater severity, than a citizen of
the Confederate States, or of such State, Territory or nation would be,
if he had committed the same offence.

Horses or other ARTICLE XIII. It is hereby further agreed that the Chiefs of the
property stolen to Quapaw Tribe shall use every exertion in their power to recover any
be returned to horses or other property that may be stolen from any citizen of the Con-
owner. federate States, or from any member of any other Indian nation or tribe
under the protection of the Confederate States, by any person or persons
whatever, and found within the limits of their country; and the property
so recovered shall be forthwith delivered to the owner or to the agent to

Proceeding be restored to him. If, in any case, the right to the property claimed
where right to pro- is contested by the person in possession, the agent shall summarily inves-
perty is contested. tigate the case, and, upon hearing the testimony of witnesses, shall decide
the right to the property, and order it to be detained or delivered up

Appeal. accordingly. Either party may appeal from his decision to the Superintendent, whose decision shall be final in all cases, the property in the

Where restora- meantime remaining in the custody of the agent. If, in any case, the
tion cannot be exertions of the Chiefs to cause the restoration of stolen property prove
made, the value of ineffectual, and the agent is satisfied from the testimony that it was
the property stolen
to be deducted actually stolen, or received with knowledge of its being stolen, by any
from the annuity of person belonging to the Quapaw Tribe, he shall so report to the Super-
the tribe. intendent, with a copy of the testimony, which shall, for that purpose,
be always reduced to writing; and the Superintendent shall, if satisfied
from the testimony, deduct from the annuity of the Tribe a sum equal
to the value of the property stolen.

When the value ARTICLE XIV. The Confederate States hereby guarantee full and fair
of the property payment, to the owner, of the actual and full value of all horses and
stolen will be paid
by the C. S. to the other property stolen from any person or persons belonging to the
owner. Quapaw Tribe, by any citizen of the Confederate States, or by any
Indian of any other nation or tribe under their protection, in case the
same cannot be recovered and restored, and upon sufficient proof being
made before the Superintendent, or any agent of the Confederate States,
for any such nations or tribes, that such property was actually stolen by
a citizen or citizens of the Confederate States, or by an Indian or Indians
of any nation or tribe under their protection.

Agent and In- ARTICLE XV. An agent for the Great and Little Osage Tribes, the
terpreter. Quapaws, Senecas, and Senecas and Shawnees shall be appointed by the
President, and an Interpreter for the Quapaw Tribe for their protection,
and that their complaints may be heard by and their wants made known

Where to reside. to the President. The agent shall reside continually in the country of
one or the other of said tribes or bands, and the interpreter shall reside

continually amongst the Quapaws, and neither of them shall ever be absent from their posts, except by permission of the Superintendent. *Not to be absent without leave.*

ARTICLE XVI. None of the braves of the Quapaw Tribe shall go upon the war path, against any enemy whatever, except with the consent of the agent, or unless it be to pursue hostile bands of white men or Indians entering their country and committing murder, robbery or other outrage, when immediate pursuit is necessary; nor shall hold any talks or councils with any white men or Indians without his knowledge and consent. And they especially agree to attend no councils or talks in the country of any people, with whom the Confederate States are at war; and in case they do so, all the benefits secured to them by this treaty shall immediately and forever cease. *No war to be waged or councils held, except with the consent of the agent.*

ARTICLE XVII. The Confederate States will not permit any improper person to reside or be in the Quapaw country, but only such persons as are employed by them, their officers or agents, and traders, licensed by them, who shall sell to the Quapaws and buy from them, at fair prices, under such regulations as the President shall make from time to time. *Who may live in the Quapaw country.*

ARTICLE XVIII. No State or Territory shall ever pass laws for the government of the Quapaw people; and except so far as the laws of the Confederate States are in force in their country, they shall be left free to govern themselves. and to punish offences committed by one of themselves against the person or property of another: *Provided*, That if one of them kills another, without good cause or justification, he shall suffer death, but only by the sentence of the Chiefs, and after a fair trial, all private revenge being strictly forbidden. *The Quapaws left free to govern themselves.*

Proviso.

ARTICLE XIX. Every white man who marries a woman of the Quapaws, and resides in the Quapaw country, shall be deemed and taken, even after the death of his wife, to be a Quapaw and a member of the tribe, so far as to be subject to its laws in respect to all offences committed in its country against the person or property of another member of his tribe, and *as* not to be considered a white man committing such offence against the person or property of an Indian, within the meaning of the acts of the Congress of the Confederate States. And all negroes or mulattoes, bond or free, committing any such offence in said country, shall in like manner be subject to the laws of the tribe. *White man who marries a woman of the Quapaws deemed to be a Quapaw so far as to be subject to the laws of the tribe.*

Negroes and mulattoes in like manner subject to the laws of the tribe.

ARTICLE XX. The Confederate States shall have the right to establish, open and maintain such military and other roads through any part of the Quapaw country, as the President may deem necessary, without making any compensation for the right of way, or for the land, timber or stone used in constructing the same; but if any other property of the tribe, or any other property or the improvements of an individual be used or injured therein, just and adequate compensation shall be made. *Military and other roads.*

ARTICLE XXI. The Confederate States may grant the right of way for any railroad through any part of the Quapaw country; but the company to which any such right may be granted shall pay to the tribe therefor such sum as shall, in the opinion of the President, be its fair value; and shall also pay to individuals all damages done by the building of said road to their improvements or other property, to such amount in each case as commissioners appointed by the President shall determine. *Right of way for railroads.*

Payment of damages to individuals.

ARTICLE XXII. The agent of the Confederate States, for the Osages and other tribes, shall prevent all intrusions, by hunters and others, upon the lands of the Quapaws, and permit no white men or other Indians to settle thereon, and shall remove all such persons, calling, if necessary, upon the military power for aid; and the commanders of military posts, in that or the adjoining country, shall be required to afford him such aid upon his requisition. *Intrusions and settlement upon the land of the Quapaws to be prevented.*

The Quapaws may allow other Indians to settle among them.

ARTICLE XXIII. The Quapaws may allow persons of ony other tribe of Indians to settle among them, and may receive from them for their own benefit, compensation for such lands as they may sell or assign to such persons.

Who not to pasture stock on their lands.

Liberty given to travel in their country, and drive stock through the same.

ARTICLE XXIV. No citizen or inhabitant of the Confederate States or member of any friendly nation or tribe of Indians, shall pasture stock on the lands of the Quapaws, but all such persons shall have full liberty, at all times, and whether for business or pleasure, peaceably to travel in their country, on the roads or elsewhere, to drive their stock through the same, and to halt such reasonable time on the way as may be necessary to recruit their stock, such delay being in good faith for that purpose and no other.

Surrender of fugitives from justice.

ARTICLE XXV. Any person duly charged with a criminal offence against the laws of the Confederate States, or of any State or Territory, or of any Indian nation or tribe under the protection of the Confederate States, escaping into the Quapaw country, shall be promptly taken and delivered up by the Chiefs of the Quapaws, on the demand of the proper authority of the Confederate States, or of the State, Territory, nation or tribe within whose jurisdiction the offence shall be alleged to have been committed.

Laws declared to be in force in the Quapaw country.

ARTICLE XXVI. In addition to the laws of the Confederate States, expressly applying to the Indian country, so much of their laws as provides for the punishment of crimes amounting to felony at common law, or by statute against their laws, authority or treaties, and over which the courts of the Confederate States have jurisdiction, including the counterfeiting the coin of the United States, or of the Confederate States, or any other current coin, or the securities of the Confederate States, or the uttering of such counterfeit coin or securities; and so much of said laws as provides for punishing violations of the neutrality laws, and resistance to the process of the Confederate States; and all the acts of the provisional Congress providing for the common defence and welfare, so far as the same are not locally inapplicable; and the laws providing for the capture and delivery of fugitive slaves, shall be in force in the Quapaw country; and the district court for Chalahki district,

Jurisdiction of district court for the Chalahki district.

when established, shall have exclusive jurisdiction to try, condemn and punish offenders against ▓▓▓▓ laws, to adjudge and pronounce sentence, and cause execution thereof to be done.

Any of the Quapaws indicted in any court of the C. S. or State court entitled to process for witnesses.

Costs of process paid by C. S.

When accused may be assigned counsel.

ARTICLE XXVII. Whenever any person, who is a member of the Quapaw Tribe, shall be indicted for any offence in any court of the Confederate States, or in a State court, he shall be entitled, as of common right, to subpœna, and, if necessary, to compulsory process for all such witnesses in his behalf as his counsel may think material for his defence; and the costs of process for such witnesses, and of the service thereof, and fees and mileage of such witnesses shall be paid by the Confederate States; and whenever the accused is not able to employ counsel, the court shall assign him one experienced counsel for his defence, who shall be paid by the Confederate States a reasonable compensation for his services, to be fixed by the court, and paid upon the certificate of the judge.

Existing laws, usages and usages in regard to slavery. declared binding.

ARTICLE XXVIII. It is hereby declared and agreed that the institution of slavery in the said Quapaw Tribe is legal and has existed from time immemorial; that slaves are personal property; that the title to slaves and other property having its origin in the said tribe is to be determined by the laws and customs thereof; and that the slaves and personal property of every person domiciled in the country of said tribe shall pass and be distributed at his or her death, in accordance with the laws, usages and customs of the said tribe, which may be proved by oral

evidence, and shall everywhere be held valid and binding within the
scope of their operation. And if any slave escape from said tribe, the
laws of the Confederate States, for the capture and delivery of fugitive
slaves, shall apply to such cases, whether they escape into a State or Territory or into any Indian nation or tribe, under the protection of the
Confederate States; the obligation upon each such State, Territory, nation
or tribe to deliver up the same being in every case as complete as if they
had escaped from a State, and the mode of procedure the same.

ARTICLE XXIX. The Quapaw Tribe of Indians hereby makes itself
a party to the existing war between the Confederate States and the
United States of America, as the ally and ward of the former; and, in
consideration of the protection guaranteed by this treaty, and of their
common interests, hereby agrees to aid in defending its country against
any invasion thereof by the common enemy; and it is agreed that all
warriors furnished by it for the service of the Confederate States, and
which shall be mustered into that service, shall receive the same pay
and allowances as other troops of the same class therein, and remain in
the service as long as the President shall require.

ARTICLE XXX. The Confederate States hereby agree to furnish each
warrior of the Quapaw Tribe, who has not a gun, with a good rifle, and
also to furnish each warrior with a sufficient supply of ammunition
during the war.

ARTICLE XXXI. The Confederate States will also furnish the Quapaws, at a proper place, with such medicines as may be necessary, and
will employ a physician for them and for the Senecas and Senecas and
Shawnees, who shall reside at a convenient place in the country of one
or the other tribe, during the pleasure of the President; and any
physician employed shall be discharged by the Superintendent, and
another be employed in his place, in case of incompency or inattention
to his duties.

ARTICLE XXXII. In consideration of the uniform loyalty and good
conduct of the Quapaw Tribe, and of their necessities, arising from the
sale by them of their lands in Arkansas for a grossly inadequate price,
by the treaty of the year one thousand eight hundred and twenty-four,
the Confederate States hereby agree to expend, for the benefit of the
Quapaws, in each year, for and during the term of twenty years from
the day of the signing of this treaty, commencing with the year one
thousand eight hundred and sixty-two, the sum of two thousand dollars,
which shall be applied each year by the Superintendent to the purchase
of articles costing that sum at the place of purchase in the Confederate
States, to consist of blankets, clothing, tobacco, household and kitchen
furniture and utensils, and other articles of ease and comfort for the
Quapaws, which shall be distributed among them by the agent, as
equally as possible, regard being had in the distribution to the character
for industry or idleness, and good or bad conduct, on the part of the
recipient, as well as the necessities of each, so that the good and the
needy shall be preferred; and in determining which, the agent shall pay
due respect to the opinions and judgment of the chiefs.

ARTICLE XXXIII. The Confederate States also agree to employ a
blacksmith for the Quapaws, for and during the term of twenty years
from the date of this treaty, and an assistant, who shall be one of the
Quapaw people, and receive a compensation of two hundred and fifty dollars per annum. And they will also furnish the blacksmith with a dwelling
house, shop and tools, and supply the shop with coal, and with six hundred pounds of iron, and one hundred pounds of steel, annually.

ARTICLE XXXIV. The Confederate States will also employ one wagon-
maker and wheelwright for the Quapaws, for and during the term of

The Quapaw
Tribe makes itself
a party to the ex-
isting war and
agrees to furnish
aid.

Pay of warriors.

How long to
serve.

Rifle and ammu-
nition for each
warrior.

Medicines and
medical services.

The C. S. agree
to expend for
Tribe, $2 an-
nually, for twenty
years.

How fund to be
applied.

Blacksmith and
assistant.

Compensation.

Shop and tools.
Coal, iron and
steel.

Wagon maker
and wheelwright.

Shop, tools and materials. twenty years from the date of this treaty, and furnish him with a dwelling house, shops, tools and the necessary materials.

Grist and saw mills. ARTICLE XXXV. The Confederate States hereby agree to build and put in running order for the Quapaws, at some suitable point in their country, to be selected by the agent, a good grist and saw mill, and to deliver the same, when completed, to the Quapaw people, whose absolute property it shall at once become. And the Confederate States will also employ, for the term of ten years, an experienced miller for each mill, to be selected, if possible, from among the Quapaws, and if such millers can be had at a compensation not exceeding six hundred dollars per annum for each.

Millers.

Compensation.

Wagons and harness, oxen and horse gear. ARTICLE XXXVI. The Confederate States also further agree to purchase, for the Quapaws, four good wagons and harness for four horses for each wagon, ten yoke oxen, and ten sets of horse gear complete, to be delivered to the chiefs, and used for the general benefit of their people.

Annual payment for the education of the Quapaw children. ARTICLE XXXVII. The Confederate States also further agree perpetually to pay regularly and annually hereafter, the sum of one thousand dollars for education of their children, provided by the treaty of the thirteenth day of May, A. D., one thousand eight hundred and thirty-three, and also to add to that sum in each and every year the further sum of one thousand five hundred dollars; which sums shall be payable on the first day of January in each year, commencing with the year one thousand eight hundred and sixty-two, and shall be applied by the agent to the education of Quapaw children and youths in the Osage Manual Labor School, until an institution of learning can be, with the aid of this perpetual fund, established in the country of the Quapaws.

Annuity to the Chiefs. ARTICLE XXXVIII. Inasmuch as the Quapaws have no fund out of which to pay the salaries of their Chiefs, or the expenses of their government, the Confederate States further agree to pay to each of the present Chiefs, Wat-ti-shi-nek Kat-eh-de, the first Chief, and Ka-hi-keh-tih-te, the second Chief, for each year, and during his natural life, an annuity of one hundred dollars in money per annum, payable on the first day of January in each year, commencing with the year one thousand eight hundred and sixty-two.

Trader purchasing articles given to Quapaws, to be punished. ARTICLE XXXIX. If any trader or other person should purchase from any Quapaw any of the chattels or articles given him by the Confederate States, he shall be severely punished.

General amnesty. ARTICLE XL. A general amnesty of all past offences against the laws of the United States or of the Confederate States, committed before the signing of this treaty, by any member of the Quapaw Tribe, as such membership is defined in this treaty, is hereby declared; and all such persons, if any, charged with such offence, shall receive from the President full and free pardon, and if imprisoned or held to bail, before or after conviction, shall be discharged.

When this treaty to take effect. ARTICLE XLI. This convention shall be obligatory on the Quapaw Tribe of Indians from the day its date, and on the Confederate States from and after its ratification by the Senate or provisional Congress.

In perpetual testimony whereof, the said Albert Pike, as Commissioner, with plenary powers, on the part of the Confederate States, doth now hereunto set his hand and affix the seal of his arms; and the undersigned, Chiefs and headmen of the Quapaw Tribe of Indians, do hereunto set their hands and affix their seals.

{ SEAL. }

This done in duplicate, at the place, and upon the day, in the year first aforesaid.   ALBERT PIKE,

Commissioner of the Confederate States to the Indian nations west of Arkansas.

WAT-TI-SHI-NEK-KAT-EH-DE,   MOS-KA-ZI-KA,
Principal Chief of the Quapaws.   A-HI-SUT-TA,
GEORGE LANE,   NIK-KAT-TOH,
ELIJAH H. FIELDS,   MO-ZEK-KA-NE,
NOT-TET-TU,   S. G. VALLAR,
KA-NI,   R. P. LOMBARD.

Signed, sealed and devivered in presence of us.

WM. QUESENBURY,
Secretary to the Commissioner.
E. RECTOR,
Superintendent Indian Affairs Confederate States.
ANDREW J. DORN,
Confederate States Agent for the Quapaws, etc.
W. WARREN JOHNSON,
R. H. BEAN,
J. W. WASHBOURNE.

To the Indian names are subjoined marks.

RATIFICATION.

Dec. 21, 1861.

Resolved, (two-thirds of the Congress concurring,) That the Congress of the Confederate States of America, do advise and consent to the ratification of the articles of a convention, made by Albert Pike, Commissioner of the Confederate States to the Indian nations west of Arkansas, of the one part, and the Quapaw Tribe of Indians, by its Chiefs and warriors, who signed the same articles of the other part, concluded at Park Hill, in the Cherokee Nation, on the fourth day of October, in the year of our Lord, one thousand eight hundred and sixty-one, with the following

Ratification by Congress of the foregoing treaty with the Quapaws.

AMENDMENT:

Strike out from article twenty-seven, the following words: "or in a State court," and insert in lieu thereof the following words: "or in a State court, subject to the laws of the State."

Amendment.

NOTE.—The amendment was agreed to and ratified by the Quapaws as a part of the treaty.

TREATY WITH THE CHEROKEES.

OCTOBER 7TH, 1861.

A TREATY OF FRIENDSHIP AND ALLIANCE,

Oct. 7, 1861.

Made and concluded at Tahlequah, in the Cherokee Nation, on the seventh day of October, in the year of our Lord, one thousand eight hundred and sixty-one, between the Confederate States of America, by Albert Pike, Commissioner with plenary powers, of the Confederate States, of the one part, and the Cherokee Nation of Indians, by John Ross, the Principal Chief, Joseph Verner, Assistant Principal Chief, James Brown, John Drew and William P. Ross, Executive Councillors, constituting with the Principal and Assistant Principal Chiefs the Executive Council of the Nation, and authorized to enter into this treaty by a General Convention of the Cherokee People, held at Tahlequah, the seat of Government of the Cherokee Nation, on the twenty-first day of August, in the year of our Lord, one thousand eight hundred and sixty-one; together with Lewis Ross, Thomas Pegg and Richard Fields, Commissioners selected and appointed by the Principal Chief with the advice and consent of the Executive Council to assist in negotiating the same, of the other part.

Preamble.

The Congress of the Confederate States of America, having by an "act for the protection of certain Indian tribes," approved the twenty-first day of May, in the year of our Lord, one thousand eight hundred and sixty-one, offered to assume and accept the protectorate of the several nations and tribes of Indians occupying the country west of Arkansas and Missouri, and to recognize them as their wards, subject to all the rights, privileges and immunities, titles and guarantees with each of said nations and tribes under treaties made with them by the United States of America; and the Cherokee Nation of Indians having assented thereto upon certain terms and conditions:

Now, therefore, the said Confederate States of America, by Albert Pike their Commissioner, constituted by the President, under authority of the act of Congress in that behalf, with plenary powers for these purposes, and the Cherokee Nation by the Principal Chief, Executive Council and Commissioners aforesaid, has agreed to the following articles, that is to say:

Perpetual peace and friendship.

ARTICLE I. There shall be perpetual peace and friendship, and an alliance offensive and defensive, between the Confederate States of America and all of their States and people, and the Cherokee Nation and all the people thereof.

The Cherokees acknowledge themselves to be under the protection of the C. S.

ARTICLE II. The Cherokee Nation of Indians acknowledges itself to be under the protection of the Confederate States of America, and of no other power or sovereign whatever; and does hereby stipulate and agree with them that it will not hereafter contract any alliance, or enter into any compact, treaty or agreement with any individual, State or with a foreign power; and the said Confederate States do hereby assume and accept the said protectorate, and recognize the said Cherokee Nation as their ward; and by the consent of the said nation now here freely given, the country whereof it is proprietor in fee, as the same is hereinafter described, is annexed to the Confederate States in the same manner and to the same extent as it was annexed to the United States of America before that Government was dissolved, with such modifications, however, of the terms of annexation, and upon such conditions as are hereinafter expressed, in addition to all the rights, privileges, immunities, titles and guarantees with or in favor of the said nation, under treaties made with it, and under the statutes of the United States of America. And in consequence of the obligations imposed on the Cherokee people by this article, it is agreed on the part of the Confederate States, that they will not at any time enter into any compact, treaty or agreement with any individuals or party in the Cherokee Nation, but only with the constitutional authorities of the same, that will in any way interfere with or affect any of the national rights of the Cherokee people.

The C. S. assume the protectorate.

Cherokee country annexed to the C. S.

C. S. not to enter into compacts, except with the Constitutional authorities of the Cherokee Nation.

ARTICLE III. The Confederate States of America, having accepted the said protectorate, hereby solemnly promise the said Cherokee Nation never to desert or to abandon it, and that under no circumstances will they permit the Northern States or any other enemy to overcome them and sever the Cherokees from the Confederacy; but that they will, at any cost and all hazards, protect and defend them and maintain unbroken the ties created by identity of interests and institutions, and strengthened and made perpetual by this treaty.

Protection promised.

ARTICLE IV. The boundaries of the Cherokee country shall forever continue and remain the same as they are defined by letters patent therefor given by the United States to the Cherokee Nation on the thirty-first day of December, in the year of our Lord, one thousand eight hundred and thirty-eight; which boundaries are therein defined as follows:

Boundaries of the Cherokee country.

Beginning at a mound of rocks four feet square at base, and four and a half feet high, from which another mound of rocks bears south one chain, and another mound of rocks bear west one chain, on what has been denominated the old western Territorial line of Arkansas Territory, twenty-five miles north of Arkansas river; thence south twenty one miles and twenty-eight chains, to a post on the northeast bank of the Verdigris river, from which a hackberry, fifteen inches diameter, bears south sixty-one degrees thirty-one minutes east, forty-three links, marked C. H. L. and a cottonwood forty-two inches diameter, bears south twenty-one degrees, fifteen minutes, east, fifty links, marked C. R. R. L.; thence down the Verdigris river, on the north east bank, with its meanders to the junction of Verdigris and Arkansas rivers; thence from the lower bank of Verdigris river; on the north bank of Arkansas river, south, forty-four degrees, thirteen minutes, east, fifty-seven chains, to a post on the south bank of Arkansas, opposite the eastern bank of Neosho river, at its junction with Arkansas, from which a red oak thirty-six inches diameter, bears south seventy-five degrees, forty-five minutes, west, twenty-four links, and a hickory twenty-four inches diameter bears south eighty-nine degrees, east, four links; thence south fifty-three degrees west, one mile, to a post from which a rock bears north fifty-three degrees east, fifty links, and a rock bears south, eighteen degrees, eighteen minutes west, fifty links; thence south eighteen degrees, eighteen minutes west, thirty-three miles, twenty-eight chains, and eighty links, to a rock, from which another rock bears north eighteen degrees, eighteen minutes east, fifty links, and another rock bears south fifty links; thence south four miles, to a post on the lower bank of the north fork of Canadian river, at its junction with Canadian river, from which a cotton wood, twenty-four inches diameter bears north eighteen degrees east, forty links, and a cotton wood fifteen inches diameter, bears south nine degrees east, fourteen links; thence down the Canadian river on its north bank to its junction with Arkansas river; thence down the main channel of Arkansas river to the western boundary of the State of Arkansas at the northern extremity of the eastern boundary of the lands of the Choctaws, on the south bank of Arkansas river, four chains and fifty-four links east of Fort Smith; thence north seven degrees twenty-five minutes west with the western boundary of the State of Arkansas, seventy-six miles, sixty-four chains and fifty links to the southeast corner of the State of Missouri; thence north, on the western boundary of the State of Missouri eight miles, forty-nine chains and fifty links, to the north bank of Cowskin or Seneca river, at a mound six feet square at base and five feet high, in which is a post marked on the south-side Cor. Ch. Ld.; thence west on the northern boundary of the lands of the Senecas, eleven miles and forty chains, to a post on the east bank of Neosho river, from which a maple eight eighteen inches diameter bears south thirty-one degrees east, seventy-two links; thence up Neosho river, with its meanders, on the east bank, to the southern boundary of Osage lands, thirty-six chains and fifty links, west of the southeast corner of the lands of the Osages, witnessed by a mound of rocks on the west bank of Neosho river; thence west on the southern boundary of the Osage lands to the line dividing the Territory of the United States from that of Mexico, two hundred and eighty-eight miles, thirteen chains and sixty-six links, to a mound of earth six feet square at base, and five and a half feet high in which is deposited a cylinder of charcoal, twelve inches long and four inches diameter; thence south along the line of the Territory of the United States and of Mexico, sixty miles and twelve chains to a mound of earth six feet square at base and five and a half feet high, in which is deposited a cylinder of charcoal, eighteen inches long and three inches diameter; thence east, along the northern boundary of Creek lands, two hundred and seventy-three miles, fifty-five chains and sixty-six links, to the beginning; containing within the survey thirteen millions five hundred and seventy-four thousand one hundred and thirty-five acres and fourteen hundredths of an acre.

Title of the U. S. in the Cherokee country vested in the C. S. ARTICLE V. The Cherokee Nation hereby gives its full, free and unqualified assent to those provisions of the act of Congress of the Confederate States of America, entitled "An act for the protection of certain Indian tribes," approved the twenty-fourth day of May, in the year of our Lord, one thousand eight hundred and sixty-one, whereby it was declared that all reversionary, and other interest, right, title and proprietorship of the United States in, unto and over the Indian country, in which that of the said Cherokee Nation is included, should pass to and vest in the Confederate States, and whereby the President of the Confederate States was authorized to take military possession and occupation of all said country; and whereby all the laws of the United States with the exception thereinafter made, applicable to and in force in said country, and not inconsistent with the letter or spirit of any treaty stipulations entered into with the Cherokee Nation were enacted, continued in force, and declared to be in force in said country, as laws and statutes of the Confederate States: *Provided,*

Proviso. *however,* And it is hereby agreed between the said parties, that whatever in the said laws of the United States contained, is or may be contrary to or inconsistent with any article or provision of this treaty, is to be of none effect henceforward, and shall, upon the ratification hereof, be deemed and taken to have been repealed and annulled as of the present date, and this assent, as thus qualified and conditioned, shall relate to and be taken to have been given upon the said day of the approval of the said act of Congress.

ARTICLE VI. The Confederate States of America do hereby solemnly guarantee to the Cherokee Nation, to be held by it to its own use and behoof in fee simple forever, the lands included within the boundaries defined in article four of this treaty; to be held by the people of the Cherokee Nation in common as they have heretofore been held, if the said nation shall so please, but with power of making partition thereof and dispositions of parcels of the same by virtue of laws of said nation duly enacted, and approved by a majority of the Cherokee people in general convention assembled; by which partition or sale, title in fee simple absolute shall vest in parceners and purchasers whenever it shall please said nation, of its own free will and accord and without solicitation from any quarter, to do so; which solicitation the Confederate States hereby solemnly agree never to use; and the title and tenure hereby guaranteed to the said nation is and shall be subject to no other restrictions, reservations or conditions, whatever, than such as are hereinafter specially expressed. *Partition and sale of lands.*

ARTICLE VII. None of the lands hereby guaranteed to the Cherokee Nation shall be sold, ceded or otherwise disposed of to any foreign nation or to any State or government whatever; and in case any such sale, cession or disposition should be made without the consent of the Confederate State, all the said lands shall thereupon revert to the Confederate States. *Lands not to be sold or ceded to any foreign nation, or to any State or government.*

ARTICLE VIII. The Confederate States of America do hereby solemnly agree and bind themselves that no State or Territory shall ever pass laws for the government of the Cherokee Nation; and that no portion of the lands guaranteed to it shall ever be embraced or included within or annexed to any Territory or Province; nor shall any attempt ever be made, except upon the free, voluntary and unsolicited application of said nation, to erect its said country, by itself or with any other, into a State or any other territorial or political organization, or to incorporate it into any State previously created. *No State or Territory to pass laws for the Cherokees.* *Not to be incorporated into any other territorial or political organization.*

ARTICLE IX. All navigable streams of the Confederate States and of the Indian country shall be free to the people of the Cherokee Nation, who shall pay no higher toll or tonnage duty or other duty than the citizens of the Confederate States; and the citizens of that nation living upon the Arkansas river shall have, possess and enjoy upon that river, the same ferry privileges, to the same extent in all respects, as citizens of the Confederate States on the opposite side thereof, subject to no other or a different tax or charge than they. *Navigable streams free to the Cherokees.* *Ferry privileges upon the Arkansas river.*

ARTICLE X. The Cherokee Nation may by act of its legislative authorities receive and incorporate in the nation as members thereof, or permit to reside and settle upon the national lands, such Indians of any other nation or tribe as to it may seem good; and may sell them portions of its land, and receive to its own use the consideration therefor: and the nation alone shall determine who are members and citizens of the nation entitled to vote at elections and share in annuities: *Provided*, That when persons of another Indian nation or tribe shall once have been received as members of the nation, they shall not be disfranchised or subjected to any other restrictions upon the right of voting than such as shall apply to the Cherokees themselves. But no Indians not settled in the Cherokee country shall be permitted to come therein to reside, without the consent and permission of the legislative authority of the nation. *Indians of other nations or tribes may be received as members.* *Who entitled to vote at elections and share in annuities.* *Proviso.*

ARTICLE XI. So far as may be compatible with the Constitution of the Confederate States and with the laws made, enacted or adopted in conformity thereto, regulating trade and intercourse with the Indian tribes, as the same are modified by this treaty, the Cherokee nation shall possess the otherwise unrestricted right of self-government and full jurisdiction, judicial and otherwise, over persons and property within its limit, excepting only such white persons as are not by birth, adoption or otherwise; mem- *Right of self-government and full jurisdiction over persons and property.* *Exception.*

bers of the Cherokee Nation; and that there may be no doubt as to the mean-

White person who marries a Cherokee woman, or is permanently domiciled in the Cherokee country, taken to be a member of the nation.

ing of this exception, it is hereby declared that every white person who, having married a Cherokee woman, resides in said Cherokee country, or who, without intermarrying, is permanently domiciled therein with the consent of the authorities of the nation, and votes at elections, is to be deemed and taken to be a member of the said nation within the true intent and meaning of this article; and that the exception contained in

Exception in the law for the punishment of offences committed in the Indian country, extended and enlarged.

the laws for the punishment of offences committed in the Indian country, to the effect that they shall not extend or apply to offences committed by one Indian against the person or property of another Indian, shall be so extended and enlarged by virtue of this article when ratified and without further legislation, as that none of said laws shall extend and apply to any offence committed by any Indian, or negro, or mulatto, or by any white person, so by birth, adoption or otherwise a member of the Cherokee Nation against the person or property of any Indian, negro, or mulatto, or any such white person when the same shall be committed within the limits of the said Cherokee Nation as hereinbefore defined; but all such persons shall be subject to the laws of the Cherokee Nation, and to prosecution and trial before its tribunals, and punishment according to such laws, in all respects like native members of the said nation.

Intruders to be removed.

ARTICLE XII. All persons not members of the Cherokee Nation, as such membership is hereinbefore defined, who may be found in the Cherokee country, shall be considered as intruders, and be removed and kept out of the same either by the civil officers of the nation under the direction of the executive or legislature, or by the agent of the Confederate States for the nation, who shall be authorized to demand, if neces-

Exceptions

sary, the aid of the military for that purpose; with the following exceptions only, that is to say : Such individuals with their families as may be in the employment of the Government of the Confederate States; all persons peaceably travelling, or temporarily sojourning in the country, or trading therein under license from the proper authority; and such persons as may be permitted by the legislative authority of the Cherokee Nation to reside within its limits without becoming members of the said nation.

Reservation of land for Indian agency.

ARTICLE XIII. A tract of two sections of land in the said nation, to be selected by the President of the Confederate States, or such officer or person as he may appoint, in conjunction with the authorities of the Cherokee Nation, at such a point as they may deem most proper, is hereby ceded to the Confederate States, for the purpose of an agency; and when selected shall be within their sole and exclusive jurisdiction, except as to offences committed therein by one member of the Cherokee Nation

Proviso.

against the person or property of another member of the same : *Provided*, That whenever the agency shall be discontinued, the tract so selected therein shall revert to the said nation, with all the buildings that may

Further proviso.

be thereupon : *And provided also*, That the President, conjointly with the authorities of the nation may at any time select in lieu of said reserve, any unoccupied tract of land in the nation, and in any other part thereof, not greater in extent than two sections, as a site for the agency of the nation, which shall in such case constitute the reserve, and that first selected shall thereupon revert to the Cherokee Nation.

Forts and military posts, and military and post roads.

ARTICLE XIV. The Confederate States shall have the right to build, and establish and maintain such forts and military posts, temporary or permanent, and such military and post roads as the President may deem necessary in the Cherokee country; and the quantity of one mile square of land, including each fort or post, shall thereby vest as by cession in the Confederate States and be within their sole and exclusive jurisdiction, except as to offences committed therein by members of the Cherokee Nation against the persons or property of other members of the same, so long as such fort or post is occupied; but no greater quantity of land beyond one mile square shall be used or occupied, nor any greater quantity of timber felled than of each is actually requisite; and if in the establishment of such fort, post or road, or of the agency, the property of any individual member of the Choctaw Nation, other than land, timber, stone and earth, be taken, destroyed or impaired, just and adequate compensation shall be made by the Confederate States.

ARTICLE XV. No person shall settle or raise stock within the limits of any post or fort or of the agency reserve, except such as are or may be in the employment of the Confederate States, in some civil or military capacity; or such as, being subject to the jurisdiction and laws of the Cherokee Nation, are permitted by the commanding officer of the fort or post to do so thereat, or by the agent to do so upon the agency reserve. *No person to settle or raise stock within certain limits.*

ARTICLE XVI. An agent of the Confederate States for the Cherokee Nation, and an interpreter shall continue to be appointed, both of whom shall reside at the agency. And whenever a vacancy shall occur in either of the said offices, the authorities of the nation shall be consulted as to the person to be appointed to fill the same; and no one shall be appointed against whom they in good faith protest, and the agent may be removed, on petition and formal charges preferred by the constituted authorities of the nation, the President being satisfied, upon full investigation, that there is sufficient cause for such removal. *Agent and interpreter. Vacancy; in either of said offices, how filled.*

ARTICLE XVII. The Confederate States shall protect the Cherokees from hostile invasion and from aggression by other Indians and white persons, not subject to the laws and jurisdiction of the Cherokee Nation; and for all injuries resulting from such invasion or aggression, full indemnity is hereby guaranteed to the party or parties injured, out of the Treasury of the Confederate States, upon the same principle and according to the same rules upon which white persons are entitled to indemnity for injuries or aggressions upon them committed by Indians. *Protection from invasion and aggression. Indemnity for injuries.*

ARTICLE XVIII. It is further agreed between the parties that the agent of the Confederate States, upon the application of the authorities of the Cherokee Nation, will not only resort to every proper legal remedy, at the expense of the Confederate States, to prevent intrusion upon the lands of the Cherokees, and to remove dangerous or improper persons, but he shall call upon the military power if necessary; and to that end all commanders of military posts in the said country shall be required and directed to afford him, upon his requisition, whatever aid may be necessary to effect the purposes of this article. *Prevention of intrusion upon the lands of the Cherokees, and removal of improper persons.*

ARTICLE XIX. If any property of any Cherokee be taken by citizens of the Confederate States, by stealth or force, the agent, on complaint made to him in due form by affidavit, shall use all proper legal means and remedies in any State where the offender may be found to regain the property or compel a just remuneration; and on failure to procure redress, payment shall be made for the loss sustained, by the Confederate States upon the report of the agent, who shall have power to take testimony and examine witnesses in regard to the wrong done and the extent of the injury. *Property taken by stealth or force. Remedy.*

ARTICLE XX. No person shall be licensed to trade with the Cherokees except by the agent, and with the advice and consent of the National Council. Every such trader shall execute bond to the Confederate States in such form and manner as was required by the United States, or as may be required by the bureau of Indian affairs. The authorities of the Cherokee Nation may, by a general law, duly enacted, levy and collect on all licensed traders in the nation, a tax of not more than one *License to traders. Bond. Tax on licensed traders.*

half of one per cent. on all goods, wares and merchandise brought by them into the Cherokee country for sale, to be collected whenever such goods, wares and merchandise are introduced, and estimated upon the first cost of the same at the place of purchase, as the same shall be shown *Appeal from de-* by the copies of the invoices filed with the agent. No appeal shall here-*cision refusing li-* after lie from the decision of the agent or council, refusing a license, to *cense.* the Commissioner of Indian Affairs, or elsewhere, except only to the *Who may trade,* superintendent, in case of a refusal by the agent. And no license shall *and what articles* be required to authorize any member of the Cherokee Nation to trade in *may be sold with-* the Cherokee country; nor to authorize any person to sell flour, meats, *out license.* fruits and other provisions, or stock, wagons, agricultural implements or *What goods are* arms brought from any of the Confederate States into the country; nor *forfeited when ex-* shall any tax be levied upon such articles or the proceeds of the sale *posed to sale with-* thereof. And all other goods, wares and merchandise, exposed to sale *out license.* by a person not qualified, without a license, shall be forfeited, and be delivered and given to the authorities of the nation, as also shall all wines and liquors illegally introduced.

Restrictions on ARTICLE XXI. All restrictions contained in any treaty made with the *the right of the* United States, or created by any law or regulation of the United States, *Cherokees to sell* upon the limited right of any member of the Cherokee Nation to sell *and dispose of per-* and dispose of, to any person whatever, any chattel or other article of *sonal property, re-* personal property, are hereby removed; and no such restrictions shall *moved.* hereafter be imposed, except by their own legislation.

May take, hold ARTICLE XXII. It is hereby further agreed by the Confederate States, *and pass lands, by* that all the members of the Cherokee Nation, as hereinbefore defined, *purchase or des-* shall be henceforward competent to take, hold and pass, by purchase, or *cent.* descent, lands in any of the Confederate States, heretofore or hereafter acquired by them.

Cherokee coun- ARTICLE XXIII. In order to secure the due enforcement of so much *try erected into a* of the laws of the Confederate States in regard to criminal offences and *judicial district to* misdemeanors as is or may be in force in the said Cherokee country, and *be called the Cha-* to prevent the Cherokees from being further harrassed by judicial pro-*lah-ki district.* ceedings had in foreign courts and before juries not of the vicinage, the said country is hereby erected into and constituted a judicial district, to be called the Cha-lah-ki district, for the special purposes and jurisdic-*District court for* tion hereinafter provided; and there shall be created and semi-annually *such district;* held, within such district at Tah-le-quah, or in case of the removal of *where to be held.* the seat of Government of the nation, then at such place as may become the seat of Government, a district court of the Confederate States, with the powers of a circuit court, so far as the same shall be necessary to *Jurisdiction co-* carry out the provisions of this treaty, and with jurisdiction co-exten-*extensive with the* sive with the limits of such district, in such matters, civil and criminal, *limits of the dis-* to such extent and between such parties as may be prescribed by law, *trict.* and in conformity to the terms of this treaty.

Laws declared to ARTICLE XXIV. In addition to so much and such parts of the acts *be in force in the* of Congress of the United States enacted to regulate trade and inter-*Cherokee country.* course with the Indian tribes, and to preserve peace on the frontiers as have been re-enacted and continued in force by the Confederate States, and as are not inconsistent with the provisions of this treaty, so much of the laws of the Confederate States, as provides for the punishment of crimes amounting to felony at common law or by statute, against the laws, authority or treaties of the Confederate States, and over which the courts of the Confederate States have jurisdiction, including the coun-terfeiting the coin of the United States or of the Confederate States, or the securities of the Confederate States, and so much of the said laws as provides for punishing violators of the neutrality laws, and resistance to the process of the Confederate States, and all the acts of the provisional Congress, providing for the common defence and welfare, so far as the same are not locally inapplicable shall hereafter be in force in the Cherokee country, and the said district court shall have exclusive jurisdiction to try, condemn and punish offenders against any such laws, to adjudge and pronounce sentence, and cause execution thereof to be done in the same manner as is done in any other district court of the Confederate States.

ARTICLE XXV. The said district court of the Confederate States of America for the district of Cha-lah-ki shall also have the same admiralty jurisdiction as other district courts of the Confederate courts against any person or persons residing or found within the district; and in all civil suits at law or in equity when the matter in controversy is of greater value than five hundred dollars, between a citizen or citizens of any State or States of the Confederate States or any Territory of the same, or an alien or aliens and a citizen or citizens of the said district, or person or persons residing therein; and the Confederate States will, by suitable enactments, provide for the appointment of a judge and other proper officers of the said court, the clerk and marshal being members of the Cherokee Nation, and make all necessary enactments and regulations for the complete establishment and organization of the same, and to give full effect to its proceedings and jurisdiction. *Admiralty jurisdiction of the district for the Cha-lah-ki district. Jurisdiction in civil cases. Appointment of judge and other officers of the court.*

ARTICLE XXVI. The said district court shall have no jurisdiction to try and punish any person for any offence committed prior to the day of the signing of this treaty; nor shall any action in law or equity be maintained therein, except by the Confederate States' or one of them, when the cause of action shall have accrued before the same day of the signing hereof. *The court to have no jurisdiction in cases where the offence was committed, or the course of action accrued prior to the signing of this treaty.*

ARTICLE XXVII. If any citizen of the Confederate States or any other person, not being permitted to do so by the authorities of said nation or authorized by the terms of this treaty, shall attempt to settle upon any lands of the Cherokee Nation, he shall forfeit the protection of the Confederate States, and such punishment may be inflicted upon him, not being cruel, unusual or excessive, as may have been previously prescribed by law of the nation. *Punishment of person for attempting, without authority, to settle on the lands of the Cherokees.*

ARTICLE XXVIII. No citizen or inhabitant of the Confederate States shall pasture stock on the lands of the Cherokee Nation, under the penalty of one dollar per head, for all so pastured, to be collected by the authorities of the Nation; but their citizens shall be at liberty at all times, and whether for business or pleasure, peaceably to travel the Cherokee country; and to drive their stock to market or otherwise through the same, and to halt such reasonable time on the way as may be necessary to recruit their stock, such delay being in good faith for that purpose. *Who not to pasture stock on their lands. Liberty given to travel in their country, and drive stock through the same.*

ARTICLE XXIX. It is also further agreed that the members of the Cherokee Nation shall have the same right of travelling, driving stock and halting to recruit the same, in any of the Confederate States, as is given citizens of the Confederate States by the preceding article. *Cherokees may travel, drive stock, &c., in any of the C. S.*

ARTICLE XXX. If any person hired or employed by the agent or by any other person whatever, within the agency reserve, or any post or fort, shall violate the laws of the nation in such manner as to become an unfit person to continue in the Cherokee country, he or she shall be removed by the superintendent, upon the application of the executive of the nation, the superintendent being satisfied of the truth and sufficiency of the charges preferred. *How persons employed within the agency reserve may be removed.*

ARTICLE XXXI. Any person duly charged with a criminal offence against the laws of either the Creek, Seminole, Choctaw or Chickasaw Nations, and escaping into the jurisdiction of the Cherokee Nation, shall *Surrender of fugitives from justice.*

26

be promptly surrendered upon the demand of the proper authority of the
nation within whose jurisdiction the offence shall be alleged to have
been committed; and in like manner, any person duly charged with a
criminal offence against the laws of the Cherokee Nation, and escaping
into the jurisdiction of either of the said nations, shall be promptly
surrendered upon the demand of the proper authority of the Cherokee
Nation.

ARTICLE XXXII. The Cherokee Nation shall promptly apprehend
and deliver up all persons duly charged with any crime against the laws
of the Confederate States, or of any State thereof, who may be found
within its limits, on demand of any proper officer of the State or of the
Confederate States; and in like manner any person duly charged with a
criminal offence against the laws of the Cherokee Nation, and escaping
into the jurisdiction of a State, shall be promptly surrendered, on demand
of the executive of the nation.

Any of the Che-
rokees indicted in
any court of the C.
S. or State court
entitled to process
for witnesses.

ARTICLE XXXIII. Whenever any person, who is a member of the
Cherokee Nation, shall be indicted for any offence in any court of the
Confederate States, or of a State, he shall be entitled, as of common
right to subpœna, and, if necessary, to compulsory process for all such
witnesses in his behalf as his counsel may think necessary for his

Costs of process,
and fees and mile-
age of witnesses.

defence; and the cost of process for such witnesses and of service thereof,
and the fees and mileage of such witnesses shall be paid by the Confederate States, being afterwards made, if practicable, in case of conviction,

When accused
may be assigned
counsel.

of the property of the accused. And whenever the accused is not able
to employ counsel the court shall assign him one experienced counsel for
his defence, who shall be paid by the Confederate States a reasonable
compensation for his services, to be fixed by the court, and paid upon
the certificate of the judge.

Rendition of fu-
gitive slaves.

ARTICLE XXXIV The provisions of all such acts of the Congress of
the Confederate States as may now be in force, or as may hereafter be
enacted for the purpose of carrying into effect the provisions of the
Constitution in regard to the redelivery or return of fugitive slaves, or
fugitives from labor and service, shall extend to and be in full force within
the said Cherokee Nation; and shall also apply to all cases of escape of
fugitive slaves from the said Cherokee Nation into any other Indian
nation, or into one of the Confederate States; the obligation upon each
such nation or State to redeliver such slaves being in every case as complete as if they had escaped from another State and the mode of procedure the same.

Cherokees com-
petent as witnesses
in the courts of the
C. S.

ARTICLE XXXV. All persons, who are members of the Cherokee
Nation, shall hereafter be competent as witnesses in all cases, civil and
criminal, in the courts of the Confederate States, unless rendered incompetent from some other cause than their Indian blood or descent.

Faith and credit
given to official
acts of judicial
officers.

ARTICLE XXXVI. The official acts of all judicial officers in the said
nation shall have the same effect and be entitled to the like faith and
credit everywhere, as the like acts of judicial officers of the same grade

Authentication
of records, laws,
&c.

and jurisdiction in any of the Confederate States; and the proceedings
of the courts and tribunals of the said nation and copies of the laws
and judicial and other records of the said nation shall be authenticated
like similar proceedings of the courts of the Confederate States, and the
laws and office records of the same, and be entitled to like faith and
credit.

Existing laws,
usages and cus-
toms in regard to
slavery, declared
binding.

ARTICLE XXXVII. It is hereby declared and agreed that the institution of slavery in the said nation is legal and has existed from time
immemorial; that slaves are taken and esteemed to be personal property;
that the title to slaves and other property having its origin in the said
nation shall be determined by the laws and customs thereof; and that

the slaves and other personal property of every person domiciled in said nation shall pass and be distributed at his or her death in accordance with he laws, usages and customs of the said nation, which may be proved like foreign laws, usages and customs, and shall everywhere be held binding within the scope of their operations.

ARTICLE XXXVIII. No *ex post facto* law, or law impairing the obligation of contracts shall ever be enacted by the legislative authority of the Cherokee Nation; nor shall any citizen of the Confederate States, or member of any other Indian [nation,] or tribe be disseized of his property or deprived or restrained of his liberty, or fine, penalty, or forfeiture be imposed on him in the said country, except by the law of the land, nor without due process of law; nor shall any such citizen be in any way deprived of any of the rights guaranteed to all citizens by the Constitution of the Confederate States. *No ex post facto law, or law impairing the obligation of contracts to be enacted. Rights of personal liberty and private property, secured.*

ARTICLE XXXIX. It is further agreed that the Congress of the Confederate States shall establish and maintain post-offices at the most important places in the Cherokee Nation, and cause the mails to be regularly carried, at reasonable intervals, to and from the same, at the same rates of postages and in the same manner as in the Confederate States; and the postmasters shall be appointed from among the citizens of the Cherokee Nation. *Post-offices. Appointment of postmasters.*

ARTICLE XL. In consideration of the common interest of the Cherokee Nation and the Confederate States, and of the protection and rights guaranteed to the said nation by this treaty, the Cherokee Nation hereby agrees that it will raise and furnish a regiment of ten companies of mounted men, with two reserve companies, if allowed, to serve in the armies of the Confederate States for twelve months; the men shall be armed by the Confederate States, receive the same pay and allowances as other mounted troops in the service, and not be moved beyond the limits of the Indian country west of Arkansas without their consent. *Cherokees to furnish a regiment, &c., to serve in the army of the C. S. Arms. Pay and allowances.*

ARTICLE LXI. The Cherokee Nation hereby agrees to raise and furnish, at any future time, upon the requisition of the President, such number of troops for the defence of the Indian country, and of the frontier of the Confederate States, as he may fix, not out of fair proportion to the number of its population, to be employed for such terms of service as the President may determine; and such troops shall receive the same pay and allowances as other troops of the same class in the service of the Confederate States. *Troops for the defence of the Indian country and frontier of the C. S. Pay and allowances.*

ARTICLE XLII. It is further agreed by the said Confederate States that the said Cherokee Nation shall never be required or called upon to pay, in land or otherwise, any part of the expenses of the present war, or of any war waged by or against the Confederate States. *Cherokees to pay no part of expenses of present or any future war.*

ARTICLE XLIII. It is further agreed that after the restoration of peace, the Government of the Confederate States will defend the frontiers of the Indian country, of which the Cherokee country is a part, and hold the forts and posts therein, with native troops, recruited among the several Indian nations included therein, under the command of officers of the Confederate States, in preference to other troops. *C. S. to defend frontiers of the Indian country and hold the forts and posts.*

ARTICLE XLIV. In order to enable the Cherokee Nation to claim its rights and secure its interests without the intervention of counsel or agents, it shall be entitled to a delegate to the House of Representatives of the Confederate States of America, who shall serve for the term of two years, and be a native born citizen of the Cherokee Nation, over twenty-one years of age, and laboring under no legal disability by the law of the said nation; and each delegate shall be entitled to the same rights and privileges as may be enjoyed by delegates from any territories of the Confederate States to the said House of Representa- *Delegate to Congress.*

tives. Each shall receive such pay and mileage as shall be fixed by the
First election for Congress of the Confederate States. The first election for delegate
delegate. shall be held at such time and places, and shall be conducted in such
manner as shall be prescribed by the Principal Chief of the Cherokee
Nation, to whom returns of such elections shall be made, and who shall
declare the person having the greatest number of votes to be duly elected,
and give him a certificate of election accordingly, which shall entitle
Subsequent elec- him to his seat. For all subsequent elections, the time, places and man-
tions. ner of holding them, and ascertaining and certifying the result, shall be
prescribed by the Confederate States.

Debt due by the ARTICLE XLV. It is hereby ascertained and agreed between the
U. S. to the Cher- parties to this treaty, that the United States of America, of which the
okee Nation. Confederate States of America were heretofore a part, were, before the
separation, indebted, and still continue to be indebted to the Cherokee
Nation, and bound to the punctual payment to them of the following
sums annually on the first day of   in each year, that
is to say : It was agreed by the tenth article of the treaty of the twenty-
ninth day of December, A. D., one thousand eight hundred and thirty-
five that the sum of two hundred thousand dollars should be invested by
the President of the United States, in some safe and most productive
public stocks of the country for the benefit of the whole Cherokee Nation,
in addition to the annuities of the nation theretofore payable, to constitute a permanent general fund, and that the nett income of the same
should be paid over by the President annually to such person or persons
as should be authorized or appointed by the Cherokee Nation to receive
the same, whose receipt should be a full discharge for the amount paid
to them, the same interest to be applied annually by the council of the
nation to such purposes as they might deem best for the general interests
of their people; and it was agreed by the eleventh article of the same
treaty, that the permanent annuity of ten thousand dollars of the Cherokee Nation should be commuted for the sum of two hundred and fourteen thousand dollars, and that the same should be invested by the President of the United States, as a part of the said general fund of the
nation, which thus became four hundred and fourteen thousand dollars.
And it was agreed by the tenth article of the same treaty, that the
President of the United States should invest in some safe and most productive public stocks of the country, the further sum of fifty thousand
dollars, to constitute a permanent orphan's fund; and that he should pay
over the nett income of the same annually to such person or persons as
should be authorized or appointed by the Cherokee Nation to receive
the same, whose receipt should be a full discharge for the amount paid
to them; which nett annual income should be expended towards the
support and education of such orphan children of the Cherokees as might
be destitute of the means of subsistence. And it was agreed by the tenth
article of the same treaty, that the further sum of one hundred and fifty
thousand dollars should be invested by the President of the United States
in some safe and most productive public stocks of the country for the benefit of the whole Cherokee Nation, which should constitute, in addition to the
existing school fund of the nation, a permanent school fund, the nett income
whereof the President should pay over annually to such person or persons
as should be authorized or appointed by the Cherokee Nation to receive
the same, whose receipt should be a full discharge for the amount paid to
them ; and that the interest should be applied annually by the council of
the nation for the support of common schools and such a literary institution of a higher order as might be established in the Cherokee country;
and it was estimated by the eleventh article of the same treaty that the then
existing school fund of the nation amounted to about fifty thousand dollars

which, it was thereby agreed, should constitute a part of the permanent school fund aforesaid. And it is also further agreed between the said parties to this treaty, that the United States of America while the said Confederate States were States of the said United States, did invest the whole of the said several principal sums of money, except the sum of five thousand dollars, in stocks of the States hereinafter named, and of the United States, to the amount hereinafter named in each, that is to say : Investment of the principal sums in stocks.

The Permanent General Fund of the Nation.

Permanent general fund.

In seven per cent. stock of the State of Florida, seven thousand dollars, ($7,000.)

In six per cent. stock of the State of Georgia, one thousand and five hundred dollars, ($1,500)

In five per cent. stock of the State of Kentucky, ninety-four thousand dollars, ($94,000.)

In six per cent. stock of the State of Louisiana, seven thousand dollars, ($7,000.)

In six per cent. stock of the State of Maryland, seven hundred and sixty-one [dollars] and thirty-nine cents, ($761 39.)

In six per cent. stock of the State of Missouri, fifty thousand dollars, ($50,000.)

In six per cent. stock of the State of North Carolina, twenty thousand dollars, ($20,000.)

In six per cent. stock of the State of South Carolina, one hundred and seventeen thousand dollars, ($117,000.)

In five per cent. stock of the State of Tennessee, one hundred and twenty-five thousand dollars, ($125,000.)

In six per cent. stock of the State of Tennessee, five thousand dollars, ($5,000.)

And in six per cent. stock of the State of Virginia, ninety thousand dollars, ($90,000.)

Making the whole capital so invested, five hundred and seventeen thousand two hundred and sixty-one dollars and twenty-nine cents; the nett annual income whereof was and is twenty-eight thousand nine hundred and fourteen dollars and ninety-one cents.

The Permanent Orphan Fund.

Permanent orphan fund.

In six per cent. stock of the State of Virginia, forty-five thousand dollars, ($45,000.)

The nett annual income whereof was and is two thousand and seven hundred dollars; leaving the sum of five thousand dollars uninvested and which still so remains.

The Permanent School Fund.

Permanent school fund.

In seven per cent. stock of the State of Florida, seven thousand dollars, ($7,000.)

In six per cent. stock of the State of Louisiana, two thousand dollars, ($2,000.)

In five and a half per cent. stock of the State of Missouri, ten thousand dollars, ($10,000.)

In six per cent. stock of the State of Missouri, five thousand dollars, ($5,000.)

In six per cent. stock of the State of North Carolina, twenty-one thousand dollars, ($21,000.)

In five per cent. stock of the State of Pennsylvania, four thousand dollars, ($4,000.)

In six per cent. stock of the State of the South Carolina, one thousand dollars, ($1,000.)

In six per cent. stock of the State of Tennessee, seven thousand dollars, ($7,000.)

In the United States six per cent. loan of 1847, five thousand eight hundred dollars, ($5,800.)

And in six per cent. stock of the State of Virginia, one hundred and thirty-five thousand dollars, ($135,000.)

Making the whole capital so invested, of the said permanent school fund, one hundred and ninety-seven thousand eight hundred dollars; the nett annual income of whereof was and is eleven thousand eight hundred and forty-eight dollars.

All of which stocks the said United States now and do still continue to hold, or ought to have, in their hands.

Interest due on the principal sums and arrearages thereof.
And it is also hereby ascertained and agreed between the parties to this treaty, that there will be due to the Cherokee Nation on the first day of January, in the year of our Lord, one thousand eight hundred and sixty-two, for and on account of the said annually accruing interest on the said principal sums, and of arrearages thereof, the sum of sixty-five thousand six hundred and forty-four dollars and thirty-six cents, as follows, that is to say:

For the instalments of interest on the permanent general fund, as invested, for July, 1860, and January and July, 1861, forty-three thousand three hundred and seventy-two dollars and thirty-six cents, ($43,372 36.)

For the instalments of interest on the permanent orphan fund, as invested and uninvested, for July, 1860, and January and July, 1861, four thousand five hundred dollars, ($4,500.)

For the instalments of interest on the permanent school fund, as invested, for July, 1860, and January and July, 1861, seventeen thousand seven hundred and seventy-two dollars, ($17,772.)

And it not being desired by the Confederate States that the Cherokee Nation should continue to receive these annual sums of interest or the said arrearages, from the Government of the United States or otherwise have

The C. S. assume the payment for the future, of the interest and arrearages.
any further connection with that Government: therefore, the said Confederate States of America do hereby assume the payment for the future of the annual interest on the said sum of five thousand dollars, part of the permanent orphan fund, which was never invested, and on so much and such parts of said principal sums as, having once been invested, may now be in the hands of the United States uninvested; and also of the annual interest on so much and such parts of the said several principal sums as may have been invested in stocks of the United States or in the bonds or stocks of any of the States other than the said Confederate States; and do agree and bind themselves regularly and punctually hereafter, on the first day of July in each and every year, to pay the same; and they do also agree and bind themselves to pay to the treasurer of the Cherokee Nation immediately upon the complete ratification of this treaty the said sum of sixty-five thousand six hundred and forty-four dollars and thirty-six cents for such interest and arrearages now due and which will be due on the first day of January, A. D., one thousand eight hundred and sixty-two, as are above stated.

Also the duty of collecting and paying over the money accruing from the bonds of the States of this Confedera-
And the said Confederate States of America do hereby assume the duty and obligation of collecting and paying over as trustees to the said Cherokee Nation all sums of money not hereby agreed to be assumed and paid by them, accruing whether from interest or capital of the bonds of the several States of the Confederacy now held by the Government of the

United States as trustee for the Cherokee Nation; and the said interest c · held by the U. and capital, as collected, shall be paid over to the said Cherokee Nation. S. as trustee.

And the said Confederate States will request the several States of the Confederacy whose bonds are so held, to provide by legislation. or otherwise that the capital and interest of such bonds shall not be paid to the Government of the United States, but to the Government of the Confederate States in trust for the said Cherokee Nation.

Request to the States of this Confederacy to pay their said bonds to the C. S., in trust for the Cherokee Nation.

And the said Confederate States of America do hereby guarantee to the said Cherokee Nation the final settlement and full payment, upon and after the restoration of peace and recognition of their independence, as of debts in good faith and conscience as well as in law due and owing on good and valuable consideration by the said Confederate States and other of the United States jointly before the secession of any of the States, of any and all parts of the said several principal sums of money which may have remained uninvested in the hands of the United States, or which may have been again received by them after investment and may now be held by them; and do also guarantee to the said Cherokee Nation the final settlement and full payment, at the same period, of the capital of any and all bonds or stocks of any State not a member of the Confederacy and of any and all stocks of the United States in which any of the Cherokee funds may have been invested.

The C. S. guarantee to the Cherokee Nation final settlement and full payment of all the principal sums of money due from the U. S.

ARTICLE XLVI. All the said annual payments of interest and the arrearages shall be applied under the exclusive direction of the legislative authority of the Cherokee Nation to the support of their Government, to the purposes of education, to the maintenance of orphans, and to such other objects for the promotion and advancement of the improvement, welfare and happiness of the Cherokee people and their descendants, as shall to the legislature seem good, the same being in accordance with treaty stipulations and maintaining unimpaired the good faith of the Cherokee Nation to those persons and in regard to those objects for whom and which it has become trustee. And the capital sums aforesaid shall be invested or reinvested with any other moneys hereby guaranteed, after the restoration of peace, in stocks of the States of the Confederacy at their market price and in such as bear the highest rate of interest, or shall be paid over to the Cherokee Nation, after reasonable notice, to be invested by its authorities as its legislature may request. And no department or officer of the Government of the Confederate States shall hereafter have power to impose any conditions, limitations or restrictions on the payment to the said nation of any [of] said annual sums of interest, or of any arrearages, or in any wise to control or direct the mode in which such moneys when received by the authorities of the nation, shall be disposed of or expended.

How the annual payments of interest and the arrearages to be applied.

Investment of the capital sums.

No conditions or restrictions to be imposed on the payment of interest, &c., to the Cherokees.

ARTICLE XLVII. Whereas, by the treaty of the twenty-ninth day of December, A. D., one thousand eight hundred and thirty-five, the United States of America, in consideration of the sum of five hundred thousand dollars, part of the *of the* sum of five millions of dollars agreed by that treaty to be paid to the Cherokee Nation for the cession of all their lands and possessions east of the Mississippi river, did covenant and agree to convey to the Cherokees and their descendants by patent in fee simple the certain tract of land between the State of Missouri and the Osage reservation, the boundary line whereof it was provided should begin at the southeast corner of the said Osage reservation and run north along the east line of the Osage lands fifty miles to the northeast corner thereof; thence east to the west line of the State of Missouri; thence with that line south fifty miles; and thence west to the place of beginning: which tract of country was estimated to contain eight hundred thousand acres of land; and whereas, the same has been seized and settled upon by lawless intruders from the northern States and may become totally lost to the Cherokees:

Land sold by the U. S. to the Cherokees.

Boundaries.

Settled on by intruders from the northern States.

Payment for the land, should it be lost to the Cherokees, guaranteed to them by the C. S.

Now, therefore, it is further hereby agreed between the parties to this treaty, that in case the said tract of country should be ultimately lost to the Cherokees by the chances of war, or the terms of a treaty of peace or otherwise, the Confederate States of America do assure and guaranty to the Cherokee Nation the payment therefor of the said sum of five hundred thousand dollars, with interest thereon at the rate of five per cent. per annum from the said twenty-ninth day of December, A. D., one thousand eight hundred and thirty-five, and will either procure the payment of the same by the United States, or pay the same out of their own treasury, after the restoration of peace.

Advancement to the Cherokee Nation after the ratification of this treaty.

ARTICLE XLVIII. At the request of the authorities of of the Cherokee Nation, and in consideration of the unanimity and promptness of their people in responding to the call of the Confederate States for troops, and of their want of means to engage in any works of public utility and general benefit, or to maintain in successful operation their male and female seminaries of learning, the Confederate States do hereby agree to advance to the said Cherokee Nation, immediately after the ratification of this treaty, on account of the said sum to be paid for the said lands mentioned in the preceding article, the sum of one hundred and fifty thousand dollars, to be paid to the treasurer of the nation, and appropriated in such manner as the legislature may direct; and to hold in their hands as invested for the benefit of the said nation, the further sum of fifty thousand dollars, and to pay to the treasurer of said nation interest thereon, annually, on the first day of July in each year, at the rate of six per cent. per annum, which shall be sacredly devoted to the support of the said two seminaries of learning, and to no other purpose whatever.

Treaty of the 6th Aug. 1846, with the U S. negotiated and concluded with three parties, to wit: the Cherokee Nation, the "treaty party" and the "western Cherokees, or "old settlers."

ARTICLE XLIX. It is further ascertained and agreed by and between the Confederate States and the Cherokee Nation that the treaty of the sixth day of August, A. D., one thousand eight hundred and forty-six, was negotiated and concluded with the United States, by three several parties, that is to say, the Cherokee Nation, by delegates appointed by its constituted authorities; that portion of the nation known as "the treaty party," being those who made and those who agreed to the treaty of the year one thousand eight hundred and thirty-five; and "the western Cherokees," or "old settlers," being those who had removed west prior to the date of that treaty, and were then residing there. That the said three parties, by their delegates, after the making of the said treaty, of the year one thousand eight hundred and forty-six, borrowed from Corcoran and Riggs, bankers in the city of Washington, the sum of sixty thousand dollars, upon agreement endorsed by the Secretary of War, by which the same was to be repaid, with interest, when the moneys payable under said treaty should be appropriated, as follows, that is to say; twenty-five thousand dollars by the treaty party, twenty thousand dollars by the western Cherokees or old settler party, and fifteen thousand dollars by the Cherokee Nation. That at the session of Congress next after the making of that treaty, the sum of twenty-seven thousand dollars, for the Cherokee Nation, was appropriated under the eighth article of the same, and the sum of one hundred thousand dollars, under the sixth article, for the treaty party; but no appropriation was made for the western Cherokees or old settler party, under the fourth article, (whereunder only any moneys were payable to them,) the amount due them, and which was to be wholly paid per capita, under that article, not having as yet been ascertained; that consequently the sum borrowed as aforesaid, with the accrued interest, was repaid out of the two appropriations aforesaid, one half of the principal and interest which should have been paid by the western Cherokees or old settler party, being deducted from and paid out of the appropriation made for each of the others; and there being thus paid, out of the moneys so appropriated under

Money borrowed by the three parties from Corcoran and Riggs, bankers of Washington city.

Appropriation of moneys paid under the treaty.

the eighth article, for various purposes, for the whole nation, over and above its proportion, the sum of ten thousand three hundred dollars; and out of the moneys appropriated under the sixth article, for those of the treaty party who had sustained losses and damage in consequence of the treaty of the year one thousand eight hundred and thirty-five, over and above the proportion of that party, a like sum of ten thousand three hundred dollars. That when afterwards the amount ascertained to be due to the western Cherokees or old settlers, under the fourth article, was appropriated, the whole amount was paid to and distributed among them *per capita*, and no part of the sum so advanced for them, out of the other and previous appropriations, was reserved, nor has any part thereof whatever hitherto been re-imbursed to those entitled to receive the same, by the western Cherokees, or by the United States, or otherwise howsoever.

Therefore, it is further hereby agreed that the Confederate States will pay, upon the ratification of this treaty, to the Cherokee Nation, the sum of ten thousand three hundred dollars; and will also appropriate and place in the hands of the agent for the Cherokees the further sum of ten thousand three hundred dollars, to be distributed among the claimants of the treaty party, provided for by the sixth article of the said treaty, or their legal representatives under the laws of the nation, in such proportions as it shall be certified to him by Stand Watie, the only surviving member of the committee of five, appointed under that article to audit such claims, that it ought, in accordance with the allowances made by the committee, to be distributed among them. *Payments agreed to be made by the C. S. to be distributed among the claimants of the treaty party.*

And it was agreed by the said eighth article of the said treaty of the year one thousand eight hundred and forty-six, that of the sum of twenty-seven thousanddollars, provided thereby to be paid to the Cherokee Nation, the sum of five thousand dollars should be equally divided among all those whose arms were taken from them previous to their removal west, by order of an officer of the United States, and of that sum of five thousand dollars, three thousand three hundred dollars was applied to the payment in part of the proportion of the money borrowed as aforesaid, due by the Western Cherokees or Old Settler party; and as the authorities of the nation declined to receive the residue of said sum of five thousand dollars, it being but one thousand seven hundred dollars, and that residue never was paid by the United States, and still remains due by them,— *Payment for arms taken from the Cherokees.*

Therefore, it is hereby further agreed, that the Confederate States will also pay, upon the ratification of this treaty, to the treasurer of the Cherokee Nation, the further sum of one thousand seven hundred dollars; making, with the said sum of ten thousand three hundred dollars, the sum of twelve thousand dollars; and that out of the same, the sum of five thousand dollars shall, by the authorities of the nation, be distributed among those persons, and their legal representatives, whose arms were taken from them as aforesaid : and that any part of that sum finally remaining undistributed, together with the residue of seven thousand dollars, shall be used and appropriated in such manner as the national council shall direct.

ARTICLE L. It is hereby further agreed that all claims and demands against the Government of the United States in favor of the Cherokee Nation or any part thereof, or of any individuals thereof, and which have not been satisfied, released or relinquished, arising or accruing under former treaties, shall be investigated upon the restoration of peace, and be paid by the Confederate States, which do hereby take the place of the United States and assume their obligations in that regard. *The C. S. to assume the payment, upon the ratification of peace, of all claims and demands of the Cherokees against the U. S.*

ARTICLE LI. It is further agreed between the parties that all provisions of the treaties of the Cherokee Nation with the United States, *Certain provisions of the treaties* of the Cherokee Nation with the U. S., continued in force.

which secure or guarantee to the Cherokee Nation or individuals thereof any rights or privileges whatever, and the place whereof is not supplied by, and which are not contrary to the provisions of this treaty, and so far as the same are not obsolete or unnecessary, or repealed, annulled, changed or modified by subsequent treaties or laws, or by this treaty, are and shall be continued in force, as if made with the Confederate States.

One youth, a native of the Cherokee Nation, may be selected annually, to be educated at any military school of the C. S.

ARTICLE LII. In further evidence of the desire of the Confederate States to advance the individual interests of the Cherokee people, it is further agreed, that the delegate in Congress from the Cherokee Nation may, with the approbation of the President, annually select one youth, a native of the nation, who shall be appointed to be educated at any military school that may be established by the Confederate States, upon

Extension of the privilege to the Choctaw and Chickasaw and the Creek and Seminole nations.

the same terms as other cadets may be appointed. And the Confederate States also agree that the same privilege shall be exercised by the delegate from the Choctaw and Chickasaw Nations, and the Creek and Seminole Nations, respectively.

General amnesty declared.

ARTICLE LIII. A general amnesty of all past offences against the laws of the United States, and of the Confederate States, committed in the Indian country before the signing of this treaty, by any member of the Cherokee Nation, as such membership is defined by this treaty, is hereby declared ; and all such persons, if any, whether convicted or not, imprisoned or at large, charged with any such offence, shall receive from the President full and free pardon, and be discharged.

When this treaty to take effect.

ARTICLE LIV. A general amnesty is hereby declared in the Cherokee Nation ; and all offences and crimes committed by a member or members of the Cherokee Nation against the Nation, or against an individual or individuals, are hereby pardoned ; and this pardon and amnesty shall extend as well to members of the nation now beyond its limits, as to those now resident therein.

ARTICLE LV. This treaty shall take effect and be obligatory upon the contracting parties, from the seventh day of October, in the year of our Lord one thousand eight hundred and sixty-one, whenever it shall be ratified by the General Council of the Cherokee Nation, and by the provisional President and Congress, or the President and Senate of the Confederate States ; and no amendment shall be made thereto by either, but it shall be wholly ratified or wholly rejected.

In perpetual testimony whereof, the said Albert Pike, as Commissioner, with plenary powers, on the part of the Confederate States, doth now hereunto set his hand and affix the seal of his arms; and the said Principal and assistant Principal Chiefs, Executive Councillors and Special Commissioners, on the part of the Cherokee Nation, do hereunto set their hands and affix their seals.

{ SEAL. }

Thus done and interchanged in duplicate, at the place, in the year and on the day in the beginning hereof mentioned.

ALBERT PIKE,
Commissioner of the Confederate States to the Indian Nations west of Arkansas.

JNO. ROSS,
Principal Chief.
J. VANN,
Assistant Chief.
JAMES BROWN,
Executive Councillor.
JOHN DREW,
Executive Councillor.

WILL. P. ROSS,
Executive Councillor.
LEWIS ROSS,
Commissioner C. N.
THOMAS PEGG,
Commissioner C. N.
RICHARD FIELDS,
Commissioner C. N.

Signed, sealed and delivered in presence of us.

WM. QUESENBURY,
Secretary to the Commissioner.

E. RECTOR,
Superintendent Indian Affairs Confede-
rate States.

W. WARREN JOHNSON,

GEO. M. MURRELL,

RATIFICATION.

Dec. 11, 1861.

Resolved, (two-thirds of the Congress concurring,) That the Congress of the Confederate States of America do advise and consent to the ratification of the articles of a treaty made by Albert Pike, Commissioner of Confederate States to the Indian Nations west of Arkansas, in behalf of the Confederate States, of the one part, and the Cherokee Nation of Indians, by its Principal and Assistant Principal Chiefs, Executive Councillors and Commissioners, for that purpose only, authorized and empowered, of the other part, concluded at Tahlequah, in the Cherokee Nation, on the seventh day of October, in the year of our Lord, one thousand eight hundred and sixty-one, with the following

Ratification by Congress.

AMENDMENTS:

Amendments.

I. Add at the end of article xxxv. the following words: " And the Confederate States will request the several States of the Confederacy to adopt and enact the provisions of this article, in respect to suits and proceedings in their respective courts."

II. Strike out from article xliv. the following words : " The same rights and privileges as may be enjoyed by delegates from any Territories of the Confederate States to the said House of Representatives," and insert in lieu thereof the following words: " A seat in the hall of the House of Representatives, to propose and introduce measures for the benefit of the said nation, and to be heard in regard thereto, and on other questions in which the nation is particularly interested ; with such other rights and privileges as may be determined by the House of Representatives.

III. Strike out from article xxxiii. the following words: " or of a State," and insert in lieu thereof the following words: " or of a State, subject to the laws of the State."

NOTE.—The foregoing amendments were subsequently concurred in and adopted by the Cherokee Nation.

BIBLIOGRAPHY

BIBLIOGRAPHY

Alfriend, F. H. The Life of Jefferson Davis. Cincinnati, Caxton Publishing House, 1868. xvii, 645 p.

Bancroft, A. C., ed. The Life and Death of Jefferson Davis. New York, J. S. Ogilvie, 1889. 256 p.

Catton, William and Bruce Catton. Two Roads to Sumter. New York, McGraw-Hill, 1963. 285 p.

Craven, J. J. Prison Life of Jefferson Davis. New York, Carleton, 1866. x, 377 p.

Cutting, Elisabeth. Jefferson Davis, Political Soldier. New York, Dodd, Mead & Co., 1930. x, 361 p.

Davis, Burke. To Appomattox. New York, Rinehart & Co., 1959. 433 p.

Davis, Jefferson. Inaugural Address(of President Davis, Montgomery, Alabama, February 18, 1861). In Davis, Jefferson. The Rise & Fall of the Confederate Government. New York, Thomas Yoseloff, 1958. p. 232-236.

_____. Relations of States. Speech in the U. S. Senate, May 7, 1860. Baltimore, J. Murphy & Co. 15 p.

_____. Reply of Jefferson Davis to Senator Douglas on the subject of slavery, May 1860. Baltimore, J. Murphy & Co., 1860. 16 p.

_____. The Rise and Fall of the Confederate Government. New York, D. Appleton & Co., 1881. 2 v.

_____. A Short History of the Confederate States of America. New York, Belford Co., 1890. xii, 505 p.

Davis, Varina H. Jefferson Davis, Ex-President of the Confederate States of America; a Memoir by His Wife. New York, Belford Co., 1890. 2 v.

Dodd, William E. Jefferson Davis. Philadelphia, G. W. Jacobs & Co., 1907. 396 p.

Eckenrode, Hamilton J. Jefferson Davis, President of the South. New York, Macmillan, 1923. 371 p.

Freeman, Douglas S., ed. Lee's Dispatches to Jefferson Davis, 1862-1865. New York, Putnam, 1957. lxxi, 416 p.

Gordon, Armistead C.   Jefferson Davis. New York, C.
    Scribner's Sons, 1918.   viii, 329 p.

Hendrick, Burton J.   Statesmen of the Lost Cause;
    Jefferson Davis and His Cabinet.   Boston, Little
    Brown & Co., 1939.   xvii, 452 p.

Jones, Charles C., Jr.   Funeral Oration (Jefferson
    Davis), Augusta, Georgia, December 11, 1889.   17 p.

Knight, Landon. The Real Jefferson Davis. Battle
    Creek, Mich., The Pilgrim Magazine Co., 1904.   203 p.

Lee, Charles R. The Confederate Constitution.   Chapel
    Hill, University of North Carolina Press, 1963.
    viii, 225 p.

McElroy, Robert. Jefferson Davis; the Unreal and the
    Real.   New York, Harper & Brothers, 1937.   2 v.

Pollard, Edward A. Life of Jefferson Davis.   Phila-
    delphia, National Publishing Co., 1869.   viii, 536 p.

Pritchard, Benjamin. The Capture of Jefferson Davis.
    New York, J. A. Fox, 1964.   40 p.

Quyun, Russell H. The Constitutions of Abraham
    Lincoln and Jefferson Davis, a Historical and Bio-
    graphical Study in Contrasts.   New York, Exposi-
    tion Press, 1959.   304 p.

Rowland, Dunbar, ed. Jefferson Davis, Constitutional-
    ist, His Letters, Papers and Speeches.   Mississippi
    Dept. of Archives, 1923.   10 v.

Schaff, Morris. Jefferson Davis, His Life and Per-
    sonality.   Boston, J. W. Luce & Co., 1922.   277 p.

Strode, Hudson.   Jefferson Davis. New York, Harcourt
    Brace, 1955-64.   3 v.

_____, ed. Private Letters (of Jefferson Davis),
    1823-1889.   New York, Harcourt, Brace and World,
    1966.   xxi, 580 p.

Tate, Allen. Jefferson Davis: His Rise and Fall,
    a Biographical Narrative.   New York, Minton,
    Balch & Co., 1929.   311 p.

Vandiver, Frank E. Jefferson Davis and the Confederate
    State; an Inaugural Lecture at the University of
    Oxford.   Oxford, Clarendon Press, 1964.   22 p.

Wakelyn, John L. Biographical Dictionary of the
    Confederacy. Frank E. Vandiver, Advising
    Editor. Westport, Conn., Greenwood, 1977.
    xii, 603 p.

Werstein, Irving. Abraham Lincoln Versus Jefferson
    Davis. New York, Crowell, 1959.   272 p.

Wiley, Bell I. The Road to Appomattox.   Memphis,
    Memphis State College Press, 1956.   121 p.

Winston, Robert W. High Stakes and Hair Trigger;
    the Life of Jefferson Davis.   New York, H.
    Holt, 1930.   viii, 306 p.

BIBLIOGRAPHY